WHY
SCRIPTURE MATTERS

Reading the Bible in a Time of Church Conflict

JOHN P. BURGESS

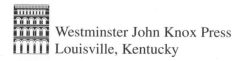

Westminster John Knox Press
Louisville, Kentucky

Scripture quotations, unless otherwise noted, are from the New Revised Standard Version of the Bible, copyright © 1989 by the Division of Christian Education of the National Council of the Churches of Christ in the U.S.A., and are used by permission.

Scripture quotations from the Revised Standard Version of the Bible are copyrighted 1946, 1952, © 1971, 1973 by the Division of Christian Education of the National Council of the Churches of Christ in the U.S.A. and are used by permission.

Grateful acknowledgment is made for permission to quote from the poem "Untergang," by Georg Trakl (5th version), in *Vor Feuerschlunden: Erfahrung mit Georg Trakls Gedicht*, by Franz Fühmann (Leipzig: Hinstorff Verlag, 1984).

Book design by Jennifer K. Cox
Cover design by Kevin Darst

First edition
Published by Westminster John Knox Press
Louisville, Kentucky

This book is printed on acid-free paper that meets the American National Standards Institute Z39.48 standard. ♾

PRINTED IN THE UNITED STATES OF AMERICA
98 99 00 01 02 03 04 05 06 07 — 10 9 8 7 6 5 4 3 2 1

Library of Congress Cataloging-in-Publication Data

Burgess, John P., 1954–
    Why Scripture matters : reading the Bible in a time of church
conflict / John P. Burgess. — 1st ed.
        p.   cm.
    Includes bibliographical references and index.
    ISBN 0-664-25708-9 (alk. paper)
    1. Bible—Evidences, authority, etc.   2. Bible—Inspiration.
3. Word of God (Theology)   I. Title.
BS480.B773   1998
220.1—dc21   98-17301

For George B. Telford, Jr., and Joseph D. Small III

CONTENTS

ACKNOWLEDGMENTS

I wrote this book as I served as Associate for Theology in the denominational offices of the Presbyterian Church (U.S.A.). While the PC(USA) in recent years has experienced considerable disagreement and conflict about basic questions of belief and practice, this position provided me remarkable opportunities to reflect with colleagues on strategies for renewing the church's theological vocation. This book bears, I hope, some of the fruit of our labors.

I am especially thankful to colleagues in the Congregational Ministries Division, and to its director, Eunice Poethig, who supported my requests for study leave. Within the division, I have been a member of the Christian Faith and Life Program Area; Anne Noss, Associate Director, has understood how important my writing is to me, and has encouraged me to speak to a wide church audience.

Within the program area, the Office of Theology and Worship has been my home. Colleagues responded to an early version of these ideas. I am also indebted to several groups of pastors who participated in theological consultations on the use of Scripture in the church. They contributed richly to my reflections, confirmed many of my intuitions, and gave me the confidence to develop my lines of thinking.

While the denominational offices have played a special role in shaping this book, I am equally grateful to colleagues in the academy from whom I have learned. My interest in Scripture and ethics first emerged in graduate seminars with James Gustafson at the University of Chicago. I have learned immensely from his skills of analysis. I am also grateful to Jon Levenson, who has been an important conversation partner since those days. In 1996,

I presented some of these ideas at the annual meeting of the Society of Christian Ethics. Members of the society helpfully pushed me to define my focus more clearly. In addition, several anonymous referees offered detailed critiques. I am especially thankful to Michael Westmoreland-White, who read the entire manuscript.

Davis Perkins, President and Publisher of the Presbyterian Publishing Corporation, first invited me to turn my ideas into a book. I have felt his support every step of the way. In addition, I am thankful to Richard Brown, Director of Westminster John Knox Press. Despite his many responsibilities, he graciously agreed to serve as my editor. At several key points, his suggestions have saved me from insufficient nuance. An anonymous reader for the press also offered helpful comments. Needless to say, I have not been able to address every concern. Errors of fact or interpretation are solely my own.

A grant for religious leaders from the Louisville Institute for the Study of American Protestantism supported a study leave in the fall of 1995 that enabled me to begin work on this project. I wish to express my appreciation to James Lewis, Director, and to the board of the institute. In 1997, a grant from Lilly Endowment Inc. enabled me to redefine my job position to provide greater time for theological work and hence the writing of this book. I am thankful to Craig Dysktra, Vice President, Religion; and Christopher Coble, Program Director, Religion.

I have reserved to the last my particular debt to the two individuals who have been my closest colleagues and mentors during my time in the denominational offices. When I was hired, George Telford was director of what was then the Theology and Worship Ministry Unit. He more than anyone else has helped me to define myself as a church theologian, one who seeks through theological reflection to make a contribution toward deepening the church's faith and life. In recent years, Joseph Small, Coordinator for Theology and Worship, has been my most important conversation partner. He cannot begin to imagine how much he has contributed to my growth theologically during my years in the offices. I have borrowed a number of his ideas in writing this book. In addition, he made invaluable suggestions for revision of the manuscript.

Finally, I wish to thank my family for letting me be first of all a husband and a father. In her care for us all, my wife Deb makes it possible for me to attend more faithfully to my theological work. My daughters Hannah, Luisa, and Rachel regularly inquired as to how the book was coming along. They also reminded me of simple truths. When I asked them one day why they thought the Bible mattered, Hannah looked at me quizzically and replied, "But, Daddy, how else will you know who Jesus is?"

To him, the Word made flesh, be all glory and honor, forever and ever.

John P. Burgess
Advent 1997

INTRODUCTION

Does the Bible really matter? From one point of view, the answer is obvious. The church is not the church without the Bible. The church's Scriptures guard the corporate memory of the people of God. They lie at the heart of the community's worship. They undergird the church's efforts to educate and form men and women in the faith. They impel the church's service in and to the world.

From another point of view, however, the answer is not self-evident. Over the last thirty years, the Protestant mainline in North America has experienced a radical decline in numbers — and, more significantly, a loss of confidence in Scripture. Efforts to enlist the Bible in defining, or redefining, the church's theology and ethics have resulted in debilitating fights, even threats of schism.

In my own denomination, the Presbyterian Church (U.S.A.), the controversy over the 1993 Reimagining Conference, an ecumenical gathering of women seeking new forms of religious ritual and language, exposed the degree to which fundamental issues of Christology (the church's teachings about Christ) were up for grabs. Similarly, continuing debates about homosexuality have demonstrated the denomination's inability to find consensus about the basic moral contours of the Christian life—whether in regard to sexuality or other pressing moral issues, such as distribution of wealth or exercise of power (both within the church and in society).

In such a time, people both inside and outside the church shake their heads in disbelief. How is it possible that Christians disagree so intensely about matters basic to their life together? Why do efforts to talk about common values, even a common language, prove so difficult, and consensus so elusive?

In a time of theological fragmentation, Christians find themselves reading the church's foundational documents in profoundly different ways. Appeals to the latest findings of historical-critical scholars—with their efforts,
for example, to reconstruct a picture of the "real," historical Jesus—have
further complicated the picture. Many people seem to be asking whether
Scripture is trustworthy—and if so, in what respect.

This book explores what it means to read the Bible as *Holy Scripture* in
a time of church conflict. If the church is divided into competing interest
groups, it is not surprising that the authority and interpretation of the Bible
are matters of contention. I believe that the church desperately needs to recover a piety of the Word—a deep-seated sense that Scripture sets forth a
Word of God. Only then might the church be able to focus again on the living God, and not just on human differences.

In a divided church, we are tempted to rush to Scripture to support our
judgments about the rightness or wrongness of each other's theology and
ethics. People on all sides, it seems, claim Scripture for their point of view.
The result, a wide variety of interpretations, sometimes confirms the cynic
in us all. It appears that people really can get whatever they want out of the
Bible.

I wish to pose an alternative. I wish to challenge the church to recover
a sense of Scripture's compelling power, in the hope that the church might
experience Scripture more as a source of life—a sacrament—than as a set
of right answers that one party wields against another. A piety of the Word
may not resolve every theological and ethical debate, but it may help to reshape the terms of the debate, making life in community possible—indeed,
necessary—despite our different readings of Scripture.

THE BROADER CONTEXT

The current battle for the Bible has at least two ironies. First, questions
of biblical authority and interpretation are rarely topics of sustained theological conversation in the church, even though we may sense that they lie
behind particular theological and ethical debates. Rather, the issue of the
day—whether homosexuality or affirmative action, the right language for
talking about God, or the nature of Christ's saving power—most often
commands our attention. We seem to prefer political fights—where the
lines are clearly drawn—to theological work, especially if it would force
us to consider nuances and ambiguities that we would rather avoid.

Second, the church's appeal to biblical authority is more often rhetori-
cal than real. Our arguments about Scripture frequently expose just how

little we really know the Bible itself. We appeal to a select handful of passages to justify our positions but lack the capacity to order Scripture as a whole. We say that the Bible matters but spend remarkably little time actually reading it.

These dynamics seem to be at work in all mainline denominations and, perhaps, in other North American churches. In recent years, historians, sociologists, and theologians alike have argued that Christians must now come to terms with profound changes in North American culture. Society no longer props up religious practice; the elimination of Christian prayer from the public schools, and the demise of blue laws, are representative of the decline of Christendom.[1] Religious pluralism is an inescapable fact of life. Our neighbors are as apt to be Muslim (or Hindu, or Jewish) as Christian; they may dabble in New Age spirituality or may switch denominations—even religions—as often as they move. A consumer society has weakened the capacity of religious traditions to transmit their distinctive beliefs and practices; the emphasis is on consumer choice, not the claims of the past. We seem condemned to the "heretical imperative," to constructing our own languages of meaning and value in a world where the Christian religion is but one option among many.[2]

North America is not necessarily becoming more secular. Gallup polls remind us that Americans still believe overwhelmingly in God, the divinity of Jesus, and even the promise of eternal life. Yet, it is clear that the language of the Bible is becoming less familiar to us both as a society and a church. Today, one is as apt to hear an Eastern Orthodox priest as a Presbyterian minister, a black Baptist preacher as a Lutheran bishop, call for basic religious education, beginning with Scripture.

A good deal of recent scholarly literature has emphasized that Scripture is the *church's* book. But this literature has argued that the challenge to the church is more than remedial education, more than getting church members to learn the contents of the Bible or to become familiar with the latest findings of historical-critical research. Rather, Christians must attend to the character of their life together. Only as we understand anew who we really are—our basic beliefs and practices, our distinctive ways of doing things—will we know how to read Scripture rightly.

Yet, little of this scholarship has paid adequate attention to the fact that the real church is fragmented. Too many scholars simply pose questions of method (How do we apply the biblical materials to the life of the church? What kind of community do we need to become in order to read Scripture rightly?). They fail to see that many people wonder why they should take Scripture seriously when it supports a host of competing, even conflicting, causes. Scholars may develop a detailed position on homosexuality or the uniqueness of Christ, but they also need to tell us why the church should care about Scripture to begin with.

THE AIMS OF THIS BOOK

While seeking to make this scholarly literature more accessible to the church, I begin not with questions of methodology, but with a theological consideration of what makes the writings of the Bible *Holy Scripture*. In developing my arguments, I take into account the fact that a fragmented church experiences significant conflict in its interpretation of Scripture. My intent is to reflect on the authority and interpretation of Scripture not as abstract theological problems, but as matters of practical theology. I am interested in how the church actually uses Scripture, and in how the church might use it more faithfully, especially in its worship.

In particular, I argue that the church desperately needs to recover practical disciplines of reading Scripture as a Word of God. We do not simply need a better method of interpretation; we need a piety, a different set of dispositions and attitudes toward Scripture. We need a reverent confidence that these words set forth a Word of God for us.

I introduce these concerns by briefly describing and assessing several significant efforts in recent theology to claim Scripture as the community's book. In my judgment, these efforts fail to pay adequate attention to the current crisis of Scripture and church. I agree that Scripture is the church's book. But the fragmentation of the church results in the fragmentation of the Bible. We cannot simply wait for the church to get its act together; we must begin now to rediscover the power of Scripture to remold us as a community of faith (chapter 1).

Recovery of a piety of the Word poses particular challenges to a church that too often seems Scripture-weary and biblically illiterate. I believe that the crisis of Scripture cannot be remedied simply by asking church members to try harder. The problem is deeper. Powerful cultural forces are undermining our ability to read Scripture as a word of life. The Scripture-weariness of the church dramatically poses questions of why the Bible matters and what makes the Bible truly *Holy Scripture* (chapter 2).

If the church is to recover a piety of the Word, I believe that the church must come to understand Scripture as a sacramental, poetic-like word, not as propositional truths, an expression of human experience, or mere information for practical living. Sacramental, poetic-like language has a unique capacity to draw us into the presence of God. It does not simply tell us who we already are, but challenges us to meditate on the One in whose hands we lie (chapter 3).

The notion of Scripture as a sacramental, poetic-like word may seem strange to people shaped by a society based on information and technology. Yet, the church has inherited a number of practices of reading Scripture sacramentally. I reflect on four disciplines in particular: reading Scripture aloud, reading Scripture in community, reading Scripture in context, and memorizing Scripture. Drawing on a range of historical resources to illustrate each point, I explore practical implications for reforming the church's use of Scripture today (chapter 4).

When these disciplines open the church to Scripture's compelling power, the church is moved to comment, to communicate Scripture's compelling power to others. Drawing once again on a wide range of historical examples, I demonstrate how translations of the Bible, creeds and confessions, art, architecture, hymnody, prophetic discourse, and even ways of packaging the Bible can function as biblical commentary (chapter 5).

Disciplines of reading Scripture sacramentally are focused with particular clarity and power in worship. Indeed, worship is perhaps the most profound kind of commentary on Scripture. Drawing both on recent work in liturgical theology and on visits with congregations representing a wide range of the Christian tradition in North America, I argue that the church's liturgical traditions have a unique capacity to evoke the power of Scripture to speak a Word of God to us. I also make practical suggestions for reforming the church's use of Scripture in worship today (chapter 6).

When worship and disciplines of reading Scripture as a Word of God deepen a piety of the Word, they might contribute to resolving concrete differences in the church's theology and ethics. I demonstrate the implications of a sacramental understanding of Scripture both for our method of applying the Bible to theological and ethical issues, and for the content of our theology (chapter 7).

In a conclusion, I offer a brief reading of one biblical story, the temptation of Jesus. I do not claim to have a method that simply needs to be applied. I do not draw on Scripture to resolve particular theological or ethical dilemmas. Rather, I wish to suggest how a piety of Scripture can unlock the riches of one biblical passage. Key images, their resonance with other parts of Scripture, and their place in the church's memory give us a lens for seeing God at work in the world, and a language for expressing our trusting response.

Finally, I append a brief bibliographic essay that reviews recent scholarship on Scripture as the community's book. I explore four issues in particular: 1) Why does an author take Scripture to be authoritative? 2) What does an author take to be authoritative in Scripture? 3) How does an author deal with the fact of diverse readings of Scripture? and 4) How does an author assess the value of the historical-critical method? I believe the church must ask itself the same questions if it is to make sense of why Scripture matters in a time of church conflict.

NOTES ON TERMINOLOGY

A major theme of Karl Barth's theology—and of subsequent efforts to write theology in light of his achievement—is the Word of God. For Barth, the Word is ultimately God's self-revelation in Jesus Christ and is to be distinguished from Scripture, which is the Word of God written. Scripture bears witness to the Word; Scripture helps to set forth the Word; Scripture becomes the Word when we encounter Christ through Scripture.

The Confession of 1967 (part of the *Book of Confessions* of the Presbyterian Church [U.S.A.]) makes a distinction between "the Word" and "the words of Scripture" (a problem not present in German, where every noun is capitalized). By contrast, I will generally use "word" when referring to Scripture's verbal or literary quality (a poetic word, a sacramental word) and "Word" when referring to Scripture as setting forth God's self-revelation (the Word of God, a piety of the Word). As will become clear, I follow Barth in insisting that the Word of God is an event, not a text. Through Scripture, we listen for God's Word to us, a Word that sets forth Jesus Christ in a specific shape and form, here and now. In this sense, however, Scripture as "word" and Scripture as "Word" are finally inseparable, and the distinction between them cannot always be made neatly.

I use the terms *Scripture, the Bible,* and *the Scriptures* interchangeably, though their nuances differ. *Scripture* (from the Latin *scriptura*) refers to the fact that these words are written. The word *Bible* (from the Greek *biblia*) refers to the importance of the *book;* the writings have been collected into one volume. The term *Scriptures* reminds us that this volume nonetheless consists of diverse writings; different hands, reflecting different historical, cultural settings, have been at work. If I most often speak of Scripture, it is because I am especially interested in the character of its words, though I believe that these words are meant to be heard, not only read. Their sacramental, poetic quality makes them truly memorable.

1

CHURCH AND SCRIPTURE
IN CRISIS

On a bookshelf at home sits my first "real" Bible. The binding is broken; several pages are torn. Although I don't use it anymore for regular study, I still feel a special attachment to it.

My Bible was one of millions, I'm sure, that Thomas Nelson published. It is an RSV (Revised Standard Version). The cover is black cardboard, and the edges of the pages are red. What impressed me most as a child were the color illustrations, four plates for the Old Testament and four for the New. I can remember Ruth gleaning the fields, Abraham and Lot looking out over the Promised Land, and Herod bringing Jesus out to the crowd. The reproductions were not very good, but those images remain etched into my memory.

On the frontispiece is an inscription: "To John, December 18, 1962, From Mom and Dad." It was my eighth birthday. I remember feeling so excited, so pleased, that I now had my own Bible. For the first few days, I took it to bed with me. I slept in a room with my two brothers, and after they had fallen asleep, I would get under my sheets and blankets, make a little tent, take a flashlight from under my pillow, and open my Bible. Even though there was much of it that I could not understand, I had the sense that this book mattered, that it would draw me into the presence of God. Like the boy Samuel in the temple, I waited for the Word of God.

Did God speak? I don't ever recall a dramatic moment like Moses and the burning bush or Isaiah in the temple. But I cannot come to Scripture today without some sense of awe and reverence, as though I were still that child discovering the Bible for the first time.

I suspect that many of us have a story about our first real Bible or about another Bible that has special, sentimental significance to us: an old family

Bible, a Bible that we received as we left for college or seminary, a Bible over whose pages we pored during a time of spiritual struggle or growth. Even if we use it no longer, it reminds us that we once experienced—and perhaps still experience—Scripture's compelling power.

SCRIPTURE AS THE
COMMUNITY'S BOOK

Such stories are not without danger, however. For one thing, they may tempt us to turn Scripture into a sentimental idea. Too often, people's sense that the Scriptures matter is little more than a sentimental attachment to something long gone, such as a childhood experience.

For another thing, stories about Scripture's compelling power too often betray a temptation to make our reading of Scripture a private affair. In a recent book, theologian Stanley Hauerwas argues that the church should take the Bible out of the hands of individual Christians.

> Let us no longer give the Bible to all children when they enter the third grade or whenever their assumed rise to Christian maturity is marked, such as eighth-grade commencements. Let us rather tell them and their parents that they are too possessed by habits far too corrupt for them to be encouraged to read the Bible on their own.[1]

Hauerwas insists that the Bible is the church's book, not the individual's. We cannot read the Scriptures rightly until we participate in the life of the church. Little boys and girls should not play with matches—nor with the Bible, it seems.

In my defense, I had already heard much of Scripture in Sunday school and in family devotions. I knew that the Bible mattered immensely to my parents because of their participation in the church. They wanted me to have the Bible because it was the church's book, not because it was a text that I could master apart from the church.

But Hauerwas's point still stands. After all, I took my Bible and went off on my own. It was in solitude, not as I heard Scripture in the church's worship or discussed it in a church Bible study class, that I waited for the Word of God. Perhaps I was tempted to believe that I could now hear God on my own—that armed with a Bible, I no longer needed the church in the same way as before.

Hauerwas challenges the assumption that one can understand the Bible by himself or herself. He argues that we always come to Scripture as members of one community or another, and that those communities, their values, and their way of life shape our interpretation of Scripture. The text has no meaning except as it means something to particular people shaped by particular social and historical forces.

Even when I read the Bible by myself, I had not really escaped the bounds of life in community. Hauerwas might well assert that I had merely switched communities! I was now living more out of the influence of the wider culture than that of the church. In believing that I could come to Scripture on its own terms, by myself and apart from the church, I was reflecting the presuppositions of a contemporary Western society shaped more by the seventeenth-century Enlightenment than by the gospel.

As North American Christians, each of us is, of course, a member not only of the church, but also of this wider community. Our society teaches us to believe that we should think for ourselves. We learn to be confident that we can free ourselves to some degree from the influences of nature and tradition. We seek to discover the eternal, unchanging truths of the cosmos, and to evaluate the wisdom of the past, so that we might sort out truth from mere myth and legend. Like the little boy I was, we assume that each of us can make sense of Scripture on our own.

But such an approach to Scripture, argues Hauerwas, inevitably makes its meaning a matter of private judgment. Each individual is encouraged to interpret the text for himself or herself, and to assert its "true" meaning. A diversity of readings appears, each clashing and competing with the other. Ironically, we end up making truth relative to the opinions and beliefs of each individual, even as we claim that truth is objective and universal.[2]

ASSESSING HISTORICAL-CRITICAL STUDY OF THE BIBLE

The assumption that each individual must search for truth on his or her own contrasts with Hauerwas's assertion that the individual must first participate in the life of the church if he or she is to read Scripture rightly. While Hauerwas puts his own spin on this position, it is represented more broadly today both in the church and among theologians, as they reflect on the character of Christian community.

This new interest in the relationship of community and Scripture is in part, I believe, a reaction against historical-critical study of the Bible. If we now hear church leaders and theologians asserting so vociferously that the Bible is the church's book, it is because they want to insist that Scripture is not merely the university's or academy's book. The Bible does not belong to biblical scholars with advanced degrees; rather, it is the foundational document of a community of faith that listens to it in the confidence that it sets forth the Word of God.

In its origins, historical criticism was largely a Protestant movement. Historical critics sought to determine the objective meaning of the text, and to free it from an overlay of obscuring church tradition. Like the Reformers, they wanted to listen to Scripture alone.

But historical critics seemed to take the principle of *sola scriptura* (Scripture alone) and turn it against the Reformers themselves. Although Luther and Calvin pitted Scripture against the traditions of the Roman Catholic Church, they insisted that Scripture was the church's book, to be interpreted in the context of the community's faith and life. Historical critics sought to free Scripture even from these constraints. The meaning of the text was the meaning that the original author had intended in a particular historical context, not its meaning to a later generation. This principle of moving to the "real" meaning of the text could even be extended. Soon the original intent of the author was not as important as reconstructing the events that had given rise to the composition of the text in the first place.

The underlying assumption of historical criticism seemed to be that the texts of Scripture were like any other literary product: historically conditioned, rather than divinely inspired. Such a method of interpretation might seem antithetical to the needs of the church. Yet, Protestant (and later Catholic) scholars came to believe that it could help the church to speak to the questions and doubts of people shaped by the Enlightenment. In wielding the method for their own purposes, Christians tried to use a method grounded in the Enlightenment search for scientific truth to defend Christianity against the Enlightenment assault on religion.

No longer would the church have to defend a premodern view of the world. It would not have to insist that the miracles of Jesus really took place or that the universe was a three-tiered heaven, earth, and hell. The historical-critical method enabled Christians to strip away the poetic, metaphorical, mythical language of the text, and to reconstruct a history behind the text in which they saw God at work.

The story of the Exodus with its plagues and a miraculous crossing of the Red Sea could now be understood as a mythical explication of an historical fact: God's deliverance of the people of Israel from oppression in Egypt. The accounts of the resurrection of Jesus Christ, with their details about angels and a stone rolled away from the tomb, lent themselves to similar treatment. The point was not that Jesus' body had defied the laws of nature but that the disciples had experienced personal transformation. If there had been a miracle, it was their ability to believe that Jesus was still at work in their lives, even after his death on the cross.

But the promise of historical criticism to establish scientifically verifiable, unassailable truths was never realized. For one thing, reconstructing the history behind the text proved to be far more difficult than first imagined. Historical critics differed among themselves on what had really happened. The single truth that the text should yield proved elusive.

Second, it soon became clear that the theological and philosophical commitments of the interpreter deeply influenced his or her interpretation of this reconstructed history. In seeing God's hand at work in Israel and Jesus, Protestant biblical scholars were not simply stating objective facts that the text established. Rather, they were importing ideas out of their faith, ideas that to their critics seemed as fanciful and mythical as the original texts themselves.[3]

A good deal of recent scholarship has analyzed and assessed the implicit presuppositions of historical criticism and Christian use of it.[4] These critiques have established that historical criticism is not a neutral enterprise. Rather, it tends to reduce the texts to the history behind them. By itself, it cannot establish why this history is any more significant than any other segment of human experience past or present. The philosophical assumptions on which historical criticism is based implicitly challenge, even undermine, the Christian notion that the Bible witnesses authoritatively to God's self-revelation in history.

Attempts to enlist historical criticism for theological purposes tend to overlook these problems. But even if one could separate the method from this tendency to reduce the text to the history behind it, one would still find that different theologies yield different results when employing the same historical-critical tools.

Another way to put it is simply to reiterate Hauerwas's point. We always bring to the text an interpretative framework that has been shaped by particular traditions and communities. Different interpretive communities will use historical criticism to different ends. The secular historian will see the history behind the Exodus as nothing more than secular history; the liberation theologian, by contrast, will interpret it as a historical moment with decisive, continuing import, in which God's essential character as liberator of the oppressed has been revealed.

THREE APPROACHES TO SCRIPTURE AS THE COMMUNITY'S BOOK

If one of the temptations of historical critics is to reduce each text to one right meaning, one of the temptations of those who now wish to reclaim Scripture as the church's book is to open the text to an unlimited number of meanings, as though the text means nothing more than what it means to a particular community at a particular time. There is no fixed message, no right interpretation once and for all.

If Hauerwas and others who emphasize that Scripture is the church's book have in fact not taken this tack, it is because they clearly believe that some manifestations of Christian community are more faithful than others, and therefore that some readings of Scripture are more faithful than others. But then the question simply shifts from what is the "real" meaning of Scripture to what is the "real" church. Which beliefs or practices make for a right reading of Scripture? Which communities best embody them?[5]

Here I wish to explore three major options that appear both in the church today and in recent theological reflection on Christian community. While all three lift up the significance of Scripture as the community's book, each also reflects a fundamentally different understanding of the character of Christian community. These differences challenge us to consider whether one vision of Christian community is more faithful to the gospel than another, and what we must do when different communities claiming to be faithful to the gospel read the Scriptures in different, even conflicting, ways.

The first position defines the church as an alternative community in a world of violence and mistrust. The church has its own story, and this story shapes a way of life distinctive from the wider culture. The second position defines the Christian community in terms of feminist commitments to mutuality, interconnectedness, and the flourishing of women. The challenge to the church is not the wider culture in general, but patriarchy in particular. The third position defines the church in terms of obedience to the church's confessional tradition. The inheritance of the past preserves truths about God and world that call us to repentance and a new way of life.

These three positions need not be mutually exclusive. In the church today, they frequently overlap and combine. Nonetheless, it is useful to highlight their distinctive features for the sake of contrast and comparison.

Hauerwas offers a compelling development of the first approach. Deeply influenced by Anabaptist and other peace churches that have understood the gospel as a call to radical nonviolence, Hauerwas argues that the Christian community should engage in distinctive practices that embody

Christ's way of reconciliation, peace, and peacemaking. What matters is not an intellectual mastery of biblical texts, but a living out of Christian discipleship, participation in the living Christ. Especially in the eucharist "we learn of God's unrelenting desire to be reconciled to us, thus making it possible for us to be a community of peace in a violent world."[6]

At the same time, these practices teach us to turn to Scripture in the expectation that God speaks to us through Scripture. The Bible illustrates the kind of community that God calls us to be. When we hear Scripture rightly, it helps us to remember who God really is and who we really are. Rather than giving us a truth to defend, it issues us a challenge to live more faithfully. The Sermon on the Mount is not a collection of laws but "a description of the virtues of a community that embodies the peace that Christ has made possible among those who have been baptized into his death and resurrection."[7] Similarly, apocalyptic texts of the impending end of the world are not blueprints of the course of history. Rather, they remind us that God's purposes will ultimately triumph, enabling us to become a community of forgiveness, even when the way of forgiveness rather than resistance may mean our death.[8]

Such an interpretive framework helps us to sort out Scripture theologically. It provides a means for weighing the value of different passages, and for interpreting problematic ones. Those portions that represent a radical call to discipleship, such as the Sermon on the Mount, come to the fore. Other portions, such as New Testament diatribes against the Jews, remind us that Christians have sometimes appealed to Scripture in ways that violate this discipleship.

Whether one agrees entirely with Hauerwas or not, the point is clear: For many Christians today, the church is about discipleship. They define faith in terms of a way of life that follows from the example of Jesus, and that flows out of the power of the living, resurrected Christ. For such people, Scripture is not to be read literally. Nor is every part equally useful. But the Bible does help to illustrate this way of discipleship, and to make it vivid, concrete, and real.

Elizabeth Johnson, a Roman Catholic feminist theologian, offers a particularly compelling example of the second position. For Johnson, the essential character of the Christian community is best described in terms of mutual respect, reciprocal valuing of each other's lives, and sharing in solidarity with the dispossessed. This understanding of Christian community has emerged out of women's discovery of God in their own experience. The flourishing of women has become an essential precondition for the flourishing of all creatures in their diversity.

7

Johnson believes that the classical Christian tradition is coherent with these feminist concerns. Christianity does not provide the only language, nor even the best language necessarily, for expressing these concerns. On the contrary, because every religious tradition speaks to the mystery of the divine that we experience in the mystery of our own being, we must be open to insights from a variety of sources. But Christian language, if not absolute, is nonetheless "apt" (to use Johnson's term) for articulating feminist concerns. It provides symbolic depth to these concerns and helps to shape an alternative order to patriarchy.[9]

These theological commitments shape a way of reading Scripture. Johnson believes that the historical-critical method, guided by feminist concerns, can purify Scripture of its tendencies to value men more than women. The historical-critical method allows us to reconstruct the founding experiences of the Jewish and Christian communities. What emerges is a compelling, transforming picture of the liberating God of Israel and Jesus, whom women have already experienced for themselves through their participation in communities committed to the radical equality of men and women.

From this perspective, biblical passages that affirm the value of women (such as such Genesis 1 and Galatians 3) are of central importance.[10] Biblical symbols that provide emancipatory language for God and humans emerge with new clarity: Shekinah (a Hebrew term with female resonance, referring to the God who dwells within and among us), Wisdom, Mother, Spirit. These symbols complement and rub up against more traditional ways of thinking about God, break open our language about God, and point to the mystery of God. This biblical affirmation of diverse symbols for God is a safeguard against monolithic ideologies that would make one way of thinking about God absolutely "right," and that would claim God for a human agenda that justifies one group's oppression of another.[11]

Again, one need not agree entirely with Johnson to acknowledge that she has put her finger on the pulse of a significant part of the church today. For this part of the church, we best come to the Scriptures through human experience, not the Christian tradition. Only the experience of God's liberating power in our own lives will enable us to interpret Scripture rightly, such that Scripture affirms and deepens our experience, rather than justifying oppressive structures in church and society. If for the first part of the church, Scripture illustrates a way of life, this second part of the church sees Scripture as an important resource, though only one among many, for symbolizing the mystery of God, whom we encounter in every moment of life.

David Wells, an evangelical Protestant theologian, represents the third position. At first glance, Wells appears to offer a sharp contrast to either Hauerwas or Johnson. Wells calls for a rediscovery of the God who speaks in Scripture. He seems not to envision a particular form of Christian community that must first be recovered if we are to read Scripture rightly, but to insist that Scripture alone can tell us the truth about God and ourselves. Scripture is an external authority. It provides us objective truth about God's intrusion into history and offers us authoritative interpretation of that truth.[12]

Yet, Wells makes his case not in the abstract nor to a universal audience. He is speaking to the church, and to a church that in his view has lost its bearings. Wells argues that the church must rediscover its doctrinal heritage. The church's classic confessions and creeds distill Scripture's objective truth, thereby making it possible for us to read Scripture rightly.[13] Such a church will learn that to go to Scripture is to open itself to the God whose ways are not ours. This church will approach the Bible not as a mere historical record nor as a list of rules, but as a living witness to the God who confronts us in holiness.

Like Hauerwas and Johnson, Wells captures the feeling of a major part of the church today. For these people, the future of the church depends on its ability to return to basic theological and ethical truths for which our forbears fought. These truths of the Christian tradition are a priceless heritage that we threaten to play away, unless we immerse ourselves in them, teach them to our children, and stand by them in the midst of social and cultural change. These truths enable us to read Scripture as a witness to the living God who claims our lives for his purposes.

In sum, all three positions, despite their differences, affirm that we have to be a certain kind of community if we are to read Scripture rightly. Whether grounded in practices of nonviolence, or in a commitment to mutuality, or in doctrines about the nature of God and truth, the shape of the community— its character—determines the way in which it will read Scripture.

When such priority is given to the community, however, I believe that Scripture begins to lose its edge as a critical principle. The community too easily finds in Scripture confirmation of what it already takes itself to be. We succumb to the danger of simply reading the interests of our part of the church into Scripture. But then it is no longer clear why we need Scripture in the first place. We have already made up our minds who we are.

To be sure, none of the theologians to whom we have just turned would draw this conclusion. Each believes that the Scriptures are critically necessary to the life of the community. For Hauerwas, Scripture is constantly reminding us that God's way of peace and forgiveness will triumph over a world of violence and vengeance. For Johnson, Scripture (in particular, its powerful symbols of God) helps to translate feminist concerns into lived reality. For Wells, Scripture confronts us with the reality of a holy God who acts in human history. In each case, Scripture illustrates, prods, stirs, and corrects. It is more than a sentimental idea whose power we rob to justify our own agenda.

Hauerwas, Johnson, and Wells would seem to agree with theologians Stephen Fowl and Gregory Jones, who have eloquently argued that the church best demonstrates its faith and faithfulness in its readiness to open itself to Scripture's correction. Because hospitality is key to the Christian community, the church will want to listen to outsiders, who can help it to live more faithfully. When, in contrast, "distortions of character enter and deeply permeate the life of any Christian community, that community loses its ability to read Scripture in ways that would challenge and correct its character."[14]

Nonetheless, it is still the case that community takes priority over Scripture in the three positions that we have examined. It does not seem possible that the Scriptures could ever call radically into question Hauerwas's vision of community, or Johnson's, or Wells's. In each case, particular theological commitments result in their playing up certain parts of Scripture only to play down, even to dismiss, other parts. Hauerwas has no place for the warrior God; Johnson, for the patriarchal God; Wells, for the God who is too often absent from human history.

Each of these three visions of Christian community claims to be faithful to God's plans and purposes. Yet, none wrestles seriously with the fact of the other. We are simply left with diverse communities with diverse ways of interpreting Scripture. We seem to have no way to choose between them, except to consult our own conscience and experience.

THE COMMUNITY IN CONFLICT

Scripture is the church's book. But it turns out that there are different ways of thinking about the church. The situation that we find when we compare Hauerwas, Johnson, and Wells is more than academic, more than a debate among professors. It seems to describe our experience of a church that is divided and frequently in conflict. Again and again, we find that we belong to different communities of interpretation that read the same biblical passages in fundamentally different ways.

These differences relate both to belief and to practice. In recent years, the issue of greatest contention in mainline Protestant denominations has been ordination of homosexual persons. Those who oppose ordination of gay and lesbian persons argue that Scripture consistently rejects homosexual practice as a distortion of God's intentions. Those who support ordination of gay and lesbian persons argue that the Bible's views on homosexuality are historically and culturally conditioned, like its views on women and slaves.

I have been to more than one denominational meeting in which the two sides have trotted out their biblical experts to explain the "real meaning" of the passages in question. Under these circumstances, debate is truly interminable. Each side accuses the other of using Scripture to support a position that it has already taken on other grounds. Those who support ordination of gay and lesbian persons are said to subordinate Scripture to reason or experience. Their opponents accuse them of revising Scripture in light of contemporary historical and cultural circumstances. Those who oppose ordination of gay and lesbian persons are said to equate Scripture with traditional positions that are themselves historically and culturally conditioned and no longer applicable to the present. They claim that Scripture is revealed truth, but people on the other side of the ordination issue accuse them of reducing Scripture to a dead letter.

While issues of practice are often the lightning rod for debate, differences of belief are also present. One of the most contentious issues has been Christology. Much of the recent scholarship in search of the historical Jesus (such as the Jesus Seminar) has challenged traditional notions of Jesus as the Son of God. Some feminist theologians have dismissed traditional doctrines of the atonement, arguing that Jesus was killed because he challenged an oppressive religious and political system, not because his death was part of God's plan to reconcile humans to God and each other. Awareness of the vitality of other religions has raised questions about what makes Jesus distinctive and whether there are other ways to salvation. In each case, different interpretive communities with different theological commitments read the biblical texts in profoundly different ways, sorting out the wheat from the chaff.

Although these different communities all appeal to the authority of Scripture, one is frequently left with the impression that Scripture, in fact, doesn't matter all that much. It appears that one really can get whatever one wants out of the Bible. We've heard many times, "Even the devil quotes Scripture." The crisis in the church's use of Scripture inevitably suggests that the church itself is in crisis. The church apparently has no commonly held sense of the faith by which to sort out legitimate from illegitimate readings of Scripture. Rather, it seems that the church is merely composed of different groups with different political interests.

This situation is not new. Christians have always proposed different, even conflicting, readings of Scripture. Certain kinds of diversity can even be welcomed. Different readings of Scripture may emerge as Christians seek to embody the faith in different historical and cultural circumstances. Different readings of Scripture may also emerge as the church in one time and place seeks to test what ways of life in community best build up the church as the body of Christ.

The fact of different readings of Scripture becomes a problem when Christians do not experience a basic unity in Christ and a basic sense of a shared faith, a malaise that in recent years has particularly afflicted the Protestant mainline. The drumbeat of a steady flow of analyses and critiques has been the contention that these denominations' declining numbers and influence reflect issues of theology, not simply demographics or marketing.[15] The mainline churches have accommodated themselves to a secular, therapeutic culture. They have lost any distinctive identity grounded in the beliefs and practices of the Christian tradition. The culture wars are being fought from within, as different wings of the church struggle to redefine the church for their own purposes.

As theologian George Lindbeck has argued, today "there seems to be less and less communal sense of what is or is not Christian."[16] There is not even a "generally intelligible and distinctively Christian language within which disagreements can be expressed and issues debated."[17] In a time of an enfeebled *sensus fidelium* (referring to a sense of the *faith,* a sense among *those* who are faithful, and a sense of *what* is faithful), different readings of Scripture further enervate the church and undermine its authority. In such a time, different readings of Scripture also have the effect of undermining the authority of Scripture itself. If Scripture can be enlisted for any number of different causes, it is unclear why one should bother with it at all.

THE REFORMATION TENSION

Another way into these issues is to examine a tension that emerges from the Reformation understanding of Scripture. Textbook summaries of church history frequently contrast Protestant and Catholic approaches to Scripture. The Reformers insisted on *sola scriptura,* while their Catholic opponents insisted that the church had faithfully received and transmitted an oral tradition that was of equal authority. On closer examination, however, one finds that the Reformers, while dismissing an independent oral tradition, did not dismiss tradition. Next to *sola scriptura* stood the principle that the historical church alone could interpret Scripture.

On the one hand, the Reformers believed that Scripture imposed itself on the church. It stood over the church; it judged the church. None of the church's traditions or interpretations, however ancient or precious, could take precedence over the plain meaning of the text. But the authority of Scripture was not primarily an abstract theological point. Rather, it was a matter of lived piety. As the Reformers and their followers read Scripture, they found it to speak with immediacy and clarity. They did not hear a whir of confusing, conflicting voices, but a word of truth that ordered and judged all other voices. Its authority was self-authenticating. Like Augustine, they heard a voice that said, "Take, read," and when they did, they believed that they heard God himself speaking.[18]

A friend of mine tells of growing up in a family that never went to church or read the Bible. In his late teens, he picked up a Bible and leafed through it. As he began reading the book of Revelation, he found that he could not put it down. Soon he was reading other parts of the Bible. The book as a whole began to reshape his life. He became active in a church and was eventually called into the ministry. Scripture imposed itself on him. It claimed him.

So, it seems, the Reformers thought. If only they could get Scripture into the hands of the people, the people would hear God's Word. The Reformers therefore insisted on translating the Bible into the language of the people, and on educating them, so that the people could read the Bible for themselves.

On the other hand, the Reformers believed that one would only interpret Scripture properly if one was guided by an authoritative theological tradition nurtured by a faithful church. In the words of the Second Helvetic Confession, Scripture had to be interpreted according to the church's "rule of faith and love."[19] The Bible could not simply be left in the hands of the people. There needed to be pastors who were authoritative teachers, who knew the original languages and were able to interpret Scripture theologically. In the end, Scripture did not simply stand over the church; it had to be read in the context of the community, its worship, and its teaching authority.

As one of my seminary professors used to say, Calvin's understanding of the authority of Scripture in Book I of the Institutes ("The Knowledge of God the Creator," where Calvin treats the question of revelation) is incomplete without his understanding of the church in Book IV ("The

External Means or Aids by which God Invites Us into the Society of Christ and Holds Us Therein"). Scripture does not simply interpret itself; rather, it is the Holy Spirit working in the church that opens Scripture to our understanding.

The Westminster Confession of Faith makes a similar point:

> We may be moved and induced by the testimony of the Church to an high and reverent esteem for the Holy Scripture; the heavenliness of the matter, the efficacy of the doctrine, the majesty of the style, the consent of the parts, the scope of the whole (which is to give all glory to God), the full discovery it makes of the only way of man's salvation, the many other incomparable excellencies, and the entire perfection thereof, are arguments whereby it doth abundantly evidence itself to be the Word of God; yet, notwithstanding, our full persuasion and assurance of the infallible truth and divine authority thereof, is from the inward work of the Holy Spirit, bearing witness by and with the Word in our hearts.[20]

Without the leading of the Spirit, we cannot understand Scripture rightly. We may read it, know it backwards and forwards, even memorize it, but biblical literacy by itself proves nothing. An ability to recite names and dates, to give story lines and character biographies, is not the same as hearing Scripture as God's Word. The Spirit who guided the authors of Scripture must guide those of us who would interpret Scripture.

But the Spirit that opens the meaning of Scripture to us is also the Spirit that binds us to Jesus Christ and to one another. The Spirit is above all the animating principle of the church in its life as the body of Christ. To live in the Spirit is to live in Christian community, building up the body with one's own gifts and receiving the gifts of others. Through the Spirit, Scripture belongs to the community of faith.

As some contemporary theologians have put it, the best evidence for the authority of Scripture is the existence of a church whose life is shaped by the reading of Scripture.[21] Recovery of the authority of Scripture is, then, not primarily a matter of how to develop a better and "higher" doctrine of Scripture but of how to use Scripture more fully and persuasively in the church's life and worship. The authority of Scripture can only be established to the degree that the community uses it as though it were in fact authoritative. The point that contemporary theologians keep making—that Scripture is the *church's* book—has roots in this Reformation understanding of Word and Spirit.

But, again, what happens to Scripture when the church is in crisis, with different parts of the church reading Scripture in different ways? If we believe that the Holy Spirit binds the body of Christ together, what happens when Christ and his body appear to be divided? How can Scripture speak with compelling power if it can be used to justify contradictory understandings of faith and practice?

If we overemphasize Scripture's self-authenticating character, we may fail to recognize that we inevitably bring certain assumptions to the act of interpretation. We will too easily make the interpretation of Scripture a private matter, assuming that we know what it really means; too easily claim that Scripture's position on one controversial issue or another is self-evident and therefore beyond debate. If we overemphasize the idea that Scripture is the church's book, we will run into similar problems. We too casily end up using Scripture for our own purposes. We lose the sense that Scripture may prove us wrong, and that it may require us to change our minds. We may then find ourselves stuck, unable to make sense of the messy reality, namely, that different communities interpret Scripture in different, competing, and even contradictory ways.

SCRIPTURE AS THE WORD OF GOD

As Lutheran theologian Carl Braaten notes, "When people cease to believe in the church, they will soon cease to believe in the church's Book. . . . For the Bible by itself . . . can be invoked to support a multiplicity of confessions."[22] Braaten concludes that the recovery of the authority of Scripture is unlikely until "the divided churches resolve their differences into a larger unity of the church."[23]

I would like to propose that the converse is equally true. It may be necessary to recover a sense of the authority of Scripture if the church is to recover a sense of the church's unity, and of the church's rightful authority.[24] For this reason, I believe that it is necessary but not sufficient to think of Scripture as the church's book. The authority of Scripture cannot depend solely on whether the church commands authority. The authority of the church also depends to some degree on whether Scripture commands authority.

The Reformers sometimes gave too much emphasis to Scripture's self-authenticating character, and too little to Scripture's authority as the church's book, because they believed they needed to defend Scripture from a Catholic Church all too confident about the church's authority. The Scots Confession could therefore insist that "those who say the Scriptures have no other authority save that which they have received from the Kirk are blasphemous against God and injurious to the true Kirk, which always hears and obeys the voice of her own Spouse and Pastor, but takes not upon her to be mistress over the same."[25]

Similarly, in a time in which we are all too aware of the church's divisions and crisis of faith, we need to recover a confidence that Scripture has a life beyond us—that it retains a capacity to break forth with new power, and to stir the church to new life. We need to recover a sense of awe and reverence before Scripture, a sense that it is strange to us and not under our control, and yet that it exercises a claim on us.

As the Jewish biblical scholar Franz Rosenzweig once wrote, "The voice of the Bible is not to be enclosed . . . in the inner sanctum of a church . . . Rather, this voice seeks again and again to resound from outside . . . as a foreign and unfamiliar sound."[26] Together with Martin Buber, Rosenzweig worked on a translation of the Bible that he hoped might again open readers to the voice of God, even in a time in which belief had become difficult if not impossible. Buber and Rosenzweig believed that Scripture was written in such a way that a reader with the right key to reading it could be confronted with its power and not escape its claim on his or her life.

More recently, another Jewish biblical scholar, Jon Levenson, has argued that historical criticism can in fact contribute to this necessary discovery of Scripture's "otherness." Historical-critical methods have the result of playing up the contradictions in the text. We see things in the text that don't fit the interpretive framework that we normally employ. Historical-critical work can remind us that the text is not simply there to confirm what we already claim to know about God and God's ways.[27] As Rosenzweig and Buber might hope, historical-critical tools at their best help us to hear Scripture in its own voice—not to strip it of its power, but to provide for the possibility of a genuine encounter between God and God's people.[28]

We cannot come to Scripture without an interpretive framework shaped by the commitments and traditions of particular communities. But we can become more aware of, and more open to, the ways in which the Scriptures never wholly fit our schemes. In actually reading the Bible, we may find ourselves having to revise the assumptions that we brought with us. Scripture is the church's book, but it is above all the Word of God for which we must ever listen anew.

A Piety of the Word

We have a tendency in the church today simply to assume that Scripture matters. It is not an unreasonable assumption. Scripture is the church's book not only in theory but in fact. Christian communities continue to use Scripture in worship, to insist on the importance of Bible study, and even to put Scripture into the hands of third graders! Every Christian community implicitly feels the need to justify its theology and ethics by Scripture. The relation of the church and Scripture is so close that one could almost say that to be the church is to have the Bible.

When we simply assume that Scripture matters, it seems as though the problem is not so much the authority of Scripture but the interpretation of Scripture. Scripture matters—the question is how. The key questions seem to focus on our hermeneutics, that is, our methods of interpretation. How will we draw on the Bible to think of God, or to address issues of sexuality or politics or economics? Which parts of Scripture will we select to make our case? How will we relate the divergent voices that we encounter in the Bible? How will we relate these voices to the dictates of reason, and to experience?

Every year, dozens of new books claim to have found a hermeneutical key that will unlock the true meaning of Scripture. They debate the central themes of Scripture, the meaning of particular texts, and the right way to relate Scripture to the Christian life today. Similarly, preachers throughout the country step into their pulpits Sunday after Sunday and explicate Scripture in the confidence that it speaks to us and has the capacity to reshape our lives. Few theologians or preachers feel as though they have to establish the authority of Scripture before they begin to interpret it.

But it is precisely this assumption that, I believe, requires reexamination. When the church simply assumes that Scripture matters, the church too often ends up using Scripture for its own purposes. This problem is exacerbated in a time in which theological and ethical divisions among Christians are sometimes deep. We are all too tempted to run to Scripture to justify our own points of view, our own personal and communal biases, our own causes. We too often appeal to Scripture's authority in an effort to enhance our own authority. The result is that we empty Scripture of its power. We are left with little more than sentimental fantasies about the Bible. In polite company, we continue to say all the right things about the Scriptures—about their majesty and ultimacy and authority—but deep within we grow increasingly skeptical that they truly have a Word of God for us.

Under these circumstances, we cannot simply assume that Scripture matters. Rather, we must become much more intentional about opening ourselves to Scripture, so that we may receive it as God's Word, a Word that is not under human control, a Word that offers us grace and judgment, surprise and dismay, hope and terror. We must become much more intentional about resisting the temptation to wield Scripture simply as a weapon—to lift it up and wave it at our opponents—and more intentional about learning instead how to open Scripture as we would a good gift, standing before it together and in anticipation of hearing God's voice. We must cultivate a piety of the Word that respects Scripture more as a source of life than as a set of right answers to be applied to whatever problem we choose.

Scripture matters. That very assertion invites us to reflect on what makes Scripture *Scripture*, and to develop disciplines of reading Scripture as the Word of God.

2

WHATEVER HAPPENED TO THE COMPELLING POWER OF SCRIPTURE?

Fifty years after the fall of Jerusalem, Cyrus, the king of Babylon, allowed a group of exiles to return to Judah. The books of Ezra and Nehemiah record the efforts of the people to rebuild the temple and the walls of Jerusalem. In a dramatic moment, the people gather in a city square and ask Ezra, the priest, to read the book of the law of Moses. From morning to midday, Ezra reads, as others interpret. As the words sink in, the people weep (Neh. 8:9).

This incident parallels the reading of the book of the law in the time of Josiah, nearly a hundred years earlier. Josiah, the last of the righteous kings of Judah, is determined to restore the temple to its former glory. Hilkiah, the priest, rummages through the temple treasury and comes across the long-lost book of the law of Moses. When Josiah hears its words, he tears his clothes, "for the wrath of the Lord that is poured out on us is great, because our ancestors did not keep the word of the Lord" (2 Chron. 34:21).

The renewal of the community of faith has always been linked to the rediscovery of Scripture. It was an encounter with Scripture that decisively influenced Augustine, Martin Luther, and John Wesley, and the movements they led. More recently, new ways of reading Scripture have impelled the development of liberationist and feminist theologies and communities. As Scripture has spoken with new power, as Christians have found their story in Scripture's, Scripture has set forth God's Word, a Word that the community could not avoid, but that brought it new life.

Scripture has also been a source of personal renewal, as depicted with particular power in Fyodor Dostoyevsky's writings. In *The Brothers Karamazov*, for example, a distressed and anguished Alyosha nearly reaches a breaking point. With the death of Father Zossima, his father in the faith, and the scandal relating to the quick corruption of his body, Alyosha begins to question God and God's ways. In exhaustion, he falls to the ground. Out of nowhere, he dreams of Jesus and the wedding at Cana, and suddenly experiences release. He understands that he too, even with all his doubts, has a place at the banquet table, that the whole of creation is invited into the kingdom.[1]

Historically and personally, Scripture matters. It has compelling power. It reshapes people's lives. It is nothing less than the Word of God. But the fact that God's people have constantly needed to rediscover Scripture's power reminds us that they have also lived through times in which "the word of the Lord was rare" (1 Sam. 3:1). Scripture spoke with power to Josiah and Ezra, but only after the people of Israel had lost and ignored it for generations. Scripture spoke with power to the Reformers, but only after years of neglect.

G. G. Coulton, an English historian, wrote earlier this century of the sorry state of affairs in the Middle Ages. Clergy and laity alike had a low level of education. Many peasants could not even recite the Lord's Prayer or the Creed. The only part of worship in the vernacular was the sermon, and often the people either could not hear it or paid no attention to it. What was known of Scripture was distorted by the survival of pagan beliefs and practices. Coulton observes that "it was only heretics who possessed anything beyond the merest smatterings of Bible knowledge."[2]

Despite the rediscovery of Scripture in the Reformation, a church that insists on "Scripture alone" can also lose touch with Scripture as a living word. In the twentieth century, German theologian Dietrich Bonhoeffer wrote of a church whose language about God had become tired and impotent. Until the day "when men will once more be called so to utter the word of God that the world will be changed and renewed by it . . . the Christian cause will be a silent and hidden affair."[3] While not speaking directly of Scripture, his comments apply equally well to a church in which Scripture has become tired and impotent.

A number of years ago, biblical scholar James Smart wrote of "the strange silence of the Bible in the church."[4] In a similar vein, another biblical scholar, James Sanders, has recently suggested that Scripture is in exile. It no longer seems to speak with compelling power to the church.[5]

OUR AMBIVALENCE ABOUT SCRIPTURE

Nonetheless, even a church in crisis cannot escape Scripture entirely. As George Lindbeck has noted, Christian communities continue to assert the primacy of Scripture, despite all the divisions and disagreements between and within them that seem to undermine its authority. Even as Christians appeal to reason and experience, they still feel compelled to demonstrate that they make decisions in accord with Scripture.[6] Even if we cannot always say why, we act as though Scripture matters.

But our attitude toward Scripture is deeply ambivalent. On the one hand, we long to experience Scripture's compelling power. We want to be like an excited little boy reading the Bible under the covers at night. We long to attend worship where Scripture comes alive and cuts us to the quick. We hope to pick up our Bibles and hear God's Word.

On the other hand, we often find ourselves disappointed with Scripture, and with ourselves. Even though we want Scripture to matter, too often it does not. We resolve to plumb the depths of Scripture but seem, inevitably, to lack the patience and discipline. We claim that Scripture is our book, but too often conclude that it belongs to another time and place.

This ambivalence evidences itself in the everyday life of the church. A pastor tells of his first years of ministry in the hills of eastern Tennessee. His parishioners were people of humble origins and means, mostly uneducated, yet vibrant in faith. One Sunday afternoon, he decided to go calling. As he entered the first house in the hollow, he was warmly welcomed. The man and woman of the house invited him to sit at a table on which a beautiful, huge, family Bible lay. It was obviously well used and deeply treasured. When the pastor called on the next house, he was again astonished to find a large, beautiful Bible. Indeed, it struck him that it looked suspiciously like the one that he had seen in the first house. As he made his way to the next house, he noticed a young boy hiding behind the trees in back of the houses and running ahead of him with that Bible under his arm.[7]

We too honor the Bible. We too lay it out on the coffee table in the living room. Its expensive leather covers and fine, gold-edged paper remind us that it is a precious treasure. But too often the Bible functions as an empty icon. We revere it as a sacred object more than we open it, study it, and receive it as God's Word to us.

When I was a pastor, I would gather a group of members every year to brainstorm ideas for the adult education program. Most of the participants regularly attended Sunday school or a small group. They were among the most creative and intellectually alert members of the congregation. Inevitably, they ranked Bible study as the most important priority for the new year, and inevitably Bible study, when offered, attracted the fewest participants.

Even the use of Scripture in worship reflects our ambivalence about it. Ministers step into the pulpit and faithfully intone the chapter and verse of the passage from which they are about to read. Too frequently, it is the first time that week that they have read the passage aloud. With greater or lesser feeling and facility, they make their way through the passage, rarely looking up. If they did, they might see their listeners' eyes slowly glazing over.

Such observations suggest that much of the Bible is strange to us. Its message and meaning are hard to unravel; its names and places, hard to pronounce. "The Word of the Lord," declares the minister, as he or she concludes the reading and lifts up the book of Scripture. "Thanks be to God," responds the congregation, too often not having followed the reading. One can almost hear an audible sigh of relief as the book is closed and the minister launches into the sermon.

A Time of Biblical Illiteracy

We claim to honor Scripture, yet we ignore it. We call it the Word of God, yet we proof-text it to our own ends. We want it to grasp us and to draw us into the presence of God, yet we fear that it is nothing more than a human document, replete with all the biases and limitations of people like ourselves.

Given this ambivalence, it is not surprising that many Christians don't bother with Scripture anymore. Even if they continue to report that Scripture is authoritative, they do not read it with regularity or know its basic contents. The evidence that one really can get whatever one wants out of the Bible seems to render it an all too human document.

Jokes about biblical illiteracy abound. When a recent survey asked participants the name of Noah's wife, 10 percent answered, "Joan of Arc."[8] Even if one hesitates to draw a general principle from this one example, it nonetheless illustrates a truth that no minister, and no teacher of theology or Bible in a seminary, can avoid. One can assume little to no biblical knowledge of one's parishioners or students, even when they have grown up in the church.

It is not primarily a matter of obscure details, such as the name of Noah's wife (which Scripture does not even provide!), but of basic names, events, and concepts. As a young pastor, I asked a Sunday school class, "Who led the people of Israel across the Red Sea?" After an awkward pause, someone finally piped up, "Joshua," and I was glad that they were close, even if not right.

In recent years, controversial issues have sometimes driven the church back to Scripture, yet in a way that has not helped the church recover Scripture. It is ironic that the church has expended so much energy on a few isolated passages of the Bible traditionally understood as referring to homosexuality when too much of the church does not even know the basic biblical narrative.

This situation parallels the "practical atheism" that some observers note in Western societies. Large majorities of people continue to report that they believe in God, yet it is not clear that this belief makes any difference for the way they live their lives. Even if one argues that religion is making a comeback and that theories of secular society are overblown, one still has to acknowledge that much of this rediscovery of a religious dimension to life assumes forms that are highly private and eclectic. It seems safe to say that Christian language rooted in Scripture no longer offers North American society a common vocabulary. Even in the church, biblical language has too often been replaced by therapeutic categories. Much preaching, praying, and even singing focuses on the self, its struggles, its wounds, and its longings for healing and self-realization.

In a time of biblical illiteracy, Scripture has become little more than a sentimental idea, a vague hope for something secure, unchanging, and right. The existence of the book seems to be reassuring, even if we end up consulting it neither too often nor too closely. People will defend the Bible's authority, and in a time of personal or communal crisis will even appeal to Scripture with great passion. But they manage to live their everyday lives with little or no reference to it.

How We Actually Use Scripture

The question, then, is not simply whether people believe in the authority of Scripture, but whether Scripture is a part of their lives, a compelling force that shapes their way of looking at the world. How people actually use the Bible is a better indicator of its authority in their lives than their adherence to the idea of biblical authority. Moreover, the question is not simply how often they read Scripture, but how they hear and read it—which passages, in what context, in what way.

While little hard evidence is available, recent surveys of ministers and members of the Presbyterian Church (U.S.A.) may be representative of the situation in the Protestant mainline. When one inquires about biblical authority, Presbyterians as a whole insist "that the Bible has a central and ultimately decisive place in the ongoing life of the church and the whole Christian community. [When surveyed, Presbyterians are] almost unanimous in asserting the divine inspiration of the Bible."[9] For most Presbyterians, the issue is not whether Scripture is divinely inspired, but how to relate the divine and authoritative aspects of Scripture to the "clearly human and fallible elements . . . in the text."[10]

When surveyed, only 4 percent of Presbyterians agree with the statement that "the Bible is merely a record of the moral and religious experiences of Hebrews and Christians." At the other extreme, the statement that the Bible is "without error in all it teaches in matters of science and history, as well as in matters of theology" attracts only 14 percent. Most Presbyterians are somewhere in the middle. Forty-eight percent agree with the statement that "all of the Bible is both the inspired Word of God and at the same time a thoroughly human document." Twenty-three percent emphasize the divine elements, even at the risk of slighting the human. For them, Scripture "is trustworthy in all it teaches in matters of theology and ethics, but not necessarily in matters of science and history." A smaller percentage (11 percent) lean the other way. For them, "portions of the Bible, including some of its theological and ethical positions, may not be the inspired Word of God."[11]

A report to the church's General Assembly concluded that this "clear recognition . . . of the Bible as the unique authority in the life of the church should lead to greater use of the Bible in discussion and debate."[12] Yet, other surveys suggest that Presbyterians are better at asserting the authority of Scripture than at actually opening the Bible.

Most Presbyterians read the Bible, but few read it regularly. Fifty-eight percent of church members (that is, not officers or pastors) reported that they read Scripture at least once in the week prior to the survey, but only 38 percent regularly read Scripture at least once a week.[13] Twelve percent reported they never read Scripture.

At only one point does frequency of Bible reading clearly correspond to members' understanding of biblical authority. Of those who believe that the Bible is infallible, 35 percent read Scripture daily, as compared to 10 percent of those who do not believe the Bible is infallible. Of those who believe in infallibility, only 5 percent do not read Scripture at all, as compared to 20 percent of those who do not believe in infallibility. The causal factor, however, is unclear. Does belief in infallibility cause people to read Scripture more often, or do people who read Scripture more often find themselves more likely to affirm its infallibility?

When Presbyterians do read the Bible, they usually read it by themselves. Only 32 percent participate in a Bible study group that meets at least once a month. Of those who share a household with at least one other family member, only 11 percent have a regular time set aside for Bible reading or study. Even among pastors, a discipline of regular family devotions has largely been lost. Only 18 percent of pastors in a shared household have a regular time set aside for Bible reading with at least one other family member.

While Presbyterians use a wide variety of methods for reading Scripture, including lectionaries, devotional guides, and reading through an entire book of the Bible at a time, they most often make their selections randomly. Eighty percent of Presbyterians regularly open the Bible and browse through it until something catches their eye.

The preferred translation of church members is the King James Version (28 percent), but the Revised Standard Version/New Revised Standard Version (24 percent) and the *New International Version* (19 percent) are also widely used. These preferences correspond to generational differences. Presbyterians over forty prefer the King James Version (up to 37 percent); under forty, the *New International Version* (34 percent).

At the same time, more than two-thirds of pastors prefer the Revised Standard Version or the New Revised Standard Version. Thus, ministers and members tend to use different translations of the Bible. The translation that members most likely hear in Sunday morning worship is not the one that they are most apt to read for their own study or devotions.

The gap between members and ministers is even greater in response to the question of how often the minister bases his or her sermon on the text (or texts) that have been read in worship. Forty-three percent of members say, "every Sunday," as compared to 82 percent of ministers. Even if one changes the question to "nearly every Sunday," one still finds a significant gap. Seventy-five percent of members say their minister preaches every Sunday or nearly every Sunday on the Scriptures; 97 percent of ministers claim to do so.

These statistics are suggestive in several ways. They indicate the issue before the church is not only infrequent reading of Scripture, but the way in which Scripture is read and heard. When members read Scripture on their own, they tend to read it silently and by themselves, and thus in the same way they treat a newspaper, an office memo, or a paperback novel. They lack disciplines or practices that would train them to read Scripture as a Word of God whose character is different than the other kinds of materials that they encounter daily.

The frequency with which Scripture is read by random selection suggests that it is often read in snippets and quickly, as people squeeze Scripture reading into a busy, overcrowded day. Again, they read the Bible as though they were reading a newspaper. They browse about, looking for interesting headlines. Scripture is not ignored, but it is read through eyes trained by a modern, information society.

The fact, however, that many Presbyterians do not read Scripture regularly also reminds us that worship may be the primary place in which they receive Scripture. Most church members may become familiar with the basic narratives and concepts of Scripture not through private or family devotions, not through Sunday school or small group discussions, not through focused study or formal instruction, but as they sing hymns, pray prayers, and listen to the reading and, especially, the preaching of Scripture.

Worship offers a powerful alternative to habits of reading Scripture silently and randomly. In worship, people receive Scripture through their ears, rather than their eyes. They encounter the Bible in a way quite different from other texts, such as the newspaper.

Presbyterian churches, however, do not always effectively realize the capacity of worship to convey the power of Scripture as the Word of God. The fact that many members are not sure of the connection between the morning's Scripture texts and the sermon suggests that worship only partially succeeds in deepening people's familiarity with Scripture. The lack of a common translation may also work against a deeper appropriation of Scripture, for people become most familiar with Scripture when they hear the same phrases and words over and over.

All this evidence is at best suggestive, and further research would be required to determine whether the Presbyterian experience is applicable to other mainline denominations. Nonetheless, the issues for further investigation are clear. It may be that mainline Protestants, while honoring and revering Scripture, do not necessarily experience it as having compelling power. Scripture may remain central to the church's life, but it appears that many people have difficulty getting into the Bible, reading it, and understanding it.

Perhaps influenced by intellectual currents of the wider culture, mainline Protestants are not apt to assert the infallibility of the Bible. While it is not clear that this attitude has directly undermined their experience of Scripture's compelling power, this attitude may reflect a growing assumption that Scripture is to be read like any other text: as a collection of information. While such a text is undoubtedly of value, it is not clearly a living Word of God that transforms people's lives.

The Loss of Transcendence

In order to account for the crisis of Scripture in the modern world, we may find ourselves asking what makes Scripture *Scripture* in the first place.

In a recent book, W. C. Smith, a prominent historian of world religions, adopts an historical, comparative approach to these questions. Examining the role that sacred writings have played in the world's great religions, he argues that Scripture is more a phenomenon than an object. Scripture is not simply a collection of texts. Rather, texts become Scripture to the degree that a community finds them to mediate an encounter with the transcendent. As Smith puts it:

> Peoples have found their scriptures . . . supremely good. For indeed those involved, *engagés,* have consistently reported that their scriptures—and this is indeed those scriptures' *raison d'être*—open up a window, or constitute that window, to a world of ultimate reality and truth and goodness. Over against the mundane world of sorrow, of self-interest and its loneliness, of injustice and failure, scriptures have played a role of enabling human beings to be aware of and indeed to live in relation to the other dimension of reality that characterizes our humanity by being somehow near and within our life yet also somehow far from it. Theists have explained what has been going on in their engagement by saying that those scriptures are the word of God.[14]

Smith links the crisis of Scripture today with a loss of a sense of the transcendent. We live in a "de-transcendentalizing" world. We have little sense of transcendent ideals—that is, of ultimate principles or truths—that structure reality, make it comprehensible, and direct our behavior. As a result, Smith fears that

> modern secular culture is in danger of finding itself without a shared vocabulary to enable it corporately to live well, or even to think and talk about doing so, or its members to encourage each other to do so. The deficiency is hardly made up by the comic strips or sports pages, the commercialized television programmes, the cunning advertising presentations, that largely prevail as the common lore in society.[15]

Smith also links a loss of the transcendent with a loss of the poetic. When poetry and literature have mediated the highest ideals of human existence, they have become classics. At times, they have even assumed Scripture-like quality. In a de-transcendentalizing world, however, language loses its capacity to point beyond itself. Poetic language no longer conveys a vision of the good, the true, and the beautiful, but is reduced to language games.

These themes have been widely shared in contemporary philosophical analyses of the modern condition. Martin Heidegger, the great existentialist philosopher of the twentieth century, wrote that the gods had retreated from our world. He feared that technological ways of thinking had reduced the world to an object of human manipulation, and that humans had lost their capacity to experience awe and wonder at "being"—the fact that things are, have existence, and claim time and space, rather than not being. Heidegger strove to recover the power of the poetic to disclose alternative ways of experiencing the world. He believed that the poetic could open up a space for us to dwell thoughtfully and thankfully in the world before the mystery of our existence.[16]

More recently, British philosopher Charles Taylor has written of the emergence of the "objectifying self" in Western thought. Since Descartes, humans have thought of the world as an object that could be studied, dissected, and manipulated for human ends.[17] They have looked for meaning from within themselves, rather than in the world of nature and history.

For the "objectifying self," Scripture, like other texts, is an historical product. It can claim no special authority, no unique capacity to mediate the transcendent. It becomes an object of inquiry, set over against the human observer, rather than drawing us into the presence of ultimate reality.

The emergence of historical consciousness has left us with the "wide, ugly ditch" over which the eighteenth-century philosopher Gotthold Lessing said that he could not jump, as hard as he tried: "Accidental truths of history can never become the proof of necessary truths of reason."[18] Once we understand that Scripture is a historical product, we are no longer able to say why it is any more significant for us today than the literature of any other great tradition.

From this perspective, Christian Scripture proves to be only one instance of a more general religious phenomenon of sacred writings, each of which reflects the limitations and biases of a particular time and place. Similarly, the canon, those writings the church has declared to be its authoritative Scriptures, is no longer a given, something that Christians can accept as a firm reference point for God's activity among us. Rather, interest falls on the historical process by which the church came to its decisions about which books were "in." The canon becomes a mere historical fact, subject to historical analysis.

Feminists have argued, for example, that Scripture reflects a patriarchal world in which men push women to the margins. For these critics, Scripture is not a divine Word, free of historical distortion. Rather, Scripture must be purified, corrected, expanded. Its liberating impulses, hidden beneath layers of oppressive tradition, must be recovered.[19]

In reflecting on these challenges, Smith argues that historical consciousness need not reduce the Bible to a matter of mere historical curiosity, as though Scripture simply belonged to the past. On the contrary, as we explore history, we find that Christians and others have always understood their Scriptures to be more than a historical product. History can thus teach us to appreciate the power that most Christians for most of Christian history have found in Scripture.

But Smith still does not get Christians—or, for that matter, other religious believers—all the way over Lessing's ditch. For the question remains: Why should a modern person listen to these texts today? In a time in which we are especially aware of the need to learn from many different racial and ethnic traditions, why should we take the Scriptures of one tradition or another to be authoritative for our lives?[20] Smith himself acknowledges that his historical approach cannot ultimately rescue Scripture. On the contrary, as he notes, "there are some who see persuasive reason to consider whether our present phase of historical development may not mean that the age of scripture is coming to an end."[21]

Historical consciousness makes it impossible for Christians simply to assume that their Scriptures are authoritative. It is true that we have inherited these Scriptures by virtue of belonging to a particular religious tradition called Christianity. But in an era of multiculturalism and religious pluralism, we find ourselves increasingly free of the claims of any tradition, except the claims of a tradition shaped by historical consciousness.[22] We do not immediately perceive Scripture as standing over us, demanding our allegiance, defining us over against others. Scripture matters, but we find ourselves increasingly unsure how much it matters, and increasingly suspicious that we can do without it.

A TECHNOLOGY/INFORMATION ERA

The suggestion that the age of Scripture is coming to an end resembles a wider claim that one increasingly hears today, namely, that Western culture is now moving away from books altogether. The issue is not simply whether people will read books anymore. Rather, it is whether we will continue to be what philosopher Ivan Illich has called a "bookish" culture.[23]

Illich argues that the book has provided the root metaphor for the way we organize knowledge and understand truth. Books, at their best, transform mere information into arguments for one point of view or another. They invite us to weigh these arguments for ourselves, to enter into a dialogue with the author. When we seek deeper understanding of the world, we are confident that our repositories of wisdom are in book form. Illich and others now see us moving into an era in which the screen may structure the way we view the world.

Whether or not such a transition is actually taking place is difficult to discern. We are not yet able to assess the ways in which e-mail and the Internet are affecting or altering the character of our lives for better or worse. It is still too early for us to celebrate these technologies as fostering new forms of human community, or to damn them as further isolating us from each other. To speak either of a bookish culture or of a culture of the screen is to engage in huge abstractions that may mislead us more than enlighten us.

At times, we may believe that technology and information give us more control of our lives. We may easily conclude that the Internet is not good or bad in itself. The question, instead, is whether we locate valuable information through it or pornographic pictures, whether we widen our horizons or simply access those points of view with which we already agree. Everything seems to depend on our intentions, not on the medium itself.

Yet, it is increasingly clear that technology and information are not simply neutral phenomena, but that they profoundly shape the way we see and order our world.[24] For one thing, a technology/information society affects our understanding of expertise, though in a paradoxical manner. On the one hand, we are better able to acquire expertise, or at least a confidence to negotiate our concerns with those to whom we turn for their expertise. We have access to information that allows us to make better, more responsible choices about medicines that we need or stocks in which we wish to invest.

On the other hand, a technology/information society teaches us to put a high degree of trust in experts, especially when they can claim scientific and academic credentials. When we read or hear of new scientific findings, we tend to be gullible. We are ready to believe the latest scientific study, no matter how absurd it may seem on the surface. If someone tells us that scientists have recently established the nutritional value of certain plastics, we are apt to nod our heads in agreement, even if we decide later to track down the truth on our own.

Next to this trust in expertise is our tendency to believe that if only we had more information more quickly, we could solve our most difficult personal and social problems. Part of the appeal of computer technologies such as the Internet is their ability to help us collect, organize, and transmit vast amounts of information. Individuals, communities, and corporations with superior knowledge are judged to have superior ability to shape reality.

Historically, as cultural critic Neil Postman has noted, humans' ability to improve their well-being has often depended on their ability to gain key pieces of information. But our situation is different. What often hinders our ability to respond to pressing personal and social problems today is not a lack but an excess of information. Information inundates us. Even experts are unable to keep up with developments in their narrow fields, let alone with the bigger picture. We lack a shared narrative—a common story of who we are and what ultimately matters to us—that would enable us to sort out this information, and to determine which of it is valuable and which is merely distracting.

Take the example of the O. J. Simpson trial. The prosecution offered mountains of evidence, much of which jurors apparently dismissed. There were simply too many details to keep track of. What they wanted was a persuasive narrative that would help them to sort out this information. In the end, they bought the defense's story that a racist police department had tainted the evidence in order to frame Simpson. But American society as a whole was less persuaded. To this day, competing narratives abound, leading one to wonder whether there is a truth to the events or if they are only a matter of perspective.[25]

Because people are seeking coherence in the midst of information overload and competing social narratives, visual media, especially television, have come to play a major role in the way we interpret reality. Whereas the printed word is especially well suited for more distanced analysis and reflection, television elicits immediate emotional response. Images of war or love, mass demonstrations or personal vulnerability, grab our attention and sear themselves on our memory. Like other visual media, television captures cultural ideals, such as what constitutes beauty or health, in powerful, evocative images that help us to make immediate and compelling sense of what should matter for our lives.

But television's ability to command our immediate attention also comes at a huge cost. As Postman notes, television easily manipulates powerful cultural and religious symbols for their emotional effect, tending in the process to trivialize them and render them increasingly powerless. One has only to think of commercials that use monks with tonsures to sell copier machines, or that reduce sin and guilt to a recommendation for a certain brand of ice cream. Nor is this trivialization limited to commercials. The most dramatic and disturbing images of life and death on television too quickly become commonplace. We inure ourselves to depictions of violence; we accustom ourselves to oversimplified presentations of complex human predicaments. In response, television and other visual media keep pressing the limits to find new images that can grab our attention.

To Postman's analysis of television, one might add reflections on the other major manifestation of the screen in our time, the computer screen. A computer era seems to lift up the priority of the word as "information."[26] Word processing enables us to manipulate texts more quickly and efficiently. We can edit them, splice them, and erase any sign of their existence. We can store or retrieve millions of bytes of information with the push of a button. E-mail and the Internet further inundate us with information.

To be sure, e-mail and the Internet allow us to do more than locate or transmit information. They also help us to sort it out, to find the information that we want, so that we can make more coherent decisions. Moreover, they enable us to engage in new forms of discussion and argument. Yet, anyone who has followed an electronic meeting knows that the medium encourages one-liners and argumentative stances. It rewards provocations, but does not necessarily produce a deeper understanding of the matter at hand. The evocative image rather than the nuanced argument tends to predominate. If the screen offers us coherent meaning, it is again at the risk of oversimplifying reality.

It is worth asking whether the emergence of a technology and information era has contributed to, or at least corresponds to, the diminished sense of the poetic to which we have already referred. Neither the television screen nor the computer screen has eliminated the act of reading or the usefulness of books. While television viewing has increased drastically, people are not necessarily reading less. But what they are reading is changing. The fastest growing segments of the reading market focus on specialized interests relating to lifestyle choices and quality of life: hobbies, how-to books, health. What people seem to be seeking above all is information that assists them in making practical life choices. Classic literature and poetry are still available but constitute a smaller percentage of the total market.[27]

IMPLICATIONS FOR OUR READING OF SCRIPTURE

These trends may help to explain the contemporary church's ambivalence about Scripture, as well. They suggest that we have developed habits of thinking and reading that close us to Scripture's compelling power. We are simply unable to approach the text as mediating the transcendent, that is, an encounter with the living God and this God's will for our lives.

Our tendency to put our trust in *scientific experts* is reflected in our tendency to call upon scholars to tell us the "real meaning" of Scripture. We are not confident that Scripture has a plain sense that we can comprehend on our own. As Carl Braaten writes:

> The teaching of the Bible in theological schools is in the grip of gnosticism, the belief that it is necessary to appeal away from the plain

sense of Scripture to a higher knowledge that lies above or behind the text. The aim of biblical studies is to put students "in the know," so that they will be privy to an esoteric knowledge that even most intelligent and educated folks cannot get from their reading of the Scriptures in Hebrew, Greek, or English. The effect is paralysis on those not privy to this higher knowledge. The newly initiated are in bondage to their masters and cite their authority.[28]

Another dimension of our trust in scientific expertise is our tendency to regard the latest findings as the truest findings. Part of the success of the Jesus Seminar has been its ability to advertise itself as groundbreaking. It claims to give people in the church a new way of making sense of Scripture, based on the latest findings of scholars.

Our tendency to put our trust in experts is also reflected in our tendency to regard Scripture primarily as a collection of *information*. For some people, Scripture is primarily historical information about ancient cultures and people's experience of God long ago. For others of us, Scripture is primarily moral information, tidbits of wisdom about how to lead good lives. In either case, we tend to break Scripture down into small units, seeking the right meaning of each unit. We see Scripture as a collection of fragments and lose a sense of their larger literary context.

Yet, even as we seek the right meaning of each biblical text, we find that we have no way to sort out legitimate from illegitimate readings. As we turn to biblical experts for guidance, we quickly find ourselves with conflicting claims about the meaning of particular texts. The church, as Lindbeck notes, seems to have lost a sense of a common story, embodied in Scripture itself, that would enable it to adjudicate the various interpretations that scholars put forward.[29]

As in the wider culture, our longing to bring all this information into coherent order gives a certain power to the *screen*, the evocative image, and immediate experience. The biblical text seems less interesting and less powerful than more affective expressions of the faith. In a world in which immediacy and feeling are highly valued, the church finds people longing for ecstasy and transcendence. For many, the language of the Spirit—and the experience of the Spirit—has become more powerful than the language of the Word—and an understanding of the Word.

Visual media play a critical role in this regard. As David Wells has noted, televangelists—and much of contemporary evangelical Christianity—"capitalize on the widespread perception that 'reality is to be felt rather than cognitively recognized.'"[30] It is no surprise, then, that we also see efforts to translate the Bible itself into video. According to a recent fund-raising letter, the "Jesus" film is being translated into the languages of unevangelized peoples in remote parts of the globe. "Based totally on Scripture," the film is "so effective . . . that some people actually think the actors . . . are the real biblical characters, that the film was shot as the events happened, and that Jesus and His followers actually spoke their language!"[31] The point of the film is immediate emotional response, not meditative reflection on words pregnant with meaning and nuance.

In producing the video *Out of the Tombs,* based on Mark's account of the Gerasene demoniac (Mark 5:1–20), the American Bible Society makes a similar point.

> The music, images and narration weave closely together and reinforce one another. The images evoke powerful emotional responses . . . Through a sense of the emotional and spiritual power of this incident in Jesus' ministry, viewers open themselves to a deeper understanding of Jesus' authority, power, and grace in the lives of people.[32]

The capacity of video to evoke emotion is unique. Yet, the producers fail to see the cost at which this power is bought. What evokes deep emotion on a first viewing quickly becomes trivial, even laughable, upon subsequent viewings: the demoniac frothing at the mouth, the sound of a table saw expressing his inner torture, the use of psychedelic colors and unusual camera angles.

Moreover, the rendering of the story becomes heavily psychologized. The demoniac is depicted as a mentally, emotionally disturbed individual who finds release and calm in the presence of Jesus. Other aspects of the story—such as the fact that he recognizes Jesus as the Son of God, whereas those in their right minds do not—are underplayed.

Wells has noted more generally that much of the language of the Spirit and of personal experience that characterizes the church today is framed psychologically. Inordinate emphasis falls on the self and self-realization. Scripture, if important at all, is less a source of truth about God than an instrument for exploring the depths of the self. The gospel becomes a private, personalized message of self-help.

Some Bibles seem designed with these very factors in mind. A walk into any Christian bookstore reveals editions of Scripture, each in a different cover and color, directed towards individuals in particular life circumstances—male or female, children or older adults, newcomers to the faith or veterans. It is as though the Bible were there primarily to speak to our specific needs as defined by one aspect of the culture or another. The assumptions behind the *Serendipity Bible* are also instructive. As Wells notes, its study questions are based on the premise that Bible study can become a kind of group encounter session in which people explore their inner feelings and discover their "unlimited potential."[33]

These ways of packaging Scripture also suggest the other aspect of the screen, namely, the computer with its bytes of information. In an age such as ours, we too easily come to Scripture with the attitude that it has useful information for our lives; we need only to access it and apply it. Some of the study Bibles geared to meet this need employ elaborate indexes to assist the reader in finding particular pieces of information. Issues of great complexity—divorce, violence, wealth—are answered with a few one-liners from Scripture, rather than in the context of its greater witness to God and God's ways in the world. These study Bibles want to ensure "life application."[34]

The computer screen as organizing metaphor, and the implicit assumption that Scripture yields discrete pieces of information that require ordering, is well illustrated in the design of *The Word in Life Study Bible*. On each page, the biblical text is surrounded by charts, pictures, personality profiles, and suggestions for practical application. The layout reminds one of a computer screen with windows and interactive possibilities. An advertisement declares that this study Bible is "user-friendly." An index to key themes highlights such topics as work, economics, ethnicity, the city, and women. Another index lists jobs and occupations—accountant, actor, counselor, lawyer, and so on—that enable a person to find his or her biblical models, as though Scripture becomes more meaningful when we are able to find our own vocations represented in it.

The emphasis on information, on the one hand, and on emotional immediacy, on the other, might seem to conflict. Yet, the contemporary selling of Scripture seems to be predicated on the assumption that Scripture can have an emotional impact and work in a person's life only if its message is as clear and accessible as the information that one reads in the morning newspaper or sees and hears on the evening news. Publishers advertise new translations and editions of the Bible with the promise that they are accurate (in the judgment of scientific experts) and understandable (informative), so that the text is applicable (offers immediate, emotional coherence) to a person's life. Again, quoting from an advertisement:

> *The Word in Life Study Bible* provides the kind of information you'll need to make sense of what the biblical text is talking about. The articles and other information . . . provide the "who, what, when, where, how, and why" behind scores of passages, in an interesting,

easy-to-understand way . . . so that you can connect the words and events of biblical times with today.[35]

Such efforts to make the Bible accurate and easy to understand may reflect, and contribute to, a renewed interest in Scripture. They offer a counterweight to the role of scholarly experts in defining Scripture and invite us to discover its emotional power, rather than to suffocate under the boring, imposed interpretations that too often infect the church.

But one also wonders whether these benefits come at the cost of flattening Scripture and transforming it into a kind of literature that more closely resembles the newspaper than great poetry. The language of Scripture becomes increasingly univocal. It loses nuance and a capacity to point beyond itself, or to mediate an encounter with the transcendent. Similarly, a video like *Out of the Tombs* tends to reduce the complexity and richness of the story to a few psychological insights. These ploys may grab our attention, but one wonders whether this way of treating Scripture retains sufficient depth to transform individuals and communities radically and over a lifetime.

In a different context, Leander Keck has suggested that a technological view of language is pervasive in much of the church today. "The passion to understand how language works is driven by the desire to control its use, to manipulate it for desired goals."[36] When Scripture is seen primarily as bits of information, each univocal in meaning, it too becomes language that we begin to manipulate for our own purposes. Translations become known not only for accuracy and intelligibility, but for ideological criteria, whether the *New International Version* and its "conservative" rendering of texts or the New Revised Standard Version and its concern for "inclusivity."[37]

A TIME OF OPPORTUNITY

The roots of the biblical crisis of our time lie not simply in the fact that the church fails to attend to Scripture, but in the way we attend to it, when we do. If Scripture is primarily a collection of information, of sound bites, of clever aphorisms—if we go to it primarily for the sake of finding practical application, in the hope of giving our lives a bit more coherence—then it is hardly surprising that our experience of Scripture is so ambivalent.

While we continue to assert Scripture's authority, we read it as though it were all too mundane. We lose the capacity to encounter it as a call to imagine the world in a different way, as a summons to listen to a God who is at work in our lives and in the world around us. When Scripture is mere information, it too easily becomes ammunition for our own causes, even if draped in the rhetoric of the "Word of God."

These reductions of Scripture contribute to scandalous divisions in the body of Christ, rather than challenging them. We are unable to hear Scripture as a Word of God that calls to us from beyond ourselves into the presence of the One who is Lord and Savior. We are far too clear about what Scripture demands of us or others, and far too tone-deaf to the larger mysteries of life and death on which it meditates. The book that could help us to look at the meaning of our lives—together and apart, and in all of their joy and pain, opportunity and struggle—becomes the source of acrimony and division.

The cry for biblical literacy can itself be misleading. One might deceive oneself into believing that the renewal of the church simply depends on Christians knowing their Bible better. But the point is not for us to have a better grasp of all the information packed into Scripture. It is fully possible to know who Noah's wife really was (or wasn't!), without experiencing Scripture as a Word of God. Rather, the point is for us personally and corporately to be called into new life in Christ. As one author has said, the point is not information, but transformation.[38]

Nor, for all the confusion in the church, has this point been entirely lost. Congregations continue to hear Scripture read aloud in worship, Sunday after Sunday. Preachers continue to base their sermons on Scripture, even if the connection is not always evident. Christians continue to turn to Scripture to meditate on the deepest mysteries of life, not for only practical tips. Scripture matters. But the confusion in the church is sufficient to pose basic questions again about the nature of Scripture: Why does Scripture matter? What really makes Scripture *Scripture*? In what sense is Scripture the Word of God?

In such circumstances, it is more than a cliché to say that a time of crisis is also a time of opportunity. The church is called to rediscover the compelling power of Scripture, to find the hope of its own renewal in a Word of God that draws us into the presence of a God who declares:

> For my thoughts are not your thoughts, neither are your ways my ways, says the Lord. For as the heavens are higher than the earth, so are my ways higher than your ways and my thoughts than your thoughts. For as the rain and the snow come down from heaven, and return not thither but water the earth, making it bring forth and sprout, giving seed to the sower and bread to the eater, so shall my word be that goes forth from my mouth; it shall not return to me empty, but it shall accomplish that which I purpose, and prosper in the thing for which I sent it. (Isa. 55:8–11, RSV)

3

SCRIPTURE AS
SACRAMENTAL WORD

For many of us, learning a foreign language is a humbling venture. The language that I know best is German, but whenever I visit Germany, it takes me several weeks to recover a degree of fluency, and even then my capacity with the language is limited. I struggle to express myself; I search for words that either I have forgotten or that I never knew. When people speak clearly, I understand almost every word, but when they fall into colloquialisms and local accents, I often feel stupid. Native speakers are able to catch allusions and rhythmic patterns and associations that I completely miss.

At the same time, I do know enough German that I can "think the language" and probe its unique possibilities. Every language offers modes of expression and nuances of meaning that one cannot easily translate into another language. When I am in Germany, speaking German, a dormant side of my life is awakened. I see reality a little bit differently. Distinctive feelings, memories, and insights come back to life. The language carries particular associations and helps to bind me to particular events and people.

A trivial example is the word "Pfarrhaus." "Pfarrhaus" has no precise English equivalent. One might translate it as "pastor's house," but the English does not capture the particular set of associations that "Pfarrhaus" evokes in many a German's head: a large, rambling house with rooms for guests and community gatherings; a place of hospitality for wayfarers and local residents; a home and a place of study, often located next to the church itself.

In learning a foreign language, one learns how a whole way of thinking—and being—fits together, how certain words are used in certain contexts, how different sounds convey different meanings. The poetic character of language—its nuances and levels of meaning—comes to the fore. The language of Scripture, even in translation, is a kind of poetry too. It offers us a unique way of putting reality together. I believe that we will rediscover the compelling power of Scripture only if we allow it to speak to us as a poetic-like word that reframes our way of seeing the world and understanding our lives.

POETRY AND REVELATION

In a society that is largely tone-deaf to poetry, drawing an analogy between poetry and Scripture may be more confusing than illuminating. Many people today have little sense of the poetic, of the capacity of words to point beyond themselves. If they think of poetry at all, they regard it as a way for a person to order and express his or her confused, inner feelings. Poetry is reduced to certain therapeutic functions. It enables people to unload their frustrations, to give voice to their longings, and to discover their deeper selves.

Yet, surely, the task before the church today is to recapture the power of language, and especially biblical language—that is, its capacity to speak larger truths about our existence before God. The struggle to recover Scripture is, in a sense, the struggle to recover poetry.

In a recent series of articles for the *Christian Century,* poet and author Kathleen Norris has argued that the church must recover incarnational language, language that is full of "metaphorical resonance." The abstractions of bureaucratic jargon that predominate in our speech rob language of this power; what is needed, instead, are physical, concrete words and images "that resonate with the senses as they aim for the stars."[1] Such language "is not designed to convince the reader of a certain point of view," but "to express truths that can be revealed only through metaphor."[2]

In a similar vein, literary critic Helen Vendler has noted that poetic language employs "emotional, logical, allusive, symbolic, phonetic, syntactic and rhythmic" associations to bind words together. "This is why the language of ably written poetry seems so much more musical (as well as more dense) than the language of conversation or of journalism: many overlapping associative patterns are at work at the same time."[3]

Such associations need not be limited to the world of the immediate and finite. Poetry also has the capacity to evoke the divine, to remind us that we live our lives against the horizon of the transcendent. Poetic language can remind us that larger powers and forces impinge on our lives—that we are not simply self-made people, but that our lives make sense only as we grasp larger truths about the world and ourselves.

39

Franz Fühmann, one of East Germany's greatest writers (and a hero to a younger generation that challenged the literary taboos of the Communist Party), has offered helpful reflections on the power of poetry to redirect our vision. In the waning days of World War II, Fühmann found himself in an army hospital, recovering from battle wounds. His commanders granted him a brief visit home before he was to make his way to Dresden to rejoin the German army.

On the way home, Fühmann stopped in a used-book store and came across a volume of poetry by Georg Trakl. Trakl, an Austrian, had been drafted into his nation's army toward the end of World War I. He had suffered from mental illness and died in an army hospital from a self-administered overdose of cocaine. A gifted poet, he had both plumbed the depths of depression and scaled the heights of ecstasy.

Upon arriving home, Fühmann discovered that his father had known Trakl personally. His father told him of Trakl's tragic life and enabled him to picture the places where Trakl had lived and worked. In the process, Fühmann came to believe that his own biography was intertwined with Trakl's, that they shared a common destiny, despite all their differences. Trakl's search for meaning in a broken world became Fühmann's, in the midst of the agonizing days of uncertainty that marked the end of the Second World War.

Many years later, Fühmann wrote of the impact of one poem in particular:

> Over the white ponds
> the wild birds have set off.
> In the evening an icy wind blows from our stars.
>
> Over our graves
> stoops the shattered forehead of the night.
> Under oaks we swing on a silver raft.
>
> The white walls of the city still ring.
> Under thorn bushes
> O my brother we, the blind hands of a clock, climb up to midnight.[4]

At that very moment, much of Germany lay in ashes. Berlin had fallen; Cologne had been bombed to bits; much of Hamburg had burned to the ground. Russian and American troops had already met at the Elbe River. Trakl's poem presented Fühmann with a revelation of truth. While many Germans believed that a German victory would follow these darkest hours, Fühmann suddenly grasped that the war was lost. Germany was at midnight; devastation lay about on all sides.

Trakl had written his poetry neither as a news report of World War I nor as a prophecy of the future. Yet, his poetry helped Fühmann to make sense of the destruction that surrounded him. It awakened him both to the horror of dead bodies that he saw in the forest, as he walked toward Dresden, and to the beauty of fruit trees in blossom, as spring came. It gave him a way to comprehend the incomprehensible, to see a beginning in the midst of an ending, and to give voice to both his despair and his hope.[5]

Fühmann could not know in advance that Trakl's poetry would exert this kind of claim on him. But once it had, it guided him for the rest of his life. The power of poetry to frame life, to draw us back from the press of the moment, and to give us eyes to see the world around us in a new way is not unrelated to the power of Scripture to transform us. If the church is to rediscover the compelling power of Scripture, it must again experience the capacity of Scripture to change our lives, even as Trakl's poetry changed Fühmann's.

THREE APPROACHES TO SCRIPTURE

In the contemporary church, we are constantly tempted to read the Bible as though it were a newspaper or a technical handbook. Scripture becomes mere information—information about an ancient world or our present-day lives, information that we employ for one purpose or another, information that is fascinating or boring but in no case life-transforming.

The Bible is indeed filled with valuable information. But, as we noted in the previous chapter, what makes Scripture *Scripture* is its capacity to mediate an encounter with the transcendent. When we read Scripture as *Scripture,* we are, I believe, closer to Fühmann's experience of Trakl than to the way we read a newspaper or a technical handbook.

The church too often misses this dimension of Scripture. Even when it does note it, the church is often not of one mind about the character and content of the truths that it claims to encounter in Scripture. In the effort to combat the church's word-weariness, different parts of the church have reclaimed the power of Scripture, but in profoundly different ways.

For the "orthodox," the Bible is inspired and inerrant.[6] It sets forth truths about God. Some of these truths are theological: God is one; God's Son came into the world to save sinners; God calls us into new life in Jesus Christ. Other truths are ethical: the sixth commandment prohibits abortion; the seventh prohibits sexual relations outside the covenant of marriage, male and female. For the orthodox, the question is not whether we are able to grasp these truths. Rather, the question is whether we will assent to them. Scripture consists of revealed, propositional truths.[7]

The strength of this approach is in its insistence that Scripture has a definite content. Through Scripture, we confront the true nature of God. We know something of God's will and, therefore, of what is good and right for human life. Scripture stands over us and against us. We cannot simply use it for our own purposes.

The "progressivists," by contrast, turn to Scripture for symbols, stories, and illustrations that help to express the deepest longings of the human heart.[8] Scripture does not consist of transcendent truths; rather, Scripture gives expression to the human experience of transcending givens of nature and history. The Exodus becomes a metaphor for human liberation; the resurrection, a symbol for the triumph of the human spirit, even in a world of death and destruction. The words of Scripture are not so much God's as ours, and they tell us less about God than about ourselves. For Christians, Scripture may be a privileged language, but it is only one kind of language for describing the "mountain top," as well as the "valley of death," experiences that characterize our lives. We must revise its ethical pronouncements in light of contemporary historical and cultural circumstances.

The strength of this approach is in its insistence that we always read Scripture in the context of our own time. Even where its pronouncements appear eternally true, they are subject to interpretation and application. Scripture does not simply stand over us and against us; in a sense, we ourselves stand over and against Scripture, as we seek its meaning for our lives and weigh its relevance to our time.

While both of these positions have roots in the Christian tradition, I believe that much of the Christian tradition—and much of the Reformed tradition—has understood Scripture in yet another way. From this point of view, Scripture is more than revealed truths about God and is more than a language, however profound, for describing the heights and depths of the human condition. Rather, Scripture is a sacramental word that points beyond itself. Scripture is commentary on the reality of the risen Christ.

This approach, I believe, acknowledges dimensions of the other two, while going beyond them. Like the orthodox view, the sacramental view emphasizes that Scripture sets forth a Word of God. Scripture stands over us and against us. It communicates truths that we cannot discover on our own or from other sources. But, like the progressivist view, the sacramental view acknowledges that Scripture is more poetic than propositional, more illuminative than prescriptive. Even its propositional, prescriptive materials resist reduction to "one right meaning," for they are embedded in texts that have layers of meaning, and these texts find their ultimate embodiment in the mystery of Christ.[9]

One of the classic definitions of a sacrament is "a visible sign of an invisible grace."[10] Perhaps we should think of the words of Scripture as "an audible signal of an inaudible grace." When Scripture is read, when it is explicated in preaching, when it is incorporated into prayers of thanksgiving and lament, when it frames the celebration of the Lord's Supper, Scripture becomes a means by which Christians are gathered into the body of the living Lord. The words of Scripture become a window into the Word, Jesus Christ. As Paul says: "What no eye has seen, nor ear heard, nor the human heart conceived, what God has prepared for those who love him — these things God has revealed to us through the Spirit" (1 Cor. 2:9–10). Which things? "Jesus Christ, and him crucified" (1 Cor. 2:2).

As a sacramental word, Scripture is not only a witness, however unique or authoritative, to the revelation that has taken place in Christ; rather, Scripture as *Scripture* also sets forth the living Christ. It draws us into Christ's presence and invites us to be transformed into his image. It opens the possibility of relationship between the divine and the human.[11]

SCRIPTURE AS A SACRAMENT

To many in the church, it would seem strange to think of Scripture as a sacrament. They would, instead, contrast Word and sacrament. Indeed, those Christian groups that have lifted up Scripture have to some extent neglected the sacraments, and vice versa.

But, in speaking of the capacity of Scripture to mediate an encounter with the transcendent, W. C. Smith suggests that the term "sacrament" might best serve our purposes. It is "the trilateral term that is needed: the notion bespeaks divine initiative, and human involvement, plus the empirical object that mediates."[12] For Smith, sacraments are not magical. They possess no power in and of themselves. Rather, they give accessible form to people's awareness of involvement in transcendence, an awareness that precedes but finds expression in their lives.

While Protestants for the most part have not called Scripture a sacrament, their understanding of Scripture as the Word of God has meant much the same thing. To call Scripture the Word of God is to assert that Scripture is more than an historical record of God's words and deeds in the past, more than good advice or practical wisdom. Rather, Scripture is God's continuing revelation. Scripture draws us into the presence of the transcendent One.

Smith notes, "the more Bishops, the fewer Bibles."[13] This dictum has been especially true in the Reformed tradition, which has understood the

Holy Spirit to be at work principally in the community's encounter with Scripture, rather than in a clergy. Ministers are servants of the Word, not holy persons directly related to the Holy. They are "teaching elders," who help us to discern God's Word in Scripture.

Calvin himself wrote commentaries on nearly every book of the Bible. Moreover, he understood his major theological work, the *Institutes,* to be a guide to the Bible that might help pastors to order its different parts. Calvin believed that the words and images of Scripture were God's self-accommodation to humans, just as God had become flesh in Jesus Christ. Indeed, for Calvin, this very accommodation in Scripture was Christ, God with us.

As Alister McGrath in a recent biography of Calvin has noted:

> Christianity [for Calvin] is Christ-centered, not book-centered; if it appears to be book-centered, it is because it is through the words of scripture that the believer encounters and feeds upon Jesus Christ. . . . Calvin's preoccupation with human language, and supremely with the text of scripture, reflects his fundamental conviction that it is *here,* that it is through reading and meditating upon *this* text, that it is possible to encounter and experience the risen Christ.[14]

This understanding of Scripture as the Word of God was so central to the Reformed tradition that it received confessional status—often, indeed, as the very first article of faith. The Second Helvetic Confession, for example, begins:

> We believe and confess the canonical Scriptures of the holy prophets and apostles of both Testaments to be the true Word of God . . . For God himself spoke to the fathers, prophets, apostles, and still speaks to us through the Holy Scriptures. And in this Holy Scripture, the universal Church of Christ has the most complete exposition of all that pertains to a saving faith.[15]

Similarly, Reformed worship has lifted up the centrality of Scripture. Traditional Reformed hymnody restricted itself to Scripture, especially the Psalms. The sermon was understood to be an explication and application of Scripture, and often stood at the climax of the order of worship.[16]

The Reformed understanding of Scripture as the Word of God was not an innovation but a retrieval of a sacramental view of Scripture reaching back into Scripture itself. Monastic and mystical traditions in both Judaism and Christianity had kept this understanding of Scripture alive—and influenced Calvin's own thought.[17]

Jewish scholar Michael Fishbane argues that "one of the greatest contributions of Judaism to the history of religions is in its assertion that the divine reality makes itself humanly comprehensible through the structures of language."[18] In medieval Jewish thought,

> God is not merely present in Scripture through a kind of verbal displacement. God and Scripture are, in fact, one mysterious and inseparable Truth. Scripture is nothing less than the immediacy of God in a "verbal expression". . . . [The Torah is] the infinity of divine Being in a condensed linguistic expression.[19]

In the Christian tradition, early Benedictines understood the sacred page as a medicine that helped to restore the sinful soul into right relationship with God. The Word was nourishing, to be chewed upon until it was fully digested, uniting the soul with Christ.[20]

Similarly, Bernard of Clairveaux, the great medieval leader of the Cistercian order, emphasized that Scripture was the means by which humans might seek union with God. Scripture offers not only a vision of one's destination but also the details of the moral journey that one must undertake to get there. Transformation into the image of God entails conformation to God's will as revealed in Scripture.

Bernard is confident about God's love "and about the strict moral obligations that this entails"; he is humble "about his own (or any human being's) ability to apprehend them—let alone, to live up to them."[21] One can never empty Scripture of meaning. "What is proffered in scripture is transcendent truth. The words that we read are 'deep in mystery,' and present us with a mystery that we must struggle to explore that it is our privilege to explore."[22]

It is this tradition that Vatican II reclaimed in its Dogmatic Constitution on Divine Revelation. Here sacramental language of the Eucharist provides the best analogy for understanding the character of Scripture:

> The Church has always venerated the divine Scriptures just as she venerates the body of the Lord, since from the table of both the word of God and of the body of Christ she unceasingly receives and offers to the faithful the bread of life . . . For in the sacred books, the Father who is in heaven meets His children with great love and speaks with them; and the force and power in the word of God is so great that it remains the support and energy of the Church, the strength of faith for her sons, the food of the soul, the pure and perennial source of spiritual life.[23]

A renewed appreciation of the sacramental character of Scripture is increasingly evident both in the spirituality movement that, often borrowing from Catholic resources, has swept through mainline Protestantism in recent years and in recent academic literature on Scripture. One notes, in particular, the interest in recapturing the monastic practice of lectio divina (divine reading), devotional reading that respects Scripture's sacramental power.[24] The point is to open oneself to the living voice of God as it comes to one through the words of Scripture.

SCRIPTURE AND POETRY

To call Scripture a sacramental word that points beyond itself to the ultimate is, once again, to liken Scripture more to poetry than to a newspaper or a technical handbook. It may be even more accurate to say that Scripture is the standard and that great poetry, in comparison to a newspaper or a technical handbook, is more Scripture-like.[25]

As we saw in Fühmann's reading of Trakl, poetry can mediate larger truths. It can assume scriptural quality. Scripture and great poetry share a capacity to lift us up out of our ordinary selves, and to put us in touch with the ideal.[26] Both can help us to make sense of the deeper purposes of life, and to become more aware of the larger forces that shape us.

When we understand Scripture as a sacramental, poetic-like word, we assume a posture different from that of readers of newspapers or technical handbooks. Scripture, like great poetry, is not primarily information about things past, but a lens for looking at the present. The capacity of Trakl's poetry to help Fühmann to make sense of the end of the war is reminiscent of the famous words of John Calvin:

> Just as old or bleary-eyed men and those with weak vision, if you thrust before them a most beautiful volume, even if they recognize it to be some sort of writing, yet can scarcely construe two words, but with the aid of spectacles will begin to read distinctly; so Scripture, gathering up the otherwise confused knowledge of God in our minds, having dispersed our dullness, clearly shows us the true God.[27]

In reframing our world, Scripture, like great poetry, engages our imagination. As Fühmann argues, we do not simply understand a poem; a poem engages our capacity for phantasy.[28] Similarly, Scripture is an invitation to construe the world in a different way, to imagine it in light of God's plans and purposes.[29]

Scripture, like great poetry, is inexhaustible in meaning. One can always return to it and find something more. Different interpreters can probe the same text in different ways; the same interpreter can return to a text months or years later and find new meaning in it.

A number of recent efforts to reflect theologically on what makes Scripture *Scripture* have emphasized its "performative" character.[30] Every interpretation of a biblical text realizes ("performs") only some of the possibilities inherent in the text. But the meaning of Scripture is not arbitrary. The text itself imposes constraints. It defines a field of meaning within which some interpretations prove more compelling than others. One cannot get whatever one wants out of Scripture.[31]

The comparison to poetry is again instructive. Fühmann acknowledged that his interpretation of Trakl's poetry did not exclude other interpretations, but he insisted that he had not simply contrived a meaning as he related it to his own situation. Fühmann argued that poetry says something concrete, without having been written to say it. The poem transcends itself as soon as it offers us one meaning or another.[32] Thus, we never simply understand a poem, for it defies reduction to any single meaning.

Here the analogy of a musical score is also helpful. The score constrains the performers. They must attend faithfully to the notes as written. Yet, no single performance exhausts the meaning of the piece. Within the constraints of the score, the performers improvise, in the hope that the sheer wonder of playing and hearing the music might take over.

Thomas Levenson writes movingly of Yo Yo Ma's intense involvement with the cello suites of Bach:

> For Ma, the suites (and music in general) "are about the primary things we have to deal with, what we know and the terror and mystery of what we don't: the terror and mystery of death." . . . Expressing what he finds in the score that Bach left him requires a balancing act. On the one hand, Ma pays extremely close attention to the elaborate structure of the pieces. . . . But on the other hand, too precise a reading and the joy gets lost . . . "Perfection means that you hit every note, no scratches, playing totally reliably. But that squeezes the life out; it destroys a piece of music. The element of risk isn't there. In performance you shape, mold, and sculpt. . . . It has to breathe. Perfection to me is static."[33]

Scripture, like great poetry, is not relegated to experts. While scholars may help us to probe the text more deeply, they cannot reduce it to one meaning or another.[34] We need authoritative interpreters not because they have a correct meaning that we must simply repeat, but because they can help us to become interpreters in our own right. While they help us to hear the possibilities of the text more fully, we finally have to "perform" it for ourselves.

In comparing Scripture and great poetry, I do not mean to suggest that Scripture is only metaphorical, or that it is never to be read literally. I do mean to suggest, however, that Scripture is never to be understood only on

47

a literal level of meaning. Even biblical statements whose meaning seems patently clear and literal—for example, the Ten Commandments—resonate with other parts of the biblical witness. "Thou shalt not kill" not only tells us what to do, but points to the God with whom we ultimately have to do.

In sum, Scripture, like great poetry, points us both beyond itself and beyond ourselves. Insofar as Scripture offers us spectacles, the point is not to look *at* them but *through* them.[35] What we then see is not simply a reflection of ourselves. Rather, we are reminded of the ultimate powers that bear down on our lives. For a moment, we may even find ourselves caught up in wonder (or terror) before them. Again, it is like the moment of awe that can sweep over a person at a symphonic performance. In a way that eludes simple description—and that defies any effort to program mechanically—an audience can experience itself mysteriously yet inexorably drawn into another world, as though time itself has stopped.

When Christians have understood Scripture sacramentally, they have understood it to have the capacity to lift them up to Christ, so that we truly stand before his throne. We then see ourselves as his people, judged and redeemed, both called to obedience and blessed with faith. In Scripture, we come not simply to know about Christ but to know Christ for ourselves.

SCRIPTURE AS AN IDENTITY STORY

While a sacramental understanding of Scripture offers a way to get beyond the orthodox and progressivist impasse, a significant alternative has emerged in recent theological literature. In this view, Scripture is best understood as a kind of identity story. Scripture helps Christians to remember who they really are. It illustrates the character of the faithful community.

This perspective has been represented most persuasively by George Lindbeck. In his seminal work *The Nature of Doctrine,* Lindbeck identified three major theoretical approaches to religion—each of which, I believe, also finds expression in the church's life today.[36]

One of these models, the *expressive-experiential,* proceeds from the assumption that human experience offers access to the divine. In reflecting on the mystery of human existence, every person becomes aware of a transcendent dimension to life. We sense that our lives point to "something more," to something greater than ourselves. This common, human experience of transcendence—this sense that we can never exhaust life and its possibilities—this sense then gives birth to a multiplicity of human expressions of transcendence.

The interest in "faith journeys" that one finds today in parts of the church reflects this approach. It is assumed that each of us has a unique way of experiencing God, and that by sharing these experiences we come to a fuller understanding of God. Similar wisdom may come from other religions. Different ways of experiencing God point to the same ultimate reality, but individuals and cultures clothe these experiences in different symbols.

This approach also resembles the progressivism described above. Because the effort to give expression to religious experience is always conditioned by the particularities of nature and culture, the progressivist argues that we need to learn from the full range of religious expression. Every religious symbol enriches our understanding of the infinite mystery that finally transcends any of our efforts to express it. In this view, the Christian Scriptures offer us profound symbols of the divine, but their revelation is neither final nor complete.

A second model, the *cognitive-propositional,* proceeds from the assumption that revelation is transmitted not through a commonly accessible experience of transcendence but through propositional statements. Revelation has an intellectual content.

This perspective is reflected today in those parts of the church that call for reading the Bible literally. What sometimes emerges is a kind of bumper sticker theology: "God said it. I believe it. That settles it." This approach resembles the orthodoxy described above. The Christian Scriptures are thought to convey truths that are otherwise inaccessible to humans.

Lindbeck himself proposes a third model that is *cultural-linguistic.* For him, religions are characterized by distinctive practices and vocabularies. It is not so much the case that experience of the transcendent gives birth to religious expression but that particular ways of talking about, and relating ourselves to, the transcendent shape our experience of the transcendent in particular ways. To know God in the Christian sense is to become a member of a community that engages in particular practices and adheres to particular beliefs. Scripture is constituted less by symbols or propositions than by a basic narrative that unifies Scripture's diverse materials and shapes the community's sense of faithfulness.

As Lindbeck has argued elsewhere:

> Without a central core of privileged and familiar texts, social cohesion becomes more difficult to sustain, and depends more on bureaucratic management, the manipulation of public opinion, and ultimately, perhaps, totalitarian force. Reason in the form of science or philosophy is too restricted in scope (it neglects imagination, for example), and too contradictory and changing in its pictures of the cosmic setting of

49

human life to provide a satisfactory substitute. What is needed are texts projecting imaginatively and practically habitable worlds.[37]

This notion has been picked up and developed by Stanley Hauerwas in his claim that the Christian community has a distinctive character shaped by a distinctive narrative. For Hauerwas, as we noted in chapter 1, Scripture is primarily illustrative of the character of the community, rather than symbolic of a primordial human experience of transcendence (the experiential-expressivist model) or prescriptive of a particular content of belief or practice (the cognitive-propositionalist approach). Scripture, even in its symbolic or prescriptive materials, presents the community with a mirror of the way of life to which faith in Christ commits it.

But, as we also noted, this emphasis on community and on reading Scripture through the eyes of the community is more broadly shared, even among figures whose approach at first glance appears experiential-expressivist (Elizabeth Johnson) or cognitive-propositionalist (David Wells). For Johnson, Scripture releases its emancipatory symbols only when read through the community committed to the flourishing of women. For Wells, Scripture releases its truths about the sovereignty of God only when distilled into (Reformed) confessional formulations. Despite their differences theologically, Hauerwas, Johnson, and Wells all subordinate Scripture to the good ends of the community. Scripture reminds the community of its identity.

This perspective also finds widespread currency in the church today. The emphasis falls not simply on sharing faith journeys, or on reading the Bible literally, but on identifying the basic beliefs and practices that make Christians different from the wider culture. Scripture provides a vocabulary for telling the Christian story. It offers us a common point of orientation.

A friend, for example, tells of teaching her children the Apostles' Creed as a way of summarizing the biblical story. Her primary concern was not that her children interpret the Creed as a set of symbolic statements, or that they accept it as propositional truth, but that they know the community's vocabulary and grammar. The Creed would remind them of the community to which they belonged by virtue of their baptism.

SACRAMENTAL WORD OR IDENTITY STORY?

To think of Scripture as a sacramental word is not to deny that it can also serve as an identity story. But a sacramental view suggests that Scripture is something more.

Every community tells stories that help to define and preserve it. If I want you to know what it really means to be a Burgess, I am apt to tell you about my great-grandparents who moved to Colorado in the 1880s. Soon afterwards, my great-grandfather died of tuberculosis, leaving my great-grandmother to raise four children on her own.

I would not claim that the telling of that story has sacramental power. While it reminds me vividly of my past and sets forth an inspiring example of courage under adversity, I would not claim that it brings me into living relationship with my great-grandparents. There is no "real presence." An identity story is not the same as a sacramental word that truly mediates Christ's presence through the Holy Spirit and the gift of faith.

The distinction between Calvin and the Swiss Reformer Ulrich Zwingli in relation to the Eucharist has a parallel here.[38] Both men resisted the Catholic idea that the bread and wine really become flesh and blood. But Zwingli saw the Eucharist primarily as a memorial. It reminded believers of God's benefits in Christ and moved them to faith. For Calvin, by contrast, the Eucharist brought the believer into the real presence of Christ. It did not merely evoke faith; it fed faith and incorporated the believer into Christ's body.

When Scripture is primarily an identity story, it—like Zwingli's Eucharist—reminds us that we belong to Christ. It illustrates our faith in him and our covenant to commit ourselves to each other. It confirms the character of the faithful community.

To understand Scripture as a sacramental word is to say, by contrast, that Scripture does more than to remind us of our true identity, and that the Bible is more than a collection of memories of Christ's ministry, death, and resurrection. Rather, the Scriptures set forth a living word. In worship, in preaching and the celebration of the Eucharist, we open ourselves to the risen Christ as he is taking shape among us here and now.[39]

In this sacramental understanding, Scripture sets forth the living Christ. In his presence, we find ourselves transformed into his image and incorporated into his body, the church. We have not simply chosen the community. We are not members of it simply by virtue of the commitments that we have made to it. Rather, by God's grace, we experience the Christian community as God's gift to us in Christ.

When Benedictine monks quietly recited Scripture to themselves throughout the day, they were not simply reminding themselves that they belonged to a community identified by distinctive beliefs and practices. Rather, they understood themselves to be meditating on the presence of

God. They wished to inscribe the text on their soul, so that the Word might incorporate them into Christ.[40]

We too may be able to rediscover the capacity of Scripture to mediate the presence of the One to whom we belong. The movie *Chariots of Fire* includes a scene in which Eric Liddell, the Scottish athlete who refused to run in an Olympic event because it fell on a Sunday, stands in the pulpit to read a portion of Isaiah 40. The congregation is hushed. People wait with anticipation not merely to hear a great story but to respond in wonder to the living God who promises to bear them up with eagle wings.

I have frequently heard pastors comment on their experience of reciting the Twenty-third Psalm with Alzheimer's patients or people on their deathbed. People who have previously been unresponsive will sometimes begin to repeat the words or even race ahead of the pastor. The power in such moments seems to lie in more than a mere remembering that one belongs to God in life and death. Rather, Scripture conveys the very presence of God and God's people.[41]

THE MYSTERY
OF GOD'S SELF-REVELATION

To assert that Scripture sets forth Christ is to assert that the Bible, despite the diversity of its materials, finds its unity in Christ. But Christians have never been content to leave "unity in Christ" as an empty, formal principle. They have always sought to say something concrete about the Christ whom they encounter in the Scriptures.

In chapter 7, I will make my own proposals for how best to understand the Christ whom Scripture sets forth. At this point, I simply wish to argue that Scripture is larger than any effort to unify it. Even as we seek to know the Christ of Scripture, Scripture continually reminds us of the mystery of Christ—and Christ himself points us to the mystery of God.[42]

The mystery of God's self-revelation is reflected, first of all, in the *history of the canon*. The canon is not simply a list of books; it is a theological principle, even a confessional witness.[43] In its adherence to a canon, the church asserts that certain writings set forth Christ in a way that other writings do not.

Christians have always debated the exact limits of the canon. When they have lost confidence that particular writings in it set forth Christ, they have redefined the canon, as when the Reformers rejected the Apocrypha. Luther (and later the English Reformers) insisted that the apocryphal writings remained instructive—to use the terminology that I have developed in this chapter, they were part of the Christian identity story. But these Reformers also argued that these writings were not sacramental—they did not mediate an encounter with the living Christ.

The fact of different canons, as well as the continuing debate about the limits of the canon, should teach us humility in defining which Christian writings speak as Scripture. We are not free to alter the canon on our own; any alteration must be a confessional act of the church. But we must always be open to the possibility that we have misjudged which writings truly set forth Christ. God's self-revelation is larger than our efforts to define it canonically.[44]

At a second level, the mystery of the Christ whom Scripture sets forth is reflected in the *arrangement of the canon*. The order of the books is not wholly arbitrary. The Old Testament ends with verses in Malachi that early Christians understood to refer to John the Baptist, the one who would prepare the way for Jesus.[45] The New Testament begins with a genealogy that referred them back to the Old Testament.

Nor do individual books stand on their own. The movement from Genesis and creation through the history of Israel, to Jesus, to the history of the church, to Revelation and the end of time, suggests a coherent narrative. Scripture's different books work together to set forth the full scope of God's work in history.

Yet, on a closer look, this narrative is less smooth than first appears. The arrangement of the canon does not always have theological significance. The letters of Paul, for example, are ordered according to length, not according to theological priority.[46] In other places, the narrative coherence of the canon sometimes seems more apparent than real. What kind of narrative is interrupted by collections of prophecies, psalms, and proverbs? What kind of narrative tells the story of Jesus four times? Various Christian efforts to harmonize the Gospels cannot cover up the fact that the New Testament simply places them side by side.[47]

Thus, elements of coherence are offset by elements of difference, even discord. There is a basic story line, but also more than a story line. The arrangement of the canon suggests both the unity and diversity of Scripture. The text defies simple resolution into one scheme or another; God's self-revelation is larger than our efforts to give it a narrative order.

At a third level, the mystery of Christ has been reflected in the effort to define a *canon within the canon*. Even when Christians have been able to confess a common canon, they have debated which of its writings set forth Christ most faithfully. They have developed theologies based on certain biblical writings more than on others. A canon within the canon becomes the lens of interpretation through which Christians have valued some parts of the canon and devalued other parts.

Because Romans and justification by faith were his canon within the canon, Luther dismissed James as an epistle of straw. Contemporary feminist and liberationist theologies also sort out the wheat from the chaff—an emancipatory core from patriarchal overlays. Indeed, each of us has a picture of Christ that we use to interpret and order Scripture, to say which portions of the Bible speak compellingly, and which do not.

Yet, for every Romans, there is a James; for every motif of liberation, one of service, even servitude.[48] Every hermeneutical principle finally has to reckon with others that lift up equally compelling visions of the Christ whom we encounter in Scripture. If Scripture is to speak faithfully, we must try to order its diverse voices into a clear, coherent message of God's ways with us. Yet, we ultimately discover that we cannot neatly order Scripture by one theological criterion or another.

Indeed, to confess Scripture as *Scripture* is to confess that Scripture challenges our efforts to order it once and for all. The lenses that we bring to Scripture must constantly be readjusted; as we actually interpret the Bible, we sometimes find that we need a new prescription for our glasses. We have to listen carefully to all of Scripture, even those parts that do not make sense to us. We simply cannot know ahead of time which parts of Scripture will set forth Christ to us in our particular situation.[49]

Because Christians in the past have heard God's Word in all of these writings, we too will be open to hearing God's Word in them. We can be confident that God's self-revelation can occur through any part of Scripture. What does not speak to one generation—or to one church, or to one personality—may claim another.[50]

For this reason, we cannot automatically rule out any of the canon in advance. Because of his uneasiness with James, Luther lumped it together with other "suspect" books in the rear of his New Testament (two of which, Jude and Revelation, were already there)—and to this day, German Bibles in the tradition of Luther move the letters of John ahead of Hebrews and James. But Luther did not feel free to expurgate any of them from the canon.

The discipline of remaining open to all of Scripture also affects the way we read the Old Testament. For much of Christian history, the church has relied heavily on typological schemes, in which Old Testament figures and events were understood to prefigure ones in the New Testament. The Old Testament was "promise"; the New Testament, "fulfillment."[51] While reflecting the church's confidence that the two testaments cohere, typology often robbed the Old Testament of its power. It put it into an interpretive straitjacket.[52]

If Scripture sets forth Christ, the New Testament picture of Jesus, especially in the Gospels, has priority in Christian theology. They set forth the character of Christ more directly than any other part of Scripture and should therefore govern our interpretation of the Bible as a whole. Yet, Jesus is also the Son of God — the Logos, the Word — who has existed from the beginning of time and has ordered the world. When we understand Christ as the fullness of God's self-revelation in every time and place, we approach the Old Testament as more than "type" or "promise." It becomes commentary on the character of the God who has become incarnate in Jesus.[53] It fleshes out the nature of Christ.

Early Christians were confident that they heard God's voice to them in all of Scripture.[54] They applied the Old Testament traditions to Christ and to their own situation as followers of Christ, just as the people of Israel had continually reinterpreted earlier Hebrew traditions in light of their own context.[55] Our challenge is the same.

DISCOVERING THE REVELATORY POTENTIAL OF ALL OF SCRIPTURE

Already in 1926, Franz Rosenzweig argued that the circumstances of the modern age made it especially imperative to learn to listen to all of Scripture, not just selected portions. While Luther was able to base his translation of the Bible on a definite concept of the Christ to whom it testified,

> Our time has lost his notion of revelation; whether in greater clarity or in greater confusion, it seeks the revelation of what it considers worthy of belief in the whole range of what Luther, considering it merely a picture and pattern of life, had excluded from the firmly, visibly, and eternally circumscribed religious kernel of the Book.[56]

Rosenzweig argued that the translator had to proceed from the assumption that any part of Scripture was a "potentially revelation-bearing utterance."[57]

It is instructive to consider materials that Christians most often dismiss as irrelevant to their faith: the long lists of names in books like Numbers and Chronicles, and the detailed legal materials of Exodus and Leviticus. Is there really any way that they can speak to us today? Are they "potentially revelation-bearing utterances"?

It is still the practice in Benedictine monasteries to listen to a reading of Scripture during the common meal. I once visited a monastery whose abbot clicked on a tape-recorded reading of Scripture as we sat down to eat. The tape that day began in the middle of a long list of names in 1 Chronicles: so and so was the father of so and so, who was the father of so and so, who was the father of so and so. In what sense, I wondered to myself, could this portion of Scripture be digested spiritually even as we began physically to eat and digest our dinner?

Most genealogies and lists of names are as interesting as reading the phone book. Yet, there are times that they can be profoundly important, even moving. Once a year at my church, we have a cleanup day. People volunteer their time to weed the garden, clean the carpets, and make minor repairs. The next Sunday, the church newsletter lists the name of every person who participated.

Similarly, at Easter time, the name of every person who has donated a lily in memory of a loved one is carefully listed in the bulletin. At the annual meeting, the name of every member who has died over the past year is printed and read aloud. These lists are not perfunctory. They honor those who have given of their time and money. They remind us of the good that we can do for each other.

To look at another person's family tree can be deathly boring; to look at one's own can evoke a sense of wonder. A friend of mine who was researching her genealogy was unable to locate any records of one of her grandfathers. After many years of searching, she finally learned of a congregation to which he had once belonged. When she came across his name on an old membership roll, she was moved to tears.

When we understand that the long lists in the Old Testament name our ancestors, we may be reminded of God's providence over the generations. We may remember that God has worked through them, as God works through us, despite human faults and limitations. We may indeed remember that God is present to us—even experience God's presence among us here and now.

The intricate legal materials of Exodus and Leviticus are equally profound. At first glance, we see only ancient laws. Their content is peculiar; they seem to exert no claim on Christians' lives. If anything, we tend to use them as grounds to belittle a legalistic Judaism (or fundamentalist Christianity) that seems more obsessed with ritualistic and moralistic requirements than with God's grace.

Yet, the Old Testament legal materials describe a whole way of being in the world. They represent a kind of utopian order: the heavenly kingdom where everything is properly ordered and there are appropriate and measured responses to every situation.[58] They define patterns of life before God.

My life is no less obsessed with maintenance of order. I think of the

SCRIPTURE AS SACRAMENTAL WORD

amount of time that I spend simply keeping things in order: putting papers into the right files, returning phone calls, answering correspondence, and writing memos. When I come home to my family in the evening, a good deal of my time is spent washing dishes, picking up toys, sweeping floors, and putting out the trash.

When I get frustrated about the amount of time I lose on these daily tasks, I might do well to remember Leviticus. In response to God's gracious act of separating light and dark, earth and sea, and plants and animals according to their kind (Genesis 1), humans separate what is clean from what is unclean (Leviticus 11).[59] They put things into order, thereby participating in God's efforts to stave off the chaos that ever again threatens to engulf creation. The concern for order is the concern for life—the laws of the Old Testament set forth the God who is truly in the details of our everyday living.

Christians may never want to spend the majority of their time in 1 Chronicles or Leviticus. But we may find treasures in places where we least expected. We need disciplines of reading the Bible that open us to the fullness of God's self-revelation. A piety of the Word can teach us to respect Scripture's revelatory possibilities—its mystery, as well as its message to us here and now.

4

A PIETY OF THE WORD

The Bible has always been a part of my life. Ever since receiving my first Bible from my parents, I have read Scripture on my own. I have heard many sermons and participated in many Sunday school discussions of Scripture. In seminary, I received formal training in biblical exegesis. I learned Hebrew and Greek, so that I could begin to understand the Bible in its original languages. As a parent, I now love telling Bible stories to my children. At work and home, I keep a Bible close by. Hardly a day goes by that I don't pick it up. Scripture matters to me.

Yet, I have slowly come to realize just how intermittent my reading of Scripture really is. When inspired, I pick up the Bible for a few minutes at the beginning or end of the day. But often I am tired, and I do not get very far. I enjoy the feel of the pages; I glance over the chapter headings. Yet, over the course of days or weeks, I rarely make it through an entire book of the Bible, despite my best intentions. I have often found it more interesting to pick up a book about the Bible than to read the Bible itself.

I am probably not different from many mainline Protestants. Although we believe that the Bible sets forth the Word of God and is foundational to the Christian life, we sometimes find it easier to talk about the authority of Scripture than actually to read Scripture—and when we do pick it up, we do not always get very far.

Our difficulty in getting into Scripture may not be simply a matter of bad intentions or weak will. Rather, as Stanley Hauerwas has remarked so pointedly, we come to Scripture with habits that rob it of its ability to speak God's Word to us.[1] We have never learned how to read Scripture, how to hear it as God's Word to us.

Our worst habit, perhaps, is our tendency to use Scripture for our own purposes. We live in a church in confusion, even crisis, about basic theological and ethical issues. People on each side of one controversial issue or another turn to Scripture to support a position, after they have already made up their minds. The tendency to read Scripture as information reinforces this attitude. We go to the text, looking for those pieces of information that will support our particular cause. We reduce texts with layers of meaning to one "right meaning." We then reject this meaning, arguing that it is historically conditioned (and therefore irrelevant to our situation), or appeal to it as an authoritative word that should settle the debate once and for all.

If, however, Scripture as *Scripture* is a sacramental, poetic-like word, I believe that we will adopt a different stance. Rather than throwing Scripture like darts at each other, we will open ourselves to the possibility of encountering a Word from beyond ourselves. Our first reflex will not be to marshal biblical support for one position or another, but to dwell on the text. We will nurture a piety of the Word that respects Scripture's revelatory potential. We will humbly submit to insights and perspectives that break through entrenched positions. We will stand in awe and wonder before a word that is God's living Word, Christ himself, alive and in our midst.

Over the centuries, four disciplines in particular have helped Christians to nurture such a piety: reading Scripture aloud, reading Scripture in community, reading Scripture in context, and memorizing Scripture. These disciplines might help us to reform our bad habits. They might open us anew to Scripture as a sacrament. Each has practical implications for the life of the church.

READING SCRIPTURE ALOUD

Most mainline Protestants, if they read Scripture at all, read it silently, through their eyes. Yet, if Scripture is a sacramental, poetic-like word, we would do well to rediscover disciplines of reading Scripture aloud. Poetry is primarily for the ear, not the eye. It is important as sound. Scripture may speak a different kind of word to us if we learn how to hear.

In the early church, Christians always read Scripture aloud, even when studying it by themselves. The emphasis on the spoken word was, in part, a practical matter. In order to save space on precious papyrus or parchment, scribes crowded the words of Scripture together, so that there was literally no space between one word and the next. Reading aloud helped the reader to make sense of the text, to figure out where one word ended and the next began.[2] But early Christians also understood reading aloud as a spiritual exercise. In sounding out the text, one was reminded that it was a living word—a word borne by breath, by God's Spirit. (In Hebrew, as in Greek, the same word designates wind, breath, and spirit.)

The significance of Scripture as "sound" was particularly significant in the monastic tradition. It is important to remember that Benedictine monks spent the majority of their day in silence. Only the community's prayer, seven times a day, broke this silence. Moreover, in prayer, the sounds of the Scriptures dominated. In lifting their voices in worship, the monks gave voice to the written word. At the heart of the community's prayer were the Psalms, all 150 of which were chanted in the course of the week.

As historian Wolfgang Braunfels has noted:

> In the performance of the daily liturgy Cistercian aesthetic aspirations achieved their apotheosis. There are no available measurements of the acoustics of Cistercian churches, but every one of their choirs acts as a resonating chamber through which sound is both held and muted. Echoes were avoided, each word was to ring out firm and clear. . . . [A]n acute sensibility was developed for the melodic intervals of the chant.[3]

In his Rule for the monastic life, Benedict emphasized the importance of Scripture as sound. In asking the monks to chant the Psalms, he lifted up their vocal quality. Benedict also insisted that the monks reproduce the text exactly. Anyone making a mistake was to correct himself immediately and ask for pardon; if he did not, he was to be severely punished.[4] A modern commentary on the Rule notes the significance of these rules. Because prayer is central to the life of the community, to read Scripture "without care, without sense, without accuracy is to strike at the very heart of the community's life."[5]

The reading of Scripture at mealtime was also carefully regulated. Not just anyone should read; only "those who may uplift the listeners."[6] Nor did readers read at their own pleasure; rather, they were scheduled for a week at a time, so they could focus carefully on their assignment. Before commencing, the reader would ask for the community's prayer and blessing. Because he did not get to eat his meal until afterwards, the Rule made provision for him to have "a draught of wine . . . because it might be too long for him to fast otherwise."[7] As the modern commentary notes,

> Benedict considers reading such an important part of the meal . . . that he insists that the person doing the reading be a good reader, someone

who would inspire rather than irritate the souls of the listeners. The reading was to be an artistic event, an instructive experience, a moment of meditation.[8]

When we attend to the sound of Scripture, we may be reminded that the spoken word has a special kind of power. When someone speaks to us, we feel ourselves addressed. Their words come to us from outside ourselves. The words call us to attention; they evoke our response. Similarly, when Scripture is spoken, we are dramatically reminded that Scripture consists of more than words on a page. Scripture draws us into relationship with the living Lord.

When we read Scripture aloud, we are challenged to read thoughtfully and carefully, so that the sounds help to interpret the text, to lift up its nuances, and to impress it more firmly on our memory. Sound sets the text apart. Scripture reading takes on the character of an event, not merely of a private, mental exercise. It shapes an encounter with God.

In a word-weary world, attention to the sound of Scripture might help us to recover the miraculous quality of spoken words. I still remember the day my two-year-old daughter suddenly began speaking. Where there had only been sounds and cries, "da da" and "ma ma," there were now whole words. Within a couple of weeks, she began putting short sentences together. It was as though out of nowhere she had exploded with language.

The miraculous quality of spoken words may be most apparent in human relationships. Communication with each other can be difficult. Sometimes we use words to hurt and mislead each other. But sometimes our words can also effect healing. The right word at the right time can bring comfort, stimulate a new insight, or inspire action.

"A picture is worth a thousand words." But at times a spoken word or two is worth a thousand pictures. When my work requires me to travel away from home for days or even weeks, I am glad for the pictures of my wife and children that I carry in my wallet. But after a while, I would trade all those pictures for just a few living words, even by telephone. The spoken word conveys emotion more richly. It binds us together more powerfully than words on a page.

Similarly, the miracle of the spoken word lies at the heart of God's relationship to us. When we understand Scripture as "sound," we are reminded of the God whose Word is creative. "God said . . . and there was . . ." (Gen. 1:3). "And the Word became flesh and lived among us" (John 1:14). Just as our words to each other can reframe our way of seeing things, suddenly lifting our spirits or subduing them, God's "resounding" words restructure our reality. They offer us the promise of right relationship with each other and with the world around us.

Despite the lack of historical memory in much of the contemporary church, we still have a few reminders of the importance of the sound of Scripture. In some traditions, such as Eastern Orthodoxy, Scripture is sung in the liturgy, just as in some modern-day monasteries. For some Protestants, Scripture just doesn't sound right unless it is heard in the King James Version (just as for some Catholics, the mass—and the reading of Scripture in the mass—doesn't sound right unless it is heard in Latin). Sound matters.

I have noticed that some ministers even take on a different voice when they read Scripture in worship. Their voices become more formal, more reverent, and sometimes more affected—some American Presbyterians even begin to sound Scottish! Sound conveys the power of Scripture; Scripture has a sound of its own.

READING SCRIPTURE IN COMMUNITY

Most mainline Protestants, if they read Scripture at all, read it by themselves. Participation in study groups is widespread but is clearly secondary to personal, individual study. Yet, if Scripture is a sacramental, poetic-like word, we would do well to recover disciplines of reading Scripture in community. We need to hear Scripture together, and to discuss it with fellow believers. Scripture calls for public performance. It invites us to experience something extraordinary together, just as when we hear a great symphony.

Reading Scripture in community follows from reading Scripture aloud. A particularly dramatic example is the Jewish Yeshiva. Young men sit at tables, reading the Torah aloud.[9] Some speak quietly; others, loudly. Some rock back and forth. Others sit still. Yet others stand up and discuss points of controversy with each other. The study of Scripture is never simply a solitary pursuit. The room is abuzz with sound; the atmosphere is intensely communal.

As a communal experience, Scripture is a source of inexhaustible meaning. People find that they can turn to Scripture again and again, and apply it to new situations. Indeed, Scripture itself embodies this principle of communal reinterpretation. Later Scriptures often appropriate themes from earlier Scriptures to speak a word to their time.[10] Recent biblical scholarship has reminded us that the Gospels, for example, are less the products of particular individuals (Matthew, Mark, Luke, and John), than of early Christian communities that made sense of their experience of Jesus as Lord and Savior by reinterpreting the Hebrew Scriptures. Each Gospel reflects a debate within a community, as well as a debate between communities.

The importance of reading Scripture in light of the community's history of interpretation is reflected in medieval Jewish texts. Scribes surrounded the biblical (or talmudic) text with commentary of the great rabbis. These marginal notes included both majority and minority positions, as though to insist that the community was still debating their meaning.

The Bibles of the medieval church are similar. The margins—even the spaces between one line of text and the next—were filled with a gloss, a summarization of patristic interpretations of the passage in question. When Luther prepared biblical texts for his students, he left these margins blank! Yet, even here, his intent was not to "excise" the role of the community or to ignore the tradition. Rather, he had his students fill in the blanks with their own notes and reflections, as he lectured.[11] A "reformed" community replaced the old commentary with its own.

The Geneva Bible, the translation that the Puritans preferred, vividly illustrates this point. A printed, official commentary again fills the margins. An individual could not read the Geneva Bible without the constant reminder that it was the book of a particular community of believers.

But the fact that Christians over the centuries have found "inexhaustible meaning" in Scripture does not give Christians today the license to interpret Scripture subjectively or arbitrarily. On the contrary, Christians have insisted on reading Scripture in community to test their interpretations against the deeper wisdom of the community.

This concern for testing interpretations takes one form in Catholicism. The magisterium, the church's authoritative teaching office, is to seek the welfare of the broader community of faith. The church's bishops and teachers protect the church's theology, so that people might be rightly instructed and formed in the faith. The church's leaders discern and guard interpretations of Scripture that reflect the sense of the faithful, and that help to build up the community in the love of Christ.[12]

While the Reformed tradition has resisted the notion of a magisterium that places its seal of approval on certain writings and condemns others, it too has argued that we need more than good eyes (and ears!) and minds if we are to discern the meaning of Scripture correctly. The Holy Spirit must illuminate us, so we can receive Scripture not simply as interesting (or boring) words, but as the Word of God. For this reason, Reformed churches have traditionally included a prayer of illumination before the reading of Scripture in worship. We pray for the Spirit to open us to the Word that God would speak to us through the words of Scripture.

But the experience of the Spirit is not private; rather, the Spirit binds believers to Jesus Christ and each other. The Spirit that opens the words of Scripture to our understanding is the Spirit that creates a community of faith. To read Scripture in the leading of the Spirit is not to receive a personal revelation, but to read with others, to learn from each other's insights and questions, and to encourage each other to grow in faith and faithfulness.[13]

Martin Buber and Franz Rosenzweig strove to translate Scripture in such a way that people would experience its revelatory power. They wanted Scripture to "break out into the world of the living, pressing for 're-alization' in real life."[14] In both Judaism and Christianity, Scripture has found its primary realization in the "real life" of communities that read Scripture together. These communities do not tell people simply to go off and read the text on their own. Rather, they constantly orient their worship, decision making, and theological reflection around their common reading of Scripture.

READING SCRIPTURE IN CONTEXT

Mainline Protestants most often make their selection of Scripture for personal study simply by opening the Bible and rummaging through it until they find something interesting. At times, they may also use a concordance or an index to look up a particular verse. Yet, if Scripture is a sacramental, poetic-like word, we would do well to develop disciplines of reading particular passages of Scripture in their larger biblical context.

Great literature and poetry offer pithy sayings and striking turns of phrase to which we later refer without ever reporting their wider context. "To be or not to be, that is the question." "Life, liberty, and the pursuit of happiness." "No man is an island." But we would never claim that these one-liners plumb the depth of the piece to which they belong, anymore than humming the theme of Beethoven's Fifth Symphony evokes the awesome power of hearing it performed in its entirety. Similarly, as we read Scripture, it is not enough to rummage through the text in search of one wise saying or another. A great deal depends on reading passages in context.

Sometimes, this context has been framed by the way in which Scripture has circulated and been made available to its readers. Not until the invention of the printing press could the books of the Bible be easily bound together into one volume. Until then, the Scriptures circulated as separate books or collections of books. In the early church, a congregation might not have a complete set of Scriptures. Other congregations would then lend it their books for reading or transcription.[15] How these congregations understood one part of Scripture depended on which other parts they had.

From an early date, the four Gospels were typically bound together. This way of circulating them was not only practical—they were the four books most in demand—but theological. For one thing, it lifted up their special status as the foundational books of the Christian religion. For another, it suggested that they were integrally related to each other, that one could therefore compare them, and that together they filled out the story of Jesus.

Other ways of collecting biblical books establish other contexts. When I was a boy, I received a Gideon's pocket New Testament that appended the Psalms. This way of ordering Scripture makes a profound statement about the centrality of the Psalms to the church—and suggests that they are best understood in light of the New Testament. The Psalms become the prayers of Christ and his church.

Lectionaries, prayer books, hymnbooks, and devotional aids establish yet another way of collecting different parts of Scripture and associating them with each other. Thus, lectionaries typically assign parts of Second Isaiah (Isaiah 40–66) to the Sundays in Advent; Old Testament images of restoration are associated with preparations for Jesus' birth. Similarly, baptismal liturgies typically rehearse Old Testament accounts of the waters of creation, the flood, and the parting of the Red Sea in association with New Testament images of new life in Christ.

Scripture itself is organized in such a way as to suggest that particular passages are meant to be read in larger literary contexts. When we read a portion of Scripture, we are not reading "generic" literature, but different kinds of literature: poems, stories, law codes, prophetic discourses, parables, gospels, epistles. Each kind of literature has an integrity of its own. We cannot understand a portion of a miracle story without understanding the story as a whole. A particular law makes sense only in the context of the law code to which it belongs. If we ignore these literary units, we easily wrench particular passages out of context.

We must also respect the fact that Scripture is a collection of books. Books too have literary integrity. They are meant to be read in their entirety, so that one can discern their overarching themes. For this reason, lectio continua, the reading of a book of Scripture consecutively over several sessions, has frequently characterized Jewish and Christian liturgical and devotional use of Scripture.[16] Lectio continua helps us to hear the larger context of particular verses.

Moreover, the different books of the Bible do not stand alone; they too have been collected into larger units. The first five books of the Bible, what Jews call the Torah, is not an arbitrary division. Rather, it offers the reader a theological framework for interpreting the larger meaning of those books. As James Sanders notes, the Torah ends with Deuteronomy, not Joshua—with the people of Israel on the edge of the Promised Land, not in it. The Torah thus testifies to the Jewish understanding that the Jewish people are, in a spiritual sense, still on the edge of the Promised Land. Their relationship to God is based not on the triumphalism of conquering the land, but on the humility of waiting for God to fulfill God's purposes in God's own time.[17]

Similarly, the Prophets and the Writings, the other two major divisions of the Hebrew Bible, are not arbitrary. The sequence Torah, Prophets, Writings suggests an order of authority. The books that belong in the Prophets are secondary to the Torah and are commentary on it, and the Writings are less authoritative than the Prophets, though still Scripture.

In Christianity, too, particular divisions of Scripture frame the way one reads particular books. The most basic divisions are the two testaments. The sequence first Old Testament and then New Testament is an historical sequence. But it also has theological significance. The New Testament fulfills the Old Testament and becomes the key to reading it. The placement of the prophets at the end of the Old Testament reinforces the Christian notion that they point ahead to the New Testament (not back to the Torah, as in Judaism). The removal of historical writings from the Jewish category of the Writings and their placement in the narrative flow of the Old Testament reinforces the Christian notion that the Old Testament is history, and that this history finds its end in the birth of Christ.

Similarly, particular divisions of the New Testament frame the way one reads particular materials within it.[18] The placement of the four Gospels at the beginning of the New Testament establishes them as the foundational witness to Christ. The Acts of the Apostles and the Epistles apply this witness to particular communities, thus serving as a kind of commentary on the Gospels. The book of Revelation envisions the gospel's final and universal triumph. In contrast to Judaism, these divisions do not reflect levels of authority; nonetheless, they establish the unique and foundational authority of the Gospels.[19]

Finally, we can understand the meaning of particular books and particular divisions of Scripture only in the context of the canon as a whole. The Christian tradition has understood the canonical context in at least two ways. First, the canon traces the history of God's people from the beginning of time to its end. It is, above all, a narrative, in which one event follows another. It is a coherent story.

A second way of understanding the canonical context is in tension with this notion of an historical, narrative flow of events. Rather than history, we have simultaneity; rather than a flow of events, a collection of timeless verses, each of equal value. In Orthodox Judaism, for example, every part of the Torah is regarded as equally inspired. No part can be dismissed as something old, superseded by something later in the canon's historical flow.

Thus, rather than declaring some texts to be more authoritative than others, the Jewish rabbinic tradition has found creative strategies for harmonizing and synthesizing divergent texts. Exodus 21:20–26 provides for manumission of Hebrew slaves after six years; a slave may, however, refuse the offer, in which case he gives himself over to perpetual servitude. Leviticus 25:8–17, 29–34, by contrast, provides for manumission only in the jubilee year, every fifty years; moreover, slaves cannot refuse the offer.

The rabbinic solution was to combine and harmonize the two divergent texts. A new law, different from either Exodus or Leviticus, emerged: If a slave refused manumission after six years, he remained in servitude until the jubilee year. As biblical scholar Jon Levenson notes, neither Exodus or Leviticus was allowed to overwhelm the other; the result was a law that respected, while transcending, both. Levenson concludes, "What this complex position loses in simplicity it gains in honesty and fidelity to the tradition. For though the offensive feature [in Scripture] is transcended, it is never denied, ignored, disguised, or explained away."[20]

In Christianity, a canon within the canon has frequently functioned to eliminate "offensive" materials, those parts of Scripture that didn't seem to fit with the central affirmations of the gospel. At other times, however, Christians have insisted that the entire canon has sacramental character. Every part of Scripture, just as in the Jewish understanding of the Torah, is equally inspired. Not every part may set forth Christ on its own, but every part can be brought into relation with Scripture's testimony to him.

For this reason, Christians have argued that Scripture interprets Scripture. Parts of Scripture that are less clear (in their witness to Christ) can be illuminated by parts that are more clear. One part of Scripture can help us to hear echoes of the gospel in another part. A sensitive ear can gather divergent materials into a common witness to Christ.

Catholic historian Jean Leclercq notes, for example, that a "spontaneous play of associations, similarities, and comparisons" characterizes monastic exegesis.[21] The Benedictines understood one part of Scripture to comment on another.

> [T]he verbal echoes so excite the memory that a mere allusion will spontaneously evoke whole quotations and, in turn, a scriptural phrase will suggest quite naturally allusions elsewhere in the sacred books. Each word is a hook, so to speak; it catches hold of one or several others which become linked together and make up the fabric of the exposé.[22]

In Protestantism, the Reformed tradition has most clearly emphasized the simultaneity of Scripture as a witness to Christ. All of Scripture is of value, for Christ is present throughout all of it. Calvin, like the monks, knew Scripture so well that he frequently quoted it from memory in his writings — and easily paraphrased it and conflated different biblical texts as he sought to order Scripture into a coherent theological witness. In setting forth Christ and life in Christ, he could enlist all of Scripture.[23]

Similarly, the classic Reformed confessions not only declared that Scripture should be read in the light of Scripture but also sought to order Scripture as a whole into a coherent witness to God and God's purposes. The Westminster Confession of Faith, in a series of footnotes, includes biblical warrants for each of its sections. Today, we are apt to accuse its authors of proof-texting, of taking Scripture out of context. But they themselves surely believed that they were putting particular parts of Scripture into a canonical context. They were showing how a wide variety of passages helped to set forth the reality of Christ.

An old joke illustrates the importance of reading Scripture in context. A man once tried to get counsel for his life by opening the Bible at random and throwing his finger on the page. His first attempt yielded the verse: "Judas hanged himself." Dissatisfied, he tried again. This time, he read: "Go, thou, and do likewise." Trying once more, he was told: "What thou doest, do quickly."

While this method of getting into Scripture respects the power of every part, it results in absurdities. We must therefore learn to read Scripture in context. Christians have sometimes disputed the shape of this context, but they have rarely been content to treat Scripture as a collection of disconnected pieces of counsel.

MEMORIZING SCRIPTURE

Most mainline Protestants are able to recite little if any Scripture from memory. At most, they know the Lord's Prayer; many are also able to recite, even if haltingly, the Twenty-third Psalm (often, in some confused combination of the King James Version and a contemporary translation!). Yet, if Scripture is a sacramental, poetic-like word, we would do well to develop disciplines of memorization. Through memorization, Scripture dwells in our hearts, not just on the pages of a book. It can speak to us anytime, anywhere. As we recall the words of Scripture, Scripture recalls to us the reality of Christ among us.

Memorization depends on sound. To some degree, memorization also depends on disciplines of reading Scripture in community, for we tend to remember those words and phrases that the community guards most preciously and repeats most often. In hearing and repeating Scripture daily, early Benedictine monks memorized large portions of it. Because they would then recite Scripture to themselves as they worked, they were sometimes known as the "munchers." They munched on Scripture as though chewing the cud.[24] They seemed to take Moses literally: "The word is very near to you; it is in your mouth and in your heart for you to observe" (Deut. 30:14).

Memorization of Scripture also assisted the monks in reading Scripture in context. Because they knew Scripture so intimately, they could make connections between one part and another. They were living concordances, able to keep track of Scripture in its entirety.[25]

The traditional training of Eastern Orthodox priests included memorization of all 150 Psalms. The memorization of Scripture was long considered an essential spiritual discipline in some Protestant traditions, as well. Hughes Oliphant Old, a Presbyterian theologian, has recently noted that his "grandmother, a very proper Presbyterian lady who did her finishing school over a hundred years ago, could recite by heart the Sermon on the Mount, several chapters from the Gospel of John, some forty psalms, and much more."[26] Memorization of Scripture, more than special techniques of prayer, has been at the heart of a Reformed piety.

Those saints of the faith who have endured the trials of imprisonment and isolation often report that words of Scripture have come to them out of their memory, providing them spiritual sustenance at critical moments. For example, German theologian Dietrich Bonhoeffer, imprisoned by the Nazis, and Presbyterian missionary Benjamin Weir, kidnapped in Lebanon, found that memorized fragments of Scripture, often embedded in hymns, gave them an assurance that God had not abandoned them, that God was indeed with them.

In a word-weary world, memorization is a lost art. We are inundated with information that is valuable for the moment. Our memory is short-term. Recovering disciplines of memorization could teach us to savor Scripture, even as we savor a good joke or a witty insight. We could learn to dwell on the words, to turn them over, to allow Scripture to speak to us as no other book can.

Reading Scripture aloud, in community, in context, and for memoriza-tion—if we were to take these four disciplines seriously, they would re-shape the way we use Scripture in our congregations today. They would help us to rediscover its compelling power.

Understanding Scripture as a sacramental, poetic-like word that is meant to be read aloud would, for example, reshape the way we select translations, whether for worship or personal study, as well as the way we read Scripture in worship. We would pay far more attention to how Scrip-ture sounds, even as we seek to understand what it says.

We still do not have a worthy successor to the King James Version, which has so profoundly shaped the English language and great English lit-erature and poetry (just as the Luther Bible has shaped the German lan-guage and great German literature and poetry). The Revised Standard Version attempted as much as possible to maintain the literary quality of the King James Version, while correcting mistranslations and putting Scripture into contemporary English, but never found the same degree of acceptance.

Many biblical scholars believe that the results of the New Revised Stan-dard Version are even less felicitous. When Phyllis Trible, the feminist bib-lical scholar, was asked her opinion of the New Revised Standard Version, she replied, "Well, you've heard of New Coke and Classic Coke. I prefer Classic Coke."[27]

Many of the contemporary translations succumb to the general flattening of language that infects an information society.[28] Translators frequently boast that they have consulted the best manuscripts and have rendered Scripture in a colloquial English that is easily understood. They seem to see Scripture primarily as information that needs to be stated as plainly and ac-curately as possible, not as sounds that convey levels of meaning.

This tendency reaches an extreme in the *Contemporary English Version* (CEV), the successor to the *Good News Bible*. On the positive side, the CEV tries to avoid "insider," church language—an important considera-tion in a society that is increasingly secular and unchurched. Because the CEV aims at being understandable, it has proved attractive to many adults, even though it was originally intended for children.

On the negative side, these efforts often come at the cost of the poetic. Nobility of language is lost. The power of biblical language—and of tra-ditional renderings of Scripture—is ignored. Jesus is now born in a "feed box," not a manger (Luke 2:7, 12, 16).[29] When he comes into Jerusalem on a donkey on Palm Sunday, people continue to gather by the side of the road, but they no longer shout, "hosanna." Instead, like at a Fourth of July parade in downtown Peoria, they cry, "hooray" (Mark 11:9).

Translators have always struggled with how much to dignify scriptural language, and how much to render it in the style and manner in which it was written. Similarly, they have struggled with how best to translate the original languages into the vernacular, while "translating" the reader into biblical ways of thinking. At times, Luther, the translator, asked himself, "How does a German speak in such a case?"[30] At other times, he asked the reader to "give the Hebrew some room."[31] One cannot help but feel that a translation like the *Contemporary English Version,* by giving so much room to colloquial English, risks dumbing the Bible down. It asks so little of its readers that they may well wonder whether Christianity asks much of them.

It is unlikely that many pastors in the Protestant mainline will soon go back to the King James Version. Its language is too archaic, too inaccessible to modern people. But there are other solutions until a great, contemporary translation appears. James Sanders, for example, argues for using the Revised Standard Version and simply using good and reasonable judgment in changing its language to make it more "inclusive."[32]

In addition, some translators, thankfully, are trying to recapture a sense of Scripture's literary power. The translation of the Tanakh, the Hebrew Bible, by the Jewish Publication Society combines accuracy with poetic sensitivity—and even assumes that people are capable of occasionally using their dictionaries to look up an unfamiliar word. It is a rich resource not only for Jews, but for Christians who want to recover a sense of Scripture as a revelatory, sacramental word.[33]

Also of great importance is the recently published, stunning translation of *The Five Books of Moses,* by Everett Fox. As a reviewer notes:

> [Fox's] translation seeks to turn us into active listeners by reminding us that the Bible is not a modern but an ancient, demanding and sometimes obscure work whose meaning is inseparable from the language in which it was written. . . . The result is a work of jolting power and majestic strangeness. . . . [Fox] lays out the text in poetic lines, which create a sense of spoken phrasing. Instead of the traditional "In the beginning God created the heavens and the earth," we get the more active thrust and parry, the hovering motion of
>
> > At the beginning of God's creating
> > of the heavens and the earth,
> > when the earth was wild and waste,

darkness over the face of Ocean,
rushing-spirit of God hovering over the face of the waters.[34]

Besides new translations that successfully set forth Scripture's compelling power, we need to take more seriously the art of reading Scripture aloud.[35] The public reading of Scripture is not a matter of dramatic style. We are not faithful to the text if we believe we have to liven it up. Rather, it is a matter of reading Scripture in its own voice, and of setting forth its words with clarity and reverence, faith and conviction. As a man who records Bible texts for a German publishing company notes:

> The most important thing is to let the images speak. Usually, people try to load emotions on top of a text when they read it aloud. The feeling doesn't come from within, out of the text, but is laid on top of it. In contrast, I try to note: Ah, now it's getting sad; ah, now joyous. . . . I need awhile to get into a text. Once I'm in, I let it carry me along. It must sound as though I am telling the story for the first time.[36]

In the Eastern Orthodox tradition, those who sing Scripture in the liturgy undergo special training and testing. When Protestant mainline churches seek to include readers in worship, their ministers have a responsibility to help train them and test their abilities, as well. We do not have to go as far as Benedict in enforcing perfection; we can, however, convey the privilege of reading Scripture in the company of the faithful.

Mainline Protestants may also wish to rethink the wisdom of pew Bibles. When we follow along, even as the minister or reader reads aloud, Scripture again tends to come through the eye, rather than the ear. We need to train ourselves to become good listeners of Scripture. Music appreciation classes enable us to appreciate and enjoy a symphony of Beethoven or Brahms more deeply. Similarly, we need disciplined preparation to appreciate the richness of Scripture as a spoken, sacramental word.

Just as early Christians read Scripture aloud even when studying it by themselves, we too would do well to read Scripture aloud when we read it by ourselves. I suspect that many ministers do not read their sermon text aloud until worship on Sunday morning. The text might reveal more of its power and offer greater depth of meaning if they also read it aloud in the course of their preparations.

IMPLICATIONS FOR TODAY: SCRIPTURE IN COMMUNITY

Understanding Scripture as a sacramental, poetic-like word that is meant to be read in community would remind us that the process of interpretation involves a profound interaction between pastor and people, between prayer and study, and between a particular community of faith and the wider church, present and past. Whenever two or three gather in the name of Christ, they can read Scripture "in community." But the communion of saints also reaches across time and space.

On the one hand, the pastor is a theologian in residence. For this reason, the Reformed tradition has often referred to the pastor as a "teaching elder." Pastors have received special training that enables them to study Scripture more closely than most members of the congregation. Because they can help us hear the meaning of Scripture more clearly, we should honor them and evidence towards them what one author, following Calvin, has called "a teachable spirit."[37]

On the other hand, the Reformed tradition—and Protestantism in general—has also insisted that the meaning of Scripture is plain to anyone who reads it with the help of the Holy Spirit. Each of us—no matter our education or background—is called to interpret Scripture. Moreover, we have the responsibility to share our insights with each other, even when they seem to conflict. We must have the confidence that God can speak through our understanding of Scripture.

The role of pastor and people suggests a model for Bible study such as the following: On Sunday morning, people gather for an hour of adult study prior to worship. As the class opens, the pastor asks for prayer concerns. After prayer, people open their Bibles and together read a selection aloud. The pastor then asks people to report what in the passage makes them curious, what bothers them, what questions they have. A conversation begins. Different people notice different things. After half an hour, the pastor asks people to look for the broader theological themes in the passage. What does this passage tell us about God? What does God appear to be doing? What do God's ways tell us about our lives? Throughout, pastor and people are thinking together, all drawing on each other's gifts and insights. Disagreements sometimes emerge; a deeper understanding of the text always results. As the class ends, people pray for each other.

This way of reading Scripture in community has a devotional aspect. We do nothing wrong in reading Scripture silently and by ourselves. Yet, we also need to recover disciplines of hearing Scripture in the context of devotions with fellow Christians. Pastors might take the lead in helping church members to recover disciplines of family devotions. We might also find ways to gather regularly with colleagues or friends to pray and read Scripture together. One wonders what it would mean for the strengthening of the church not only if we read the Bible on our own more often, but if we also spent at least one hour reading the Bible with others for every hour that we spend reading it by ourselves.

Reading the Bible in community encourages us to look beyond our own narrow horizons. We need to draw on each other's perspectives in our own congregations, and we need to learn from Christians of other times and places. A diversity of readings can challenge us to read Scripture "against ourselves." Outsiders—strangers, prophets, the poor—can help us to correct our inevitable (and sinful) tendency to reduce Scripture to our own narrow interests.[38]

We also need the insights of those who have come before us and whom the Christian tradition has honored as authoritative teachers. Those of us in the Protestant mainline are apt to recognize the special place of the Augustines and Luthers and Calvins of the past. But we need to hear, as well, from those great teachers who do not belong as directly to our tradition, such as Thomas Aquinas, the great theologian of medieval Catholicism, or the great teachers of the Eastern Orthodox tradition.[39]

IMPLICATIONS FOR TODAY: SCRIPTURE IN CONTEXT

Understanding Scripture as a sacramental, poetic-like word would remind us to read Scripture in context. We would look at particular passages not in isolation from each other, but in relation to the larger biblical witness to God and God's purposes, as ultimately revealed in Christ.

Historical-critical scholarship has contributed to the tendency to read texts in isolation from one another. Historical-critical scholars typically dissolve the literary context in order to reconstruct a history behind the text. Recent biblical scholarship, however, has evidenced renewed interest in the literary character of Scripture. This scholarship draws on historical-critical insights not to dissolve the text, but to read it more closely as it stands.

A strictly historical-critical approach tends to see Genesis 22 (the binding of Isaac) as an etiology (an explanation of the origins) of the abolishment of child sacrifice in ancient Israel. A literary approach, by contrast, lifts up broader biblical themes. Rabbinic exegesis has frequently noted the parallels between the banishment of Hagar and Ishmael in Genesis 21, and the binding of Isaac in the next chapter. The repetition of particular words and phrases establishes thematic links.[40] In both cases, Abraham almost loses a son; in both cases, God intervenes and miraculously saves and blesses the son.

Jon Levenson notes the significance of this theme throughout Genesis: from Cain and Abel, to Joseph and his brothers. Again and again, the beloved son is lost, or almost lost, only to be miraculously restored. (Cain, in a sense, is replaced by Seth; Joseph, sold into slavery, reemerges as the king's right hand man.) Levenson also traces the subsequent development of this theme in Judaism and Christianity and their Scriptures—for example, Christ is the beloved son who is lost to death only to be resurrected as Lord and Savior.

For many Christians today, Genesis 22 is simply a riveting story. It stands on its own. If they place it in a larger context, they typically employ a typological interpretation: the binding of Isaac is understood as a typological foreshadowing of Christ's sacrifice on the cross. Levenson's literary approach sets both the binding of Isaac and the crucifixion/resurrection into a broader theological context. As we trace the resonance of these themes throughout the breadth of the canon, they become richer—and Scripture becomes all the more interesting and compelling.

The Song of Solomon offers a second example. A historical-critical approach reminds us that the Song is secular love poetry; the Song makes no mention of God and has no apparent religious significance. One may wonder, as did many Jews and Christians in the first centuries, whether it really belongs in the canon.

Yet, as part of the canon, the Song could be redeemed. It did not have to rest on its own. It could be connected to larger biblical themes. For Jews, the Song became an allegory of God's love for Israel; for Christians, of Christ's love for the church. By itself, the Song was questionable; as part of the canon, it resonated with other themes and evoked a sense of God's active presence in the community of faith.

A literary reading of Scripture lifts up other themes, as well. As biblical scholar Phyllis Trible has noted, the Song can be understood as a commentary on Genesis 2:18–25.[41] The Song celebrates erotic love as part of God's good creation of humans as male and female. It evokes a picture of life in the Garden of Eden prior to the Fall.

But the Song can also be read over against Hosea 2. The image is no longer the garden of innocence, but the wilderness of desire, in which Israel runs after gods who promise her prosperity. Erotic imagery is no longer a reason for celebration, but for lament. God chastises Israel for playing the whore. Hosea 2 reminds us that love and sex can go awry; desire can be misplaced.

This larger canonical context then helps to enrich a reading of Revelation 21:1–4, which celebrates the love between Christ and the church. Each of these passages (Genesis, Hosea, Revelation) comments on the other. Together, they point to larger themes of love and desire that run throughout the canon. Love and sexuality are part of the good creation, but they are easily distorted. In the new creation, the New Jerusalem coming down out of heaven as a bride adorned for her husband, they are redeemed.

Maintaining a sense of the canonical context is not easy. In the late Middle Ages, Scripture was divided into its current chapters and verses. While making it easier to locate particular passages, these divisions tempt us to dissolve Scripture into isolated units.

Lectionaries exacerbate this temptation. They tend to cut Scripture into snippets that are manageable for the limited time available on a Sunday morning, but that do not always respect larger literary units.[42] We may be tempted to see each reading as a unit unto itself, as though it had a priceless pearl that we must extract.

But not every verse of Scripture, not every chapter, sets forth Christ.[43] Verses and chapters and books need to be placed in the broader biblical narrative. Otherwise, we miss the forest for the trees. We focus on the text, rather than allowing the text to focus our sight on the living God. The homosexuality debates in the church are, again, illustrative. When we argue about the half dozen or so texts that have traditionally been understood as condemning homosexuality, we easily lose a sense of the larger biblical context. A more fruitful way into the debate would be to develop larger biblical themes about human nature and the place of sexuality in defining (or not defining) it.

Scripture is meant to be heard in larger units. When we read the Bible in snippets, we treat it as if it were a collection of favorite quotations. We tend to wrench passages out of context. Disciplines of reading Scripture in context require us to immerse ourselves in longer units of Scripture, not shorter—whether for worship, devotions, study, or for purposes of memorization. When we allow Scripture to comment on Scripture, we better explore the full contours of life in Christ—the reality of God's miraculous restoration of our own lives, and of God's promise of abiding relationship, despite our failures.

IMPLICATIONS FOR TODAY: SCRIPTURE FROM MEMORY

Understanding Scripture as a sacramental, poetic word that is meant to be memorized would remind us that Scripture's language is also ours. Scripture offers us a language for prayer and politics, personal meditation and communal formation. It can become a "second language" that we seek to master as well as our own; it even offers itself as a "first language" for the faith and life of the church.

In a church without a standard translation, let alone a great one, the memorization of Scripture poses a problem. Even if we wanted to memorize Scripture, it is not clear which version we would use, and which version we would teach our children. For texts like the Twenty-third Psalm, do we return to the King James Version, or do we use the same translation as the congregation in which we worship? (And is there even one translation here, or does it vary from week to week?)

The memorization of Scripture has also become a problem because mainline Protestants have rightfully reacted against a church in the past—and some forms of Protestantism in the present—that seemed to emphasize rote memorization at the cost of understanding what was being memorized. Too often, the memorization of Scripture became a matter of mastering one-liners by which one could demonstrate one's orthodoxy. One might be able to rattle off John 3:16 ("For God so loved the world, that he gave his only begotten Son . . ." [KJV]), yet have little sense of the awe and mystery that pervade the Gospel of John.

If, however, the literary—and theological—integrity of Scripture is to be respected, memorization will involve less emphasis on one-liners and more emphasis, as Old suggests above, on whole psalms and whole chapters.[44] Memorized Scripture then becomes a well from which the pastor and the worshipping community draw to lift up their voice to God. In much African-American worship, sermons and prayers are saturated with scriptural imagery and allusions. Because Scripture is so familiar to the congregation, it comes to constitute its primary language.

Scripture as the language of faith also offers powerful rhetoric for political engagement. In seventeenth-century England, Gerrard Winstanley, leader of the Diggers, wrote a series of radical tracts calling for common use of the land and political equality. Though lacking formal theological education, Winstanley knew Scripture inside out. Its images shaped his vocabulary to such an extent that the contemporary reader cannot easily tell where Scripture ends and Winstanley begins.[45]

Similarly, Abraham Lincoln's addresses, and the sermons and speeches of Martin Luther King, Jr., incorporate a great deal of Scripture—its words, phrases, and cadences. Lincoln and King almost seem to speak "Bible" as though it were the best language for talking about God's purposes in history and society.

These examples remind us that the memorized word need not be dead. An emphasis on memorization need not be a badge of mere "piety" (in a depreciating sense of that word). Memorization can help Scripture to become "living and active, sharper than any two-edged sword" (Heb. 4:12). It can help to bind Christians together, giving them a common vocabulary and a common set of lenses for interpreting God's presence in the world.

THE SIGNIFICANCE OF A DISCIPLINED READING OF SCRIPTURE

By themselves, these disciplines do not tell us anything about the content of God's Word to us in Scripture. They do not help us to know in specific what God asks of us. But they can open us to this Word, so that we may receive its compelling power, however it comes. Drawing on the wisdom of the Christian tradition, they nurture a piety rooted in the Word as a sacrament of Christ.

These disciplines are not spontaneous gestures. They require our effort and determination, and their rewards are not always obvious. Moreover, there is no formula for the work of the Holy Spirit. Practicing these disciplines does not guarantee us a more exciting experience of Scripture, as though every engagement with it should leave us breathless. They might, however, help us to resist our own worst habits, our reduction of Scripture to mere information that we marshal for one cause or another. They might help us to allow Scripture to stand over us and against us and to speak in its own voice. They might remind us to listen anew to all of Scripture, even those parts that are most troubling or least clear.

Poet Kathleen Norris has written eloquently of her experience of these disciplines in a Benedictine monastery where she resided for several months. Jeremiah was read aloud at morning and evening prayer, and Norris reports her anguish at being plunged day after day into Jeremiah's pain. Yet, "over time, the texts invite you to commune with them, and can come to serve as a mirror."[46] One has "the sense of being sought out, personally engaged, making it possible, even necessary, to respond personally, to take the scriptures to heart."[47]

In such moments, a disciplined reading of Scripture—aloud, in community, in context, and for memorization—speaks with compelling power. It sets forth God's presence, the Christ whose judgment and comfort we finally cannot escape. It becomes a sacrament that feeds us eternal life.

5

COMMENTARY ON SCRIPTURE

According to recent count, my wife, children, and I own at least fourteen complete English Bibles—and goodness knows how many pocket New Testaments and collections of portions of Scripture (from the five books of Moses, to the Psalms, to the letters of Paul). Each of these Bibles has a story. Some we received as gifts; others we inherited or purchased. Together, they represent a wide variety of translations and editions.

While we use only a couple of these Bibles regularly, we would not choose to give any of them away. Each has contributed in one way or another to our understanding of Scripture. Each has special associations with particular times of joy or struggle in our efforts to live the Christian life.

Americans in general are Bible collectors. Even in a biblically illiterate culture, the Bible continues to be a best-seller.[1] To walk into a Christian bookstore is to be overwhelmed by Bibles in a variety of bindings, print types, paper types, and sizes.

Each of these ways of packaging Scripture is a commentary on Scripture. Each says something about the kind of book Scripture is and the kind of authority it has. Each implicitly conveys a message about what makes Scripture *Scripture*.

Some Bibles have expensive leather covers and fine, thin, gold-edged paper. As one turns the pages for the first time, they rustle and crackle. People may be reluctant to write in such a Bible. The packaging lifts up the idea that this book is unlike any other. It is truly a "holy Bible." It is an object of beauty, made to last. It seems to set forth eternal truths. The words of Jesus may even be highlighted in red, as deserving special attention.

Other Bibles are geared to particular categories of people. One publisher offers a women's Bible in a pink hardcover and a men's Bible in blue.

Other Bibles are geared to children or adolescents. In the 1960s, the American Bible Society put out a "Blue Jean Bible," a New Testament that had a blue jean cover. I have even seen an edition of the Bible for military personnel. The camouflage colors must be more for marketing purposes than for disguise; the book itself is a flimsy paperback that would not hold up to the rigors of battle, nor stop many bullets.

When the Bible is packaged in one of these ways, we get a different message about its character. Rather than being a "holy Bible," Scripture is now presented as a book that speaks to us whoever we are, wherever we find ourselves. Scripture is not high and lifted up but down to earth; it is the book of the people, and its meaning should be accessible and relevant to each of us, no matter what our life situation.

Yet other Bibles come with special study guides: maps, indexes, notes, cross-references, introductory articles. These study Bibles explain difficult words and concepts, provide historical context, and lift up the distinctive themes of each biblical book. Their format resembles that of the annotated editions of Shakespeare's plays that many of us used in high school or college. Study Bibles remind us that Scripture belongs to a different time and place. Its meaning is not immediately accessible. One needs expert assistance in interpreting it rightly.

While these three messages may complement each other, they may also suggest our ambivalence about Scripture. Scripture is *holy;* it is not under our immediate control; it speaks God's Word to us from beyond ourselves. Yet, Scripture is God's Word *to us;* it reaches into *our* lives. Yet, Scripture is also a human, *historical* document that must be studied like any other text out of the past.

Other ways of using Scripture—of handling it, placing it (on stands, tables, and pulpits), and referring to it—also say something about the kind of text we take it to be. We do not have to develop an abstract theory of biblical authority before we actually turn to Scripture and do something with it; rather, the fact that we *use* Scripture (even if we don't always *read* it!) betrays an assumption that Scripture really does have authority in one respect or another. If today we want to recover a sense of Scripture's compelling power, we have a great deal to learn not only from our own experience of Scripture, but from those uses of Scripture that have nurtured its authority over the centuries.

THE CHARACTER OF COMMENTARY

The Reformed tradition has always understood new life in Christ both to rest on God's grace and to evoke our thankful response. We are freely justified by God's grace. We can do nothing to deserve it. We receive it by faith, which is itself God's gift. At the same time, God's grace moves us to gratitude and obedience. In response to God's grace, we wish to deepen our relationship with God, to grow in faith, and to participate in God's purposes for creation.

The Christian disciplines of reading Scripture that we have investigated—aloud, in community, in context, and for memorization—reflect these dynamics of grace and response. On the one hand, these disciplines are means of grace. While they cannot guarantee that we will hear Scripture as God's Word, they can correct our tendency to reduce Scripture to mere information. They can remind us that Scripture is larger than ourselves, that Scripture points us toward God and draws us into God's presence. They can teach us that Scripture is truly Scripture when it claims us for God and God's purposes by setting forth God's gift of new life in Christ.

On the other hand, these disciplines of reading Scripture as the Word of God, like other disciplines of faith, order our response to God's grace. They exercise our faith. They stir us to action. They are a kind of commentary on Scripture, insofar as engaging in them "comments" on the fact that Scripture matters to us. Moreover, these disciplines give birth to other forms of commentary on Scripture. They are means of drawing out, elaborating, and lifting up Scripture's compelling power.

Like great poetry or music, Scripture compels response. When one is moved by the performance of a great symphony, one jumps up at the appropriate moment and applauds and cheers. Or perhaps one responds more quietly, simply vowing to live life more fully, more thoughtfully, in the awareness that it is fleeting and precious. Or, yet again, one may feel compelled to talk about the experience, to capture it in words, hoping to communicate its power and relevance to others.

A good bit of Scripture is itself commentary on earlier, authoritative traditions. The author of Second Isaiah appropriates the language of the Exodus to describe the new thing that God is doing in his time. Eventually, Second Isaiah itself becomes Scripture and gives rise to new interpretations and applications. They, in turn, become authoritative and scriptural in their own right, such as the Christian understanding of Christ as the suffering servant.

W. C. Smith notes that a similar process characterizes other religions. The Mishnah, a commentary on the Torah, acquired an authority in Judaism as great, perhaps even greater, than the Torah itself. In Islam, the writings known as the Sunnah came to have special authority by virtue of commenting on the Quran, God's revelation to the prophet Mohammed. Indeed, the boundary between Scripture and commentary is not always clear, argues Smith, and sometimes the latter can be as decisive for the life of the community as the former.[2]

Scripture gives birth to commentary, and great commentary on Scripture frequently assumes a Scripture-like character. Great commentary is like iconography in the Eastern Orthodox tradition. It is a window into a reality beyond itself, even as it participates in that reality. Great commentary commands reverence, as though sharing in the sacral quality of Scripture. In commenting on Scripture, the community sets forth, and participates in, Scripture's compelling power—which for Christians is, ultimately, the power of Jesus Christ.

COMMENTARY AND SOUND

In chapter 4, we noted the importance of the sound of Scripture. Now, we might say that sound matters because sound comments on Scripture. Reading Scripture aloud helps to interpret Scripture. It sets forth its character as a Word of God.

I used to attend a congregation whose pastor allowed no one else to read the Scripture lessons in worship. He would slowly open the pulpit Bible, lovingly smooth out the page, and quietly focus his entire being on reading the assigned passage. He did not have to read dramatically or emotionally. Simply the care that he exercised testified to the privilege of approaching Scripture as the Word of God.

How we translate Scripture also says something about its character. Every translation is an interpretation—or, as we might now say, a commentary. Because no language can fully convey the sense and nuance of another, a translator has to decide which words most faithfully render the original. Inevitably, these selections reflect theological and ideological commitments. The translator, even if implicitly, comments on Scripture's meaning and authority by his or her choice of words.

One striking example of the significance of translation as commentary comes from the Reformation. Protestants challenged word choices in the Vulgate (the standard Latin translation of the Catholic Church) that appeared to favor Catholic theology. A good deal of the debate focused on Ephesians 5:32, where the Greek calls marriage a great mysterion (mystery). The Vulgate used the word sacramentum, reflecting and reinforcing the Catholic belief that marriage was one of seven sacraments. Protestants, by contrast, argued that marriage was not a sacrament—it had not been instituted by Christ nor did it have an evangelical word of promise (that is, the gospel of Jesus Christ) explicitly attached to it. They therefore insisted that "mystery," not sacrament, was the proper translation.[3]

More recent translations also illustrate these issues. The *New International Version* (NIV), a favorite among conservative Protestants in North America today, was composed in part as a reaction against the Revised Standard Version (RSV). In Exodus 21:22, for example, the RSV speaks of the penalty that ensues if a man so hurts a woman with child that a "miscarriage" occurs. The NIV, in contrast, refers to a pregnant women giving birth "prematurely." This word choice has the effect of more clearly giving the fetus human status; any harm that occurs does not refer simply to the woman, but also to the child. Each translation interprets the text.

The New Revised Standard Version (NRSV) also reflects particular theological commitments, for example, in its use of inclusive language. Where the Greek has "brethren," the NRSV reads "brothers and sisters." Even though the Greek word is meant inclusively, the translators argue that the English "brethren" can no longer be understood in this way. Thus, the question of accuracy in translation becomes inseparable from current social norms. But these norms are not neutral. They, as much as the biblical text that they would "correct," reflect the interests of particular groups—in this case, groups with a particular idea of equality between men and women.

The NRSV's insistence on inclusivity seems more tenuous linguistically—and even more clearly a matter of theological commentary—in Proverbs 1–9. The "son" who receives instruction now becomes the "child," even though the context clearly suggests a male boy, who has to be saved from the "loose woman" (Prov. 2:16).

Because a translation is an interpretation, it is decidedly secondary to the text in the original languages. Yet, translations as commentary tend to assume an authoritative, Scripture-like quality of their own. The NIV and the NRSV have come to represent not only two translations, but also two understandings of biblical interpretation and authority, each associated with particular communities of faith. Were you to read one of these versions rather than the other to certain audiences, you might be charged with having affronted not only your listeners, but God (himself? herself? Godself?).

In the English-speaking world, the King James Version of the Bible most clearly illustrates the capacity of a translation to become authoritative and Scripture-like in its own right. Some churches today even advertise the fact that they continue to use the "1611 King James." No matter how inaccurately, Christians in the English-speaking world will long continue to refer to Joseph's "robe of many colors," as the King James Version puts it. Those words have become "biblical," even if the Hebrew does not support them.[4]

COMMENTARY AND COMMUNITY

The discipline of reading Scripture in community also gives birth to commentary. In the Reformed tradition, the church has understood its confessions of faith to be an especially important form of commentary on Scripture. Confessions sort out legitimate from illegitimate readings of Scripture. They comment on Scripture, so that members of the community of faith can grasp its meaning more clearly.

Confessions are secondary to Scripture.[5] Yet, they too can become classics in their own right, taking on an authority almost equivalent to Scripture itself. The clearest example in the English-speaking, Reformed tradition is the Westminster Confession of Faith and the Westminster Catechisms, especially the Shorter Catechism.

The Westminster Confession of Faith was for many years the sole confession of American Presbyterianism. Whenever particular formulations in the Confession seemed outdated, efforts were made not to replace the Confession, but to amend it. Only in the late 1960s was it finally surpassed, when the northern stream of the church adopted a *Book of Confessions* that included the Westminster standards along with six other historic confessions and a new Confession of 1967. Significantly, the departure from sole reliance on Westminster (and the fact that the Confession of 1967 spoke to momentous changes in church and society) seemed to some congregations to provide sufficient grounds for leaving the denomination. The modification of the church's confessional basis seemed like an assault on Scripture itself.

Generations of Presbyterian children were encouraged to memorize the Shorter Catechism. When I was in seminary, one could still win a cash award for correctly answering a set of its questions. In the Dutch Reformed tradition, the Heidelberg Catechism has played a similar role. Indeed, rather than following a lectionary of Bible readings, much Dutch Reformed preaching has followed the order of questions in the Catechism (which the Catechism divides into fifty-two parts, one for each week of the year).

Besides confessions, particular theological figures have sometimes been understood as offering authoritative commentary on Scripture. Their writings then assumed a Scripture-like quality of their own. Catholicism after the sixteenth-century Council of Trent declared Thomas Aquinas to be the "Doctor of the Church," study of whose writings was enjoined on all theological students. At times, Lutherans have appealed to Luther—and Calvinists to Calvin—in much the same way. Their writings have shaped their followers as profoundly as Scripture itself.

COMMENTARY AND CONTEXT

The discipline of reading Scripture in context has given birth to commentary in the form of lectionaries, prayer books, and hymnbooks. Each way of framing Scripture determines how the community of faith will receive Scripture—which portions, in relation to which of the church's rituals.

Lectionaries assign the reading of particular passages of Scripture to each week of the year.[6] In Judaism,

> the annual lectionary and the seasonal festivals are co-ordinated. The new year begins each autumn with the creation of the world in Genesis; winter is related to the time of servitude in Egypt; with spring comes release from that oppression (pointed up in Passover); the summer is spent receiving the divine revelation at Sinai (marked in festival by Shavuot) and wandering in the desert (Sukkoth); the old year ends on the verge of entering the Promised Land.[7]

Similarly, many Christian lectionaries have related Scripture readings to the church year, beginning with Advent (the promises to Elizabeth and Mary, the birth and ministry of John the Baptist); moving through Christmas (the birth of Jesus), Lent and Easter (the crucifixion and resurrection), and Pentecost (the coming of the Holy Spirit); and concluding with ordinary time (lectio continua reading of one of the Gospels). If used regularly and widely, such lectionaries eventually establish an authoritative context for reading, and preaching on, particular biblical passages. They set up certain expectations of the minister. Woe to the minister who tries to preach on 1 Chronicles or 1 Corinthians during Advent, or on the Christmas story in April!

Prayer books often include not only weekly lectionaries, but also set readings for special occasions. Scripture is placed in a liturgical context; particular passages of Scripture become associated with particular rites of the church, such as baptism ("Go therefore and make disciples of all nations, baptizing them in the name of the Father and of the Son and of the Holy Spirit" [Matt. 28:19]), marriage (the wedding at Cana [John 2]), or burial ("I am the resurrection and the life" [John 11:25]), as well as celebration of the Lord's Supper, ordination, saints' days, and civic observances.

Here again the principles of commentary hold: Scripture gives birth to commentary that orders and interprets Scripture, and compelling instances of commentary assume an authoritative, Scripture-like quality of their own. In the English-speaking world, the clearest example of a classic prayer book is the Anglican *Book of Common Prayer*. Its rhythms and cadences suggest the grandeur of the King James Bible, and efforts to revise it have sometimes proved as controversial as new Bible translations (or as efforts among Presbyterians, as noted above, to write a new confession after Westminster).

In traditional Anglicanism and Catholicism, a priest was more apt to be found carrying a prayer book than a Bible.[8] Indeed, the prayer book included most of the Scriptures that he would need to serve the community: Scripture readings for each Sunday, feast day, and special occasion; and Psalms for prayer and personal devotion. The book itself, like the book of Scripture, could become an object of beauty and veneration—finely printed and bound, and handled with care.

Hymnbooks, too, have often been forms of commentary on Scripture. Not only do most people get their theology from the hymns that they sing, but hymnody also gives them much of their knowledge of Scripture. Hymns put particular words, phrases, and images of Scripture into theological context and help to make them memorable. Like prayer books, hymns can become classics in their own right, and efforts to change their words to make them more contemporary, or inclusive in their language, can meet incredulity, even resentment. A similar dynamic is sometimes at work in battles to introduce new hymnbooks in congregations.

Lectionaries, prayer books, and hymnbooks place particular biblical passages within a larger scriptural (and liturgical) context. If they become particularly influential in the communities that use them, they may assume a Scripture-like authority. Yet, as commentary, these aids to worship and study do not simply repeat Scripture. Rather, they rework Scripture and improvise on it. The classic words of the wedding service of the *Book of Common Prayer* ("Dearly beloved, we are gathered together here . . .") sound biblical, but they rely less on direct biblical quotations than on biblical images and cadences.

Similarly, as church historian Jaroslav Pelikan has noted, the hymnody inspired by the Reformation's rediscovery of biblical song

> became, already in Luther's hands, more than poetic translation of the Bible, more even than poetic paraphrase, but the free outpouring of the biblical message in creative new forms. . . . as can be perceived most strikingly in . . . the first stanza of "Ein feste Burg ist unser Gott". . . .

> [T]he first verses of Psalm 46 . . . are clearly the inspiration of the hymn but just as clearly are not its source in any simple literal sense.[9]

COMMENTARY AND MEMORY

This phenomenon—improvisation on the biblical text—is closely related to the discipline of reciting Scripture from memory. As noted in chapter 4, when Scripture is appropriated by memory, its images may come to saturate an individual's, even a community's language, as though their own words were equally biblical in inspiration and authority. We might now say that people "comment" on the compelling power of Scripture by incorporating it into their own speech. Disciplines of memorizing Scripture give birth to commentary in the form of prophetic discourse.

Like liturgical language and hymnody, this prophetic discourse does not simply quote biblical language but reworks it. Lincoln's Second Inaugural Address sounds biblical, but a closer reading reveals few direct quotations. Lincoln, to great poetic effect, incorporates and repeats a few biblical words and images: woe, offence, judgment, God's will, God's justice. But the impact of Scripture on Lincoln is more than literary; it is clearly theological. Lincoln was able to convey in powerful, poetic language his own sense of standing under God's judgment and mercy.

Martin Luther King, Jr., had a similar ability. In his last speech, he declared:

> I just want to do God's will. And He's allowed me to go up the mountain, and I have looked over, and I've seen the promised land. I may not get there with you. But I want you to know tonight that we, as a people, will get to the promised land.[10]

Jon Levenson asks why King's evocation of Moses is so memorable compared to other efforts to claim Scripture for one political cause or another. Levenson argues that King's identification with Israel in its suffering, not just its triumph, is one element. More pertinent, however, is the direction in which King moves when relating Scripture to present political issues.

> [King] does not project his own group into the past; he *brings the past, the story of Israel, to bear upon the present,* using the powerful archetype of Moses' life and death to convey the meaning of his own life and times. What makes the archetype so appropriate is the obvious analogy of the American black experience of slavery and emancipation and the experience of ancient Israel.[11]

By allowing Scripture to illuminate the present, and by refusing to impose on Scripture a political ideology foreign to it, this kind of commentary on Scripture sets forth Scripture's compelling power. The words of Lincoln and King themselves take on classic status. They acquire the capacity to move us as profoundly as Scripture moved Lincoln and King.

THE BOOK AS ICON

In addition to the ways in which these four disciplines of reading Scripture give birth to commentary, we could trace more generally how Scripture has inspired the arts and music, with the same result. Particular pieces have become authoritative and Scripture-like in their own right.[12] I wish to limit myself to two sets of examples: the book of Scripture, and church art and architecture.

We are not apt to think of modern marketing techniques as great commentary. In the past, however, some kinds of packaging have assumed a classic status. In the Middle Ages, illuminated manuscripts became works of art. In the Reformation, illustration of the Bible became a premier expression of the visual arts. Lukas Cranach and Albrecht Dürer provided remarkable illustrations to accompany Luther's translation of Scripture into the vernacular. Although they were no substitute for the text itself, these illustrations lifted up particular biblical stories and images, impressed them on the popular mind, and set forth their compelling power.[13]

In a more prosaic way, the "holy Bible" that sits on the coffee table in the living room in the suburbs is a kind of icon. Even if never opened, it still makes a statement, a public witness. Whether its owner is conscious of the fact or not, it seems to symbolize God's presence and authority in his or her home; people implicitly testify to their piety in giving the book of Scripture a place of honor that they normally reserve for guests.

Some liturgical traditions explicitly acknowledge the book of Scripture as an icon of the risen Christ. In these traditions, Scripture as physical object commands reverence. It points us beyond itself and draws us into the presence of the Holy One. It deserves veneration.

A number of years ago, I visited an Orthodox church in Russia. On the altar stood a Gospels book bound in beautiful silver covers. An intricate design had been worked into the silver; precious jewels had been embedded in it. In each corner of the front cover was an enamel icon of one of the Gospel writers. Liturgically and artistically, this book of Scripture had a place of honor. It gave the message that it was not simply another collection of words, but the Word of God.

In Orthodox services that I have attended in this country, I have noticed similar gestures. Not only is Scripture bound in fine covers and given a place of prominence on the altar (the place of greatest holiness), but the priest uses the book to make the sign of the cross over the eucharistic elements. The book itself assumes sacramental character. Moreover, prior to the reading of Scripture, the priest takes the book from the altar and processes with it (as will later happen with the eucharistic elements, as well). He comes out one of the side doors of the iconostasis (the wall of icons that separates the sanctuary from the holy area around the altar) and returns through its central gates. When it is time for the Scripture reading, the priest steps back out, stands between the people and the iconostasis, and places the book on a reading stand that the altar boys have set up for him. They then stand on either side of him, holding long poles with lighted candles, as he reads aloud.

For the Orthodox, the liturgy is understood to re-create paradise. It aims at drawing one into the New Jerusalem, heaven on earth. The jewels and finery of church furnishings and priestly attire symbolize the heavenly kingdom in which time is no more. The icons evoke the presence of the departed saints, who join from heaven in praising the holy God with the living on earth. Similarly, the liturgical gestures that surround Scripture are understood to invoke the presence of Christ himself. Scripture is not mere historical information or practical advice; it is the living word of the living Christ.

This way of understanding the book of Scripture struck me with particular force at a Christmas Eve service that I recently attended in a Roman Catholic cathedral. Prior to the mass, a cantor, a small choir, and a string ensemble led the congregation in singing Christmas carols. The music was quiet, understated. Only as the processional began did the organ and trumpets join in. The congregation rose and began singing, "O Come, All Ye Faithful." At the head of the procession, a priest carried a crucifix atop a long pole. Other priests and altar assistants—all in fine, white gowns—followed. Behind them walked another priest, holding above his head a copy of a Gospels book, again with silver covers and enamelled pictures of the Gospel writers. "O come let us adore him," resounded throughout the sanctuary, now directed toward the book, as though Christ himself had entered and was among us.

Even in Protestant traditions, Scripture can assume the status of an icon—especially in Protestant traditions that otherwise strip pictures of the saints from their church walls and windows (as though stripping away the symbols of the tradition, so that the Word itself may reign supreme). The Protestant family that leaves a fine, black, leather-covered Bible on its coffee table is apt to attend a church in which the book of Scripture also commands the center of attention.

A large, fundamentalist Baptist church that I recently visited has no symbols in the sanctuary, not even a cross, except for a carving of an open Bible on the front of the pulpit. This pulpit stands in the middle of the chancel and is the focal point of the congregation's worship. It functions less as a stand for a pulpit Bible or sermon notes, than as a platform for the preacher, who holds open a floppy, soft-leather covered Bible as he preaches. He may occasionally read a verse or two from it, but most of the time he simply uses it as an object of authority. He points to it, waves it, and lifts it up to add authority to his words.

In other churches, Scripture may sit on a stand on the communion table, opened toward the congregation. Like the Bible on the coffee table, it commands attention, even if the ministers never read from it. Again, the book of Scripture, its packaging, and its placement comment on the character of Scripture: Scripture is the Word of God; it sets forth the reality and presence of Christ, God with us.[14]

CHURCH ART AND ARCHITECTURE AS COMMENTARY

Church art and architecture have frequently been understood as commentary on Scripture, as well. Early church architecture, drawing on the example of the synagogue, gave visible expression to Christians' confidence that worship provided an encounter with God. The two foci for this encounter were the sacrament of the Eucharist and the Word—architecturally, the altar, where the Eucharist was celebrated, and the bema, a platform from which the Scriptures were read. In early Syrian churches, two lecterns were located on the bema: one on the south side of the church, for reading the Gospel; the other on the north side, for reading other Scriptures.[15] The movement of the liturgy was from west to east, from bema to altar.

In the churches of historical Byzantium, the typical form of architecture gives similar expression to Scripture. A central cupola rises above the ambo (elevated reading stand) and contains a reproduction of *Christos pantokrator* (the risen Christ as Almighty Ruler), who holds a Gospels book in his right hand.[16] Extensive iconography throughout the rest of the sanctuary emphasizes the collective and cosmic character of worship.[17]

The case in Western Christianity is no different. Church art and architecture developed in part as commentary on Scripture. Several examples suggest the range of this commentary.

(1) As the liturgy in the Middle Ages increasingly focused on the actions of the clergy (and therefore less on liturgy as "the work of the people"), architectural modifications were introduced. A screen (known as a pulpitum, rube, or rood screen) came to separate the choir (the area in the east, where the altar was located and the clergy officiated) from the sanctuary (or nave, where the people stood). In other words, a holy of holies was set apart architecturally from the holy—a notion which found precedent in, and commented on, the biblical description of the tabernacle and the temple (see, for example, Exod. 26:33).

This basic design commented on Scripture in other ways, as well. Illustration 1* is an example of a twelfth- and thirteenth-century German, Premonstratensian church. Entering the church from the west, the realm of sin and darkness, people found themselves drawn by the architecture toward the east, the realm of light and resurrection. They would first pass the baptismal font—which reminded them of their baptism, by virtue of which they belonged to Christ and to his body (the church)—and would orient themselves toward the altar, where Christ became present in the bread and wine.

Like the Cistercians, who did not allow depictions of persons in their church art, these Premonstratensians channeled their artistic impulses into architecture. Light pours through the three windows at the front and through the series of windows at the top of the nave walls. The solid pillars and the repetition of basic shapes (squares, circles, triangles) impress on the visitor the order and permanence that characterize the heavenly city.[18]

The wall that separates the nave from the choir has two arches that lead down steps into a crypt. To the sides of the wall, one sees staircases that lead to a second level, the area of the choir, where the monks celebrated the mass. This symbolic architecture joins the dead and the living in the east, where together they wait on the Christ who will someday return to judge them.

This wall also served as a lectern and pulpit. Of such churches, Catholic historian Louis Bouyer has noted, "On [this wall], the readers made their appearance in view of the whole congregation, to sing to them the epistle and the Gospel."[19] The homily too was given from this area.

Despite the medieval Catholic emphasis on the Eucharist, this architecture powerfully comments on the equally significant role of the Word. The Word was architecturally in the center. It stood between, and bridged, the clergy in the choir and the laity in the nave. In this symbolic architecture, the Word was fully incorporated into the life of the sacramental community.

(2) Illustration 2, an example of a fourteenth-century German "hall

*Illustrations follow p. 96 at the end of this chapter.

church," represents a variation on the basic medieval model that we have been considering. Here, the Gothic architecture gives the interior of the church an open, expansive feeling. Light pervades the sanctuary (in contrast to the darker, heavier feeling of Romanesque architecture, as in illustration one).

At the time of the Catholic Counter-Reformation, many of the screens that separated choir and nave were removed, in order to give the laity direct access to the altar. This church, however, never had such a screen; from the outset, it was built as an open room. This style of architecture was to become especially important to the emerging preaching orders (that is, the Dominicans and the Franciscans), for it corresponded to their tendency to secularize holy space and turn their churches into preaching halls.[20]

The reading and preaching of the Word now takes place in the area of the altar (the holy of holies!). Architecturally, Word and sacrament are closely associated. Both stand at the center of the church's life. Architecture again comments on Scripture and its sacramental character.

The pews and pulpit in this church were added at the time of the Reformation. While the Catholic preaching hall brought Word and sacrament together, it also had the effect of moving the Word back from the laity (whereas the pulpitum, as in illustration one, had brought it into their midst). The Protestant pulpit now restores the Word to a prominent place among the people. In this church, moreover, the pews between the pulpit and the altar were so constructed that the backs could be moved and members of the congregation could turn around and face the pulpit at the time of the sermon.

(3) The key significance of the Word for the Protestant congregation is further represented by the design of the pulpit. The preacher stands above the congregation; the congregation sits at the foot of the Word. Not only can the preacher be seen and heard by all, but the Word comes to the congregation "from on high." The fine carvings on the pulpit and the pictures of a Reformer with an open Bible in his hands also draw attention to the pulpit (illustration 3). Pulpit and altar are again the two foci: Word and sacrament. In both versions of this church, Catholic and Protestant, architecture comments on the centrality of the Word.

(4) Church art could also set forth the centrality of the Word. Many a medieval church was a "Bible picture book." Stained-glass windows, wall paintings, statues, and carvings on stone pillars illustrated biblical events and personages. In addition, this art included representations of the tradition's great saints, reminding the viewer of the historical church, to which

the gospel had given birth. In worship, all of Christendom, past and present, seemed to be gathered into the presence of Christ.

At times, not only artistic depictions of scriptural scenes and characters, but the text itself could become an object of artistic interest. Illustration 4, from a church in Switzerland, depicts a fourteenth-century wall painting. As a heavenly being dictates, St. Matthew writes his Gospel (in Latin!). Illustration 5 demonstrates the artistic significance of the scriptural text even more clearly. In this sixteenth-century German Gothic cathedral, scriptural scenes, characters, and words adorn the ceiling. The very shapes of the letters have sacramental significance. The words of Scripture ("For he spoke and they were made: he commanded and they were created" [Psalm 33:9, Douay]) are depicted as carefully as the pictures that they accompany.

These developments seem to reach a culmination in illustration 6, an example of an eighteenth-century German Lutheran church. Yet again, the architecture comments on the centrality of the Word. The pulpit is lifted up and dramatically framed. It is a throne for royalty. The pews wrap around the sides of the sanctuary, as though the chancel area were the stage of a theater or opera house. Everything about the architecture suggests that the reading and preaching of the Word are a matter of public performance. In addition, by placing the pulpit over the altar, the architecture reflects the eighteenth-century Lutheran tendency to emphasize Word over sacrament.

The sanctuary is devoid of pictures or statues. Written words—lettered with artistic skill—take the place of visual depiction. Where in the medieval church a Christ in glory would have been depicted on the front wall, the visitor now finds a verse of Scripture: "Ich verkündige euch grosse Freude" ("I declare to you great joy" [Luke 2:10, my translation]). No elaborate carvings or portraits appear on the pulpit itself, only a verse inscribed below its rim: "Lasst euch versöhnen mit Gott" ("Let yourselves be reconciled to God" [2 Cor. 5:20, my translation]).

During this period, it was common for something similar to happen to the portals of the church. In the Middle Ages, one would have found stone carvings of Christ enthroned in heaven, surrounded by the saints; now, instead, a verse of Scripture is inscribed above the doorway. Letters take the place of pictures; the Word is valued for its written words, whose letters can be read and reproduced.

In sum, just as the book of Scripture can become a holy object, the church that houses and lifts up the centrality of the Word can thereby become a holy space. Architecture focuses worshipers on those parts of the sanctuary in which the Word is proclaimed in preaching and is enacted in the Lord's Supper. Pictures and artistic representations comment on key biblical persons and scenes. Where pictures are no longer adequate, the printed letters of Scripture themselves assume sacramental character and point toward the living God.

SCRIPTURE AS COMMENTARY ON CHRIST

Great commentary sets forth the compelling power of Scripture. More-over, as it brings Scripture alive in a new time and place, it tends to assume scriptural character in its own right. It claims biblical-like authority and inspires commentary on itself.

But great commentary also tends to displace Scripture. Authoritative traditions easily become better known and more important than Scripture itself. In the Anglican tradition, the *Book of Common Prayer* has sometimes overshadowed Scripture. Catholic theologians have sometimes known Thomas Aquinas better than the Bible, just as some twentieth-century theologians have attended more closely to German theologian and biblical critic Rudolf Bultmann than either Scripture or the tradition.

Similarly, the Bible as icon on the coffee table can become more important than the effort to read it and grapple with its message. While great commentary refers us back to Scripture, it also tends to diffuse the compelling power of Scripture. When commentary becomes Scripture-like in its own right, the Bible is easily ignored, even forgotten.

Commentary is inevitable—and necessary. The great commentaries of the community of faith are frequently the means by which we are first awakened to Scripture's power and drawn to read it. Great translations, confessions, prayer books, hymnbooks, pieces of art, and musical compositions stimulate and expand our interaction with Scripture. They elaborate on Scripture, giving us insights that we would not otherwise have and inspiring us to live a Scripture-shaped life more faithfully.[21]

Yet, every approach to Scripture is selective.[22] Every commentary, no matter how complete, lifts up particular passages or themes; its angle of vision is restricted. No commentary, not even the most ambitious, can begin to exhaust Scripture. Scripture remains larger than any commentary on it.

The Protestant principle of *sola scriptura* does not mean that we must come as a tabula rasa to Scripture. It does mean that we are called to listen as carefully as possible to Scripture itself, rather than allowing the commentaries the community of faith has privileged to displace it. Scripture puts the community's commentary under judgment and gives birth to new commentary that sometimes displaces the old.

In setting forth a Word of God, Scripture finally defies any effort to order it once and for all. Whenever we engage Scripture, we are challenged to reexamine the lenses of interpretation that we have brought to it. Yet, the story of faith does not end in exploring the mysterious depths of Scripture, as though reading Scripture were the highest goal of the Christian life. Rather, Scripture as a sacramental word points beyond itself. In a profound and unique sense, the Bible is itself a kind of commentary—a commentary on the risen Christ.

We do not worship the Bible. Our ultimate loyalty is not to any particular formulation in Scripture, but to the One whom Scripture sets forth as Lord and Savior. As rich a literary text as Scripture may be, as much as Scripture may rightfully claim a preeminent place among the classics of Western culture, Christians believe that it is something more. Scripture draws us into the presence of Christ, the One with whom we finally have to do, whether in life or in death.

To think of Scripture as commentary on the risen Christ is to remember that the call to a Scripture-shaped life is a call to a Christ-shaped life. Just as every commentary on Scripture is finally subject to revision in the light of Scripture, every reading of Scripture is finally subject to the authority of Christ.[23]

To be sure, Christians, especially in the Reformed tradition, have insisted that Scripture alone gives us a clear picture of Christ. Scripture remains the critical criterion by which we judge all other claims to know God and God's ways. But Scripture is not an end in itself. Rather, Scripture when it is truly Scripture nurtures in us a living relationship with God in Christ.

In this sense, Scripture finally matters only to the extent that we ourselves become living commentaries on the reality of the risen Christ. We are called not simply to attend to the great commentaries of the community of faith that has shaped us, but to testify to Scripture's compelling power by the way we live as followers of Christ.[24]

LEARNING FROM THE TRADITION

In an age like our own, the assertion that Scripture is a sacramental word may not seem immediately persuasive. One might easily wonder, What in the world does it mean to say that Scripture sets forth Christ? The whole notion seems to invite us to pretend—that is, to make something magical out of texts that are simply plain, human texts, no matter how wise.

Attention to the phenomenon of "commentary" will not answer all our doubts, but it will require us to take seriously the experience of Christians over much of the tradition—and even into the present. To be sure, an historical consciousness reminds us that the traditions of the past are historically conditioned; they are not necessarily true for all time. But an historical consciousness also reminds us that the wisdom of the present is equally limited; we ourselves inevitably reflect the limitations of our time. Thus, an historical consciousness teaches us to become self-critical—and, therefore, more open to the insights of Christians from other times and places.

Scripture's compelling power is not primarily a matter of ecstatic experience. It does not require us to relinquish our critical faculties. If Scripture is indeed best understood as commentary on the risen Christ, then we will wish to investigate the social and historical conditions that both shaped and limited human response to God, as recorded in Scripture. Careful historical-critical work can save us from our innate tendency to read Scripture in ways that too conveniently ensure our own privilege and comfort.

But Scripture will ultimately matter to us not because we have successfully investigated the biblical authors or the tradition's great commentators, but because we have discovered its compelling power for ourselves. The answer to our doubts about Scripture as a sacramental word is finally a trust that God alone gives, but to which the community of faith invites us every time it gathers for worship. It is in worship that the community of faith testifies to the trustworthiness of these texts. Worship is the most profound commentary on Scripture, and other forms of commentary ultimately find their focus there.

1.
Premonstratensian cloister church. Jerichow, Germany.
12th and 13th centuries.

2.
Premonstratensian cloister church. Jerichow, Germany.
12th and 13th centuries.

3.
Pulpit, Marienkirche. Griefswald, Germany. 1587.

4.
Wall painting, Kirche Sogn Gieri.
Rhäzüns, Switzerland. 14th century.

IPSE·DIXIT &
FACTA·SVN
IPSE·MAN
DAVIT·ET
...TA.

EVANGELICAL-LUTHERAN CHURCH, ST. MARIEN; PIRNA, GERMANY

5.
Wall painting, St. Marienkirche. Pirna, Germany. 16th century.

6.
Stadtkirche. Zossen, Germany. 1739
(interior redesigned, 1875).

6

THE SEARCH
FOR A FITTING WORD

Even in our most personal and private moments, we come to Scripture as people shaped by the particular communities to which we belong, including our families, congregations, companies, civic organizations, and nations. I believe that a Christian reading of Scripture is best shaped by the *worshiping* community. The worshiping community does not simply read Scripture; it venerates Scripture and regards it as a source of life. As we read and hear Scripture in worship, we may be vividly reminded that Scripture is more than historical information or practical advice. In worship, we turn to Scripture for a Word of God.

All too often, however, our actual experience of Scripture in worship is disappointing. We frequently find ourselves lost in words, words, and more words. We may want to believe that God speaks to us, but we may not easily hear God speaking to us in the minister's reading and preaching of Scripture.

I must confess that I rarely remember last week's sermon—even when I have preached it—let alone the Scripture readings that have preceded it. I associate particular times in my life with Scripture, and with the discovery of Scripture's power. But, like my childhood encounter with Scripture, few of them have to do with worship.

One Advent, during my college years, I read through the prophet Isaiah. I will never forget Isaiah's imagery of the land. God threatens to render it desolate and waste, and God promises to restore it. But Isaiah's images of flowing streams, flowering shrubs and trees, and teeming creatures (as at the creation), played in my mind as I walked through the foothills of the Rockies, close to where I was living at the time, not as I attended church.

97

I still picture the New Testament that I bought in Germany, during a year of study abroad. I would read it on the train as I traveled from one part of the country to another. I remember, in particular, encountering the Gospel of John. The words seemed wondrous and mysterious, even though—indeed, perhaps because—I was reading them in a language not entirely my own. But I felt more like a mystic exploring the depths of Scripture on my own than a member of the church, joined with others in listening for God's Word together.

If Scripture is best experienced as a Word of God in the community's worship, how it is possible that these personal and private experiences of Scripture seem more memorable? One answer might be that worship feeds us Scripture more quietly but no less powerfully than any personal encounter with Scripture. Through worship, we gradually acquire a familiarity with Scripture, as well as an expectation that it will speak a Word of God to us in our moments of need. Worship may offer us Scripture more as daily nourishment than as unforgettable feast. The seemingly unremarkable experience of hearing Scripture in worship week after week may sustain its power at other times to speak to us more personally and dramatically.

But it might also be the case that the church—especially among mainline Protestants at the end of the twentieth century—has forgotten the capacity of worship to set forth Scripture's compelling power. Our situation may be similar to that of Charles Dickens's David Copperfield, for whom (even in the nineteenth century) listening to the country parson was comforting, but boring.[1] The reading and preaching of Scripture in the community's worship was hardly an occasion for encountering the transcendent. We too—and our children—grow sleepy in worship that too often is smug and complacent.

By contrast, Fyodor Dostoyevsky's Father Zossima (in *The Brothers Karamazov*) reflects gratefully on his childhood experience of hearing Scripture read aloud in Orthodox worship.[2] That experience had changed his life, opened him to God's guiding Spirit, and persuaded him that the redemption of the Russian people lay in hearing the great stories of Scripture. He could not have comprehended our weariness with the Bible.

Whether we participate in worship or not, whether we find worship powerful or not, our personal and private experiences of Scripture point us back to the church, which claims Scripture as its own every time it worships. If the church is to recover a sense of Scripture's compelling power, it must recover a fuller sense of worship.

WORSHIP AND SCRIPTURE'S SACRAMENTAL CHARACTER

Worship is meant to lift up Scripture's character as a sacramental word. As Louis Bouyer notes, Christian worship has its roots in the Jewish synagogue, where the congregation gathered around the Torah and waited for the "teaching of a word . . . as the word of life, in which God . . . communicate[s] Himself to his people, so as to become present in the midst of them."[3] In the reading and interpreting of Scripture in worship, Christians, like Jews, have believed themselves to encounter God.

Scripture is especially at home in worship. In the middle of the second century, Justin Martyr noted the centrality of Scripture to Christian worship. When Christians come together on Sundays, "the records of the apostles or the writings of the prophets are read for as long as there is time."[4]

Practical considerations played a role. Because Scripture did not circulate in mass-produced volumes that individuals could easily acquire, it became accessible to the community as a whole only as it was read in worship.[5] But the special place of Scripture in worship has also reflected theological considerations. Gordon Lathrop, a contemporary Lutheran liturgical theologian, argues that the reading and interpreting of Scripture are basic elements of the church's *ordo,* the fundamental pattern of worship that has shaped Christian worship from the first centuries into the present: "As if this were the principal reason for the gathering, ancients texts are read . . . The presider speaks about the meaning of the readings and the meaning of the gathering."[6]

The four disciplines that we have been investigating are at the heart of Christian use of Scripture in worship. It is in worship that Scripture is always read *aloud,* never simply silently. Even when people follow along in their Bibles, the reading of Scripture in worship is a public "sounding." The importance of Scripture as sound is further reflected in the practice of singing portions of Scripture in worship, or of surrounding the reading of Scripture with singing.

It is in worship that Scripture is always read in *community,* with fellow believers, never simply individually. Because worship is the central assembly of Christians, it is also the key occasion for the community to read and hear Scripture together. The reader does not read for his or her own benefit, but for the sake of the community as a whole. The congregation itself may sometimes sing or read the Scriptures in unison or responsively. Moreover, preaching seeks to explicate the meaning of this Word for the community. The preacher is attuned to the questions and concerns of the congregation. Even if the preacher alone speaks, the sermon is implicitly a dialogue with the members of the congregation. "The preacher is a witness who searches the Scriptures on behalf of the community and then returns to the community to speak what he or she has found."[7]

It is in worship that Scripture is always read in biblical *context,* never simply as a collection of disconnected sayings or events. While the reading of Scripture before the sermon may consist of little more than a verse or a part of a verse, the community customarily attends to longer portions of Scripture, as though to say that solitary units are inadequate. The community often reads and hears several readings, drawn from different parts of the Bible. Prayers, hymns, and celebration of the sacraments may include biblical imagery and allusions that evoke a larger biblical world. Sermons may place particular passages in the context of the book to which they belong, or in the context of larger biblical themes that the preacher develops.

It is in worship Scripture enters the community's *memory.* In worship, Scripture is not simply information for the moment that can be tossed out at the end of the day, like the newspaper. Liturgical actions are repeated. The saying of prayers, the singing of hymns, and celebration of the sacrament takes place weekly or more often. Key passages of Scripture are read at regular intervals, often in conjunction with the church year. Sermons draw memorable stories, events, and turns of phrase out of Scripture. Over a period of time, members of the community absorb a basic biblical vocabulary. They are able to recognize more of the content of Scripture, and to draw actively on key passages of Scripture as they think about their faith and relate it to their lives.

Other kinds of commentary on Scripture further confirm the assertion that Scripture as a sacramental word finds its home in worship. As noted in chapter 5, it is especially in the context of the liturgy that the book of Scripture is handled as an icon. The book is given beautiful covers. It is lifted up. It is kissed. In worship, the book of Scripture becomes an object of worship.

Similarly, church art and architecture help to gather the worshiping community around Scripture not as mere information, but as a sacramental word. Just as we say something about our lives by the pictures that we hang on our living room walls (such as our pride in our grandchildren, our loving memory of deceased family members, or our gratitude for extraordinary moments that we have been privileged to experience), the worshiping community surrounds itself with biblical pictures and words, in order to define itself as God's. Visual depictions of biblical characters, events, and verses initiate us into the biblical world, as though it were contemporary to us, not simply ancient history.

The design of the sanctuary reminds the community of faith that the reading and hearing of Scripture are primary functions of the very building in which they find themselves. Scripture is read and interpreted from a place of prominence. The book of Scripture sits in a place of honor: a pulpit, lectern, or special stand. Space is arranged so that everyone can see and hear the reader.

These gestures "comment" on Scripture's character as a Word of God. They shape the community and the expectations that it brings to the reading of Scripture, whether in worship or elsewhere. Personal disciplines of reading Scripture grow out of, and help support, a piety of the Word. They are grounded in worship, where Scripture is always read aloud, in community, in context, and for memorization.

INCORPORATING SCRIPTURE MORE FULLY INTO WORSHIP

In a time of biblical illiteracy, the role of worship in setting forth Scripture as a Word of God becomes all the more critical. Because many Christians read little or no Scripture on their own, they will encounter it primarily through worship.

One might wish that Christians knew the Bible better. But, as we have suggested, receiving Scripture primarily through worship is not at all bad. Not only does worship offer us rich opportunities for reading and meditating on Scripture, but worship also points us to Scripture's character as a sacramental word.

Since the 1960s, some mainline Protestants have argued that inherited liturgical forms are archaic, even oppressive. These critics, in their commitment to lifting up contemporary social and political issues, have sought to reform worship. Prayers of confession, if not dropped altogether, have sometimes become occasions for lamenting our insensitivity to members of other cultures, or for easing our discomfort at enjoying social privilege and power in a broken, suffering world. Hymns have focused on the activities of the self, especially its good works in the name of peace and justice. The Eucharist has become an occasion more for celebrating commendable human efforts at inclusivity, than God's victory over death and sin in Jesus Christ.

The effect on our hearing of Scripture has been at least twofold. First, congregations have received less Scripture in worship. Pastors have written their own prayers, ignoring Scriptural resources. Preachers have sought to address controversial issues, rather than explicating Scripture. Second, the loss of inherited liturgical forms has contributed to a flattening of Scripture. Claiming the Bible for one righteous cause or another has obscured its poetic character. Scripture has been used to score political points, rather than to draw us into the presence of God.

If Scripture is truly a sacramental word, we must resist these tendencies. Worship needs to incorporate more of Scripture, not less. Traditional liturgical forms suggest rich possibilities for incorporating Scripture more fully into worship, so that our words recede behind Scripture's. Indeed, recent liturgical resources are noteworthy in their interest in reclaiming ancient liturgical traditions. I will look in particular at the recent Presbyterian *Book of Common Worship,* but the worship books of other mainline denominations offer comparable possibilities.[8]

These worship books reminds us that worship can include larger units of Scripture. In lectio continua preaching—where a preacher works his or her way through an entire book of the Bible over the course of several weeks or months—it may be appropriate at times to read and interpret entire chapters of Scripture, even entire narratives, in a particular worship service. At other times, it may be possible to use larger units of Scripture as the sermon itself, such as the Sermon on the Mount or the Passion story.[9]

Worship can regularly include several passages of Scripture. As the *Book of Common Worship* notes:

> There should be readings from both the Old and the New Testament
> to ensure that the unity and completeness of God's revelation are pro-
> claimed. Both a reading from the epistles and a reading from the
> Gospels are appropriately included as New Testament readings. A
> psalm drawn from the full range of the psalms should also be in-
> cluded.[10]

In a word-weary church, the reading of so much Scripture may seem overwhelming, especially if the readings are simply strung one after another. For this reason, readers may wish to provide a brief introduction to each reading, noting its historical and narrative context. Those who plan worship may also wish to intersperse songs and responses between the readings, thus opening up space for the congregation to attend more fully to each reading. The *Book of Common Worship* notes that "the psalm appointed in the lectionary . . . is intended to be sung following the first reading, where it serves as a congregational meditation and response to the reading."[11] Similarly, an anthem, hymn, canticle, or Psalm appropriately follows the second reading.

Preaching plays a particularly important role in helping a congregation to hear Scripture more fully. The resurgence of interest in lectionary preaching in mainline Protestantism reflects a commitment to beginning with Scripture, rather than with a theme or topic that the preacher has selected out of his or her own head. Preaching at its best invites people to enter the biblical world, so that they may view their lives with greater clarity in light of God's purposes.

But the formal reading and preaching of Scripture are not the only ways to include more of the Bible in worship. Scripture can inform the language of the entire liturgy. The *Book of Common Worship* incorporates Scripture into calls to worship, confessions of sin, declarations of pardons, prayers, and responses. Recovering a particular emphasis of the Reformed tradition, it encourages the singing of Psalms—as well as biblical canticles, such as the Song of Zechariah and the Song of Mary—both as part of worship on the Lord's Day and as part of the order of daily prayer.

Another way in which Scripture can more fully inform the liturgy is in the celebration of the sacraments. The *Book of Common Worship* includes long eucharistic prayers that rehearse the Bible's history of salvation—God's constant care for the people of Israel and the church, despite their sinfulness and disobedience. Similarly, the baptismal liturgy lifts up images of water and Spirit that appear in the stories of creation, Noah, the baptism of Christ, and Pentecost; and in the letters of Paul.

Yet another possibility, as the *Book of Common Worship* emphasizes, is regular use of the church's ancient creeds in worship—the Apostles' Creed as a part of the liturgy for baptism and baptismal renewal, the Nicene Creed whenever the Lord's Supper is celebrated. Not only do these creeds connect us to the Christian tradition and other Christian churches, but they rehearse the basic outlines of the biblical story.

Particular Christian traditions will find additional possibilities, reflecting different theological emphases. A notable example is the reading of the Ten Commandments in worship. Lutherans have traditionally read the Commandments *prior* to the confession of sin; God's law convicts us and drives us to God's grace. Reformed Christians have typically placed it *after* the assurance of pardon, reflecting Calvin's "third use of the law," which spurs forgiven believers to conform their lives more fully to the image of Christ.

103

When Scripture more fully informs the liturgy in these and other ways, those disciplines that lift up Scripture's sacramental character are also more fully incorporated into worship. The liturgy provides an opportunity for the congregation to hear Scripture read *aloud*—not simply as the sermon text, but in many different parts of the worship service. The liturgy gathers a *community* that hears these texts and responds to them corporately. As Scripture is incorporated into prayers, hymns, and sacramental actions—and as the congregation hears large portions of Scripture, whether by lectio continua or by the reading of passages from different parts of the canon—the larger biblical *context* is regularly evoked. Finally, to the degree that the liturgy is saturated with Scripture, and particular biblical passages are related to particular liturgical actions (such as calls to worship, confessions of sin, assurances of pardon, eucharistic prayers, and benedictions), the community's *memory* is exercised and deepened.

BREAKING OPEN THE
COMPELLING POWER OF SCRIPTURE

A reformation of worship is no magic potion for a tired church. Only God's Spirit can ultimately renew us. Nonetheless, worship that is vital, and that connects us to Scripture and the Christian tradition, can be a means of grace. It can confront us with the reality of God. It provides us a way to respond to God in praise and thanksgiving. In worship, Scripture both sets forth God's Word to us and offers us a language for speaking a word of our own to God.

The power of Scripture in worship is not simply a matter of *how much* Scripture we incorporate, but of *how well* we incorporate it. In his book *Holy Things: A Liturgical Theology,* Gordon Lathrop argues that the church's inherited *ordo* helps to provide for this fuller appropriation of Scripture as a sacramental word.[12] The very structure of Christian worship shapes our use and understanding of the Bible.

Lathrop notes that the *ordo* has two foci: Word and table. The community first gathers around the reading and interpreting of Scripture. It then moves to the table, where it shares a meal. Through prayers and hymns, the community reflects its intention to undertake each of these actions in God's presence, to respond to God in thanksgiving, and to commit itself anew to serving the needs of the world to which God will have it return.[13]

The *ordo* might then be outlined as follows:

Gathering in one place
Reading of scriptures by a reader
Homily by the presider
Standing prayers
Setting out of the food of the eucharist
Great thanksgiving by the presider and the amen
Distribution of the food of the thanksgiving and sending to the
    absent by the deacons
Collection for the poor deposited with the presider sometime in
    the course of the meeting.[14]

The different parts of this order of worship work together to offer us meaning for our lives. In particular, the *ordo* provides for key biblical myths and symbols to be lifted up, as though they will help us to make sense of our lives.[15] Scripture is understood to set forth eternal truths to which we respond in trust and gratitude.

But the liturgy also challenges our accustomed interpretations of Scripture. It applies the biblical materials to new situations. It continually "breaks" Scripture's myths and symbols open, so that we might encounter the living God. Drawing on Paul Tillich, Lathrop notes that

> the terms of the myth and its power to evoke our experience of the world remain, but the coherent language of the myth is seen as insufficient and its power to hold and create as equivocal. The myth is both true and at the same time wrong, capable of truth only by reference to a new thing, beyond its own terms.[16]

This dynamic, says Lathrop, is present in the biblical materials themselves. Earlier traditions provide vocabulary and images that later communities apply to their experience of God in the present.[17] The liturgy reworks—"comments" on—these materials yet again, so that ancient words might "speak a new grace."[18]

> The *ordo* puts the ritual idiom under tension, counters it, breaks it . . . The world that is thereby suggested is . . . an alternative vision that waits for God, hopes for a wider order than has yet been achieved, but still embraces the present environment of our experience.[19]

This process of breaking Scripture open proceeds by means of key juxtapositions—tension points—in the *ordo*. The inherited language of Scripture is juxtaposed, for example, to the *contemporary situation of the gathered community*.

> The intention of the community in reading texts on Sunday has been not only to give us a magnificent language for our need; it has been to offer the taste of . . . grace and the presence of God in the midst of our history and our projected hopes. The intention of the liturgy is to manifest the presence of God.[20]

Another juxtaposition is the reading of Scripture and the *singing of praise to God*. In worship, "God is sung to as if present in the texts, even the texts expressing our need."[21] Texts from the past are juxtaposed to the congregation's song of praise in the present, as though these texts have a word for the present.

Different voices of Scripture are juxtaposed to each other. "On any given Sunday, the church usually hears more than one reading, the diverse words supplementing, criticizing, breaking each other."[22]

The reading of Scripture is juxtaposed to *preaching*. The biblical texts "are received with reverence, yet they are criticized and transformed. They become the environment for the encounter with God and with God's grace."[23] The preaching qualifies the texts. It causes a crisis in the words and breaks them open. But the texts also qualify the preaching. "The texts always mean more than the preaching can say."[24] Preaching never exhausts the texts.

Finally, Scripture is juxtaposed to the *celebration of the sacraments*. Baptism is a washing, yet it is accompanied by words of teaching and learning, such as the creed, that point us back to the biblical story. Similarly, text and Eucharist condition each other. On the one hand, "the religious meanings of ancient scriptures are found to have surprising new referents when set beside a meal of thanksgiving in which Christ's death is experienced as life-giving."[25] On the other, "the texts call the community to eat the meal of thanksgiving with wider meaning than it had thought possible."[26]

These tension points and juxtapositions in the liturgy help to guard Scripture's sacramental character. They "comment" on Scripture's capacity to mediate a relationship with the living God. The church's inherited *ordo* is more than an interesting historical detail. It is more than one option for contemporary worship among many. The basic structure of Christian worship is an important form of commentary on Scripture. Its persistence throughout Christian history suggests that we dare not ignore its value. The *ordo* trains us in the basic disciplines of reading Scripture as a sacramental word. Attention to the *ordo* promises us a fuller sense of Scripture's compelling power.

LETTING SCRIPTURE STAND FORTH

Even when the reading and interpreting of Scripture in worship are done with little or no skill, the structure of the liturgy still provides for the possibility of encountering God's grace in Scripture in new and surprising ways. Soon after my arrival in Germany as a student, I attended worship in a neighborhood church. A few elderly parishioners were scattered through the sanctuary. No one spoke to me, and I was too bashful to speak to any of them. At the end of the service, the pastor invited us forward for communion. It was a moment of—dare I say?—"radical juxtapositions"! The words of the service were in a foreign tongue, yet the sacramental actions were familiar. I lacked a sense of intimate community with these people, yet I firmly believed that the Eucharist symbolized our common bonds in Christ. In light of these tensions, simple words of Scripture—the body of Christ given for you, the blood of Christ shed for you—spoke powerfully to me of God's grace, even in a foreign place.

Wherever the integrity of the liturgy is not fully lost, Word and table hold forth the promise that we will encounter Christ. Perhaps for this reason, Calvin was hesitant ever to endorse church schism. Even when faults had crept into the preaching of the Word and the administration of the sacraments, he believed that, where they were present, Word and sacrament continued to mark the church as the church, the body of Christ.[27]

Like other great commentaries on Scripture, the *ordo* assumes an authoritative, sacramental-like quality of its own. Indeed, the *ordo* has become so fundamental to Christian worship that it underlies the practice of most Christian churches today, even when they are not aware of it. A church that eliminated any suggestion of this basic outline of worship would risk undermining its own life in Christ. People might no longer recognize its worship as Christian.

As great commentary, the *ordo* can threaten to obscure Scripture. When the *ordo* succumbs to aesthetic ideals, when the concern for beauty displaces the concern for faithful response to God's grace, the *ordo* ultimately becomes empty ritualism. Worship then supplants Scripture, rather than helping us to listen to Scripture. But the greater danger in our time is our failure to appreciate the capacity of the liturgy to mediate startling new encounters with God's Word. Forgetting the wisdom of the inherited *ordo,* we are all too tempted to invent worship to achieve a momentary, human end. We seek to inspire people with our dreams, move them emotionally with sentimental gestures, or persuade them of the righteousness of our cause. We fail to worship God.

Recovering the power of Scripture in worship may depend on letting the holy things of the liturgy stand forth in greater clarity.[28] I was recently speaking to a pastor of a new church development. Worship takes place in a school gymnasium. The pulpit is a black, metal music stand. The communion table is a battered old table that stands against the wall most of the time but that can be pulled forward and covered with a white tablecloth as needed. The congregation has no baptismal font; when a baptism is celebrated, a silver bowl is brought out of the closet. The readers use one of the paperback Bibles that otherwise lie beneath the chairs of the worshipers. The problem, as the pastor sees it, is not the humble surroundings or furnishings, but the fact that the congregation has no sense of worshiping with "holy things." Pulpit, font, and table have become nothing more than utilitarian objects, whose intrinsic symbolism is lost. In such circumstances, the notion of liturgical juxtapositions and tension points makes little sense. Even when Scripture is carefully read, the larger liturgical context militates against hearing it as a sacramental word. The power of the *ordo* remains latent.[29]

Recovering Scripture's sacramental character may also depend on regular celebration of the Eucharist. As the great Orthodox theologian Alexander Schmemann has written, "in separation from the word the sacrament is in danger of being perceived as magic, and without the sacrament the word is in danger of being 'reduced' to 'doctrine.'"[30] The reading and interpreting of Scripture becomes little more than an academic lecture. The opposite danger is also present. Where the Eucharist is not frequently celebrated, Scripture finds no dramatic enactment outside of the sermon. Preaching is easily reduced to a motivational address. The sermon becomes the sole opportunity to bring drama into the liturgy.

Mainline Protestants in the Reformed tradition sometimes forget that Calvin saw preaching and celebration of the Eucharist as having equal importance. For Calvin, the reading of Scripture was not complete without the effort both to explicate its meaning in preaching, and to "perform" its meaning in the celebration of the Lord's Supper.[31] Both preaching and celebration of the Lord's Supper set forth the reality and presence of Christ in a way accommodated to our earthly frame. Both help Scripture, one might say, to speak a sacramental word, not merely to serve as doctrine or illustration.

WORSHIP AS LENSES
FOR READING SCRIPTURE

However we worship, worship—like other commentary on Scripture—powerfully influences our way of understanding Scripture's intrinsic character. Worship gives us lenses for examining Scripture. It offers us a framework for making sense of God's Word to us.

As Karl Barth, one of the greatest Protestant theologians of this century, noted,

> [O]ur exposition and application of Holy Scripture . . . usually takes place . . . in a "church" which even by its architecture and furnishings more or less directly and faithfully reminds those who gather in it . . . of their "confessional position." . . . Even the order of worship can more or less definitely play the same role.[32]

If one wishes to understand how particular communities of faith understand Scripture and its authority, one would do well to examine not only their formal theological statements, but also the way Scripture actually functions in their congregations' worship. Who reads Scripture in worship, where in the sanctuary, when in the service, what portions—in each case, a particular community of faith implicitly comments on the nature of Scripture and its authority.

A range of illustrations might help to make this point. My aim is not to provide an exhaustive analysis of different liturgical traditions, but simply to suggest some of the ways in which worship sets forth—or obscures— Scripture's character as a sacramental word. I draw from my own experience of worship at several churches in Louisville, Kentucky, the city in which I live as I write.

SOUTHEAST CHRISTIAN CHURCH

Southeast Christian Church is an independent, evangelical megachurch. Like other "seeker" churches committed to reaching a nonchurched, babyboomer generation, it keeps traditional Christian symbolism to a minimum. Were it not for the cross at the peak of its roof, one could easily mistake the sanctuary for an office building. Inside, muted colors, potted plants, and unobstructed sight lines give the sanctuary the feel of a suburban shopping mall. The atmosphere feels safe. Newcomers may easily choose to remain anonymous, but a small army of volunteers is available to assist, should one have a question about any of the church's programs.

The sanctuary is theater-style, sloping towards the front; rows of individual seats wrap around a long stage. At one end of the stage sits amplification equipment. To the left, at a second story level, a baptistry is located; Plexiglas siding allows the congregation to see people move in and out of the water at the time of a baptism.

Services are carefully choreographed. A band plays; performers walk off and on stage, as needed. Music is upbeat; words to praise choruses and traditional hymns are flashed on screens that lower from the ceiling at the front of the sanctuary. Lighting is effectively used to move worshipers' attention from one area of the stage to another. The service is well paced and entertaining, clearly geared to a television generation.

The leaders of Southeast Christian would insist they have a scriptural basis for all they do. The church's statement of belief includes the assertion that "the Bible is the inspired word of God." Numerous Sunday school classes offer opportunity for in-depth Bible study.

The actual use of Scripture in worship, however, reflects a more complicated understanding of biblical authority and interpretation. In some respects, Scripture is highly emphasized. Scriptural images and phrases inform the words of the songs. An outline of the key parts of the text on which the minister will preach, as well as the text itself, are printed in a bulletin that all worshipers receive. Many worshipers bring Bibles along, often placing them in sturdy, leather covers that seem to function as badges of Christian identity, and perhaps as statements of personal adherence to Scripture.

In other respects, however, Scripture is curiously deemphasized. One finds no Bibles in the pews, not even a Bible on a pulpit. There is no processional in which Scripture is carried into the midst of the people. Nor does the arrangement of the church furnishings lift up the centrality of Scripture to the congregation's life. Only the baptistry is prominent. The communion table sits against the raised stage and is obscured from view. The pulpit is nothing more than a simple, moveable, wooden stand.

The minister sometimes comes up to the stage early in the service, welcomes people to worship, and reads the Bible passage aloud, as though setting the theme for the service. Sometimes, however, the passage is not read at all; at the time of the sermon, the minister simply begins preaching.

The Scripture passage (always in the *New International Version*) is never more than seven or eight verses, and there is never more than one. Selections, disproportionately from the Epistles, typically focus on how one practically lives the Christian life. The time of baptisms toward the beginning of the service and the thirty-minute sermon at the end are clearly the high points. Though the Lord's Supper is celebrated weekly, it is little more than a moment of private meditation prior to the sermon. There are no words of institution, no eucharistic prayers or hymns. The lights are simply dimmed, and people take the elements—sometimes together, sometimes individually.

The overall message is that Scripture is primarily a book of practical advice for Christian living. One joins the community through believers' baptism, prepares oneself through communion to hear the Word proclaimed, then receives authoritative teaching through the sermon. The liturgical juxtapositions and tension points that Lathrop describes are obscured or eliminated. Scripture does not clearly stand forth in its own right. Nonetheless, Scripture does not entirely lose its sacramental character. The congregation still anticipates hearing a Word of God for its life here and now, a vision of new life in Christ.

EVANGEL CHRISTIAN LIFE CENTER

Evangel Christian Life Center is an Assembly of God church. Like other neo-pentecostal churches, it crosses racial and class boundaries more successfully than many mainline Protestant congregations. Like Southeast Christian, it has also succeeded in reaching a baby-boomer generation. But worship at Evangel Christian Life Center has more of an edge to it. The music is high-energy. A large choir sways to the beat. People clap their hands or wave them in the air. The service begins with singing that can easily last half an hour or longer.

What strikes one most strongly at Evangel Christian Life Center is the fervency of prayer. After the initial round of singing concludes, deacons come forward, stand before the stage, and turn toward the congregation. The pastor invites people to come forward for prayer and the laying on of hands. Dozens will respond over the next half hour, while the rest of the congregation waits and music quietly plays.

When people have returned to their seats, the pastor typically asks if anyone in the congregation is experiencing — or has family members who are experiencing — cancer, heart disease, diabetes, or other serious illness. Calling on God to break the curse of the devil, the pastor prays for them, as well as for the healing of any who are suffering from poverty, depression, or sexual confusion.

Persons wishing to become members then come forward. The pastor prays over each one and blesses them. When parents bring their children forward to be dedicated, the pastor prays again and asks the congregation to hold out their hands toward each child.

As the fervency of the first part of the service begins to cool down, the pastor asks worshipers to raise their Bibles and repeat a prayer after him. He then reads one short passage (King James Version). A few Bibles sit in the pew racks; some people have brought their own. Most worshipers just listen.

The pastor reads and preaches from a simple wooden stand at the center of the stage. The sermon is typically a further explication of the power of the Holy Spirit to give people health, prosperity, and good life. The pastor refers to biblical figures and situations to the extent that they provide encouragement and strength for members of the congregation to resist the wiles of the devil today. Though the pastor speaks forcefully, the mood is quiet and relaxed. Upon concluding, he asks people to bow their heads and raise their hands if they have need for a better prayer life. They take each other's hands and repeat a prayer after him.

In this liturgical context, the authority of Scripture is important insofar as it authorizes the community's understanding of prayer. While the community's prayer includes biblical images, it takes place in the freedom of the Spirit. Scripture does not clearly stand forth on its own; it is overshadowed by the language of the Spirit. Nonetheless, through the Spirit, Scripture is understood to mediate a relationship with the transcendent. It retains a sacramental character because it points to the power of God that can break in on the community at any time.

St. Stephen Baptist Church

St. Stephen Baptist Church is an African American megachurch in an historically black neighborhood. Many of its members are young black professionals who were born in that area of town but now live in other parts of the city. The church emphasizes its members' Afrocentric identity. The church's logo includes a drawing of the African continent; banners with African textile designs and a banner of a black Jesus hang at the front of the sanctuary.

Though the church is large, there is a strong sense of community. Early in the service, guests are welcomed and asked to stand. People rise to greet each other during a time of "passing the love." When tithes and offerings are presented, people come forward by rows.

Compared to Southeast Christian Church and Evangel Christian Life Center, St. Stephen's incorporates Scripture more thoroughly into worship. The call to worship, consisting of quotations from several Psalms, is immediately followed by a responsive reading of Scripture from the back of the hymnal. Hymns and anthems have strong biblical themes.

The large, wooden pulpit is the focal point of the sanctuary, and the sermon is the high point of the service. The pastor reads a single passage (King James Version) from his own Bible; there is no pulpit Bible. The passage may come from any part of Scripture, including the Old Testament. Some members of the congregation have brought Bibles.

Preaching in the black Baptist tradition sets up a dynamic interplay between the preacher and the congregation. The sermon is filled with rhythm and punctuation, crescendos and decrescendos. A group of church officers seated on a pew near the front leads the congregation in responding to the preacher's words. As the sermon builds, nearly every line evokes a response. The congregation affirms, encourages, and coaxes the preacher; he frequently turns to them and asks them to answer him or help him out. When everything works, when the Spirit of God seems to take over, people find themselves clapping, standing up, shouting out, and even gesturing at the minister.

The preacher typically remains at the pulpit. Occasionally, he lifts his Bible to emphasize a point. More often, he simply tells the biblical story, emphasizing God's promise in the midst of human adversity.

The sermon is rich in biblical allusions. One word or phrase, story or event, sets up a chain of references. The preacher goes back and forth between testaments, and between Scripture and the present experience of the community. People may sit with their Bibles open, turn from one passage to another, or simply listen.

Particular biblical phrases may be repeated throughout the sermon, functioning as a chorus. As the sermon reaches a climax, the preacher breaks into song. The choir and organ join in. The congregation comes to its feet and claps in rhythm. The high point of worship has been reached.

Afterward, things wind down quickly. The pastor issues a short invitation to discipleship. A few people may come forward. An elder quickly and quietly concludes the service with a benediction.

What is striking at St. Stephen's is the degree to which its worship illustrates the four disciplines we have been discussing. Scripture is read aloud; its key phrases are repeated, even sung. The reading and interpreting of Scripture is a community event; the entire congregation responds to the Word. A larger biblical context is evoked; the sermon connects diverse parts of Scripture, even if only one has been read aloud previously. The community's memory of Scripture is engaged; the preaching of Scripture evokes a reservoir of images and phrases the community seems to have claimed as its own. Even though the order of worship does not let the *ordo* stand forth in all its clarity, the vitality of Scripture as a sacramental word is clear. Scripture is more than practical advice or the basis of authoritative belief or practice; it draws worshipers into the presence of Christ.

CATHEDRAL OF THE ASSUMPTION

The Roman Catholic Cathedral of the Assumption is a nineteenth-century edifice, recently renovated and wonderfully elegant in its architectural simplicity. Entering the sanctuary, one stands before a baptismal pool with running, "living" water. A few steps to the right, on a simple wooden stand, sits a fine Gospels book, turned to the Gospel reading for that day.

At the front of the sanctuary, an altar is pulled toward the front of the chancel area. Because the tabernacle with the reserved host sits on a side altar, this central altar functions primarily as a table for the actual celebration of the Eucharist. Candles on long candlesticks stand next to each of its corners. To the left, and slightly behind, stands a pulpit.

A stained glass window at the front depicts Christ placing a crown on Mary. Pictures of the stations of the cross hang on the side walls; a statue of Mary stands at the rear. Light fills the room. The atmosphere is warm and inviting. Many people cross themselves with water from the baptismal pool as they enter.

The liturgy at the Cathedral has been strongly influenced by developments in the ecumenical liturgical renewal movement of the last thirty years. The service begins with a processional. One of the lay readers carries a finely decorated Gospels book above his or her head and places it on the altar. A priest welcomes the congregation and leads it in a prayer of confession, which he reads from a prayer book that a deacon holds before him. After a declaration of pardon, a cantor leads the congregation in singing a response.

Lay readers come to the pulpit to read the lectionary texts from the Old Testament and the Epistles (*The New American Bible*). There are no pew Bibles. Missals in the pew racks provide the text of each reading, but few people follow along. Nor have many brought Bibles along.

Each reading concludes with the reader's declaration, "The Word of the Lord," and the congregation's response, "Thanks be to God." After the second reading, the congregation stands, sings an Alleluia response, and remains standing for the Gospel reading. The priest takes the Gospels book from the altar, moves to the pulpit, and introduces the reading. The people respond, "Glory to you, Lord Jesus Christ," and cross themselves. At the end of the reading, the priest lifts the opened book before the congregation and declares, "The Gospel of our Lord Jesus Christ." The people respond, "Praise be to you, Lord Jesus Christ."

A short sermon explicates and applies the Gospel. At its conclusion, the people stand and recite the Nicene Creed. After prayers of intercession, again with congregational response, an offering is collected. The altar is prepared, and the eucharistic elements are brought forward. The priest first prays quietly over the bread and the cup, then aloud, the congregation again responding in song. Lay servers come forward. During the singing of a hymn, the congregation comes forward by rows. The celebration of the Eucharist ends with the priest's declaration, "The Lord be with you," and the congregation's, "And also with you"—the same words that opened the service.

Short announcements and a benediction end the service. A lay reader retrieves the Gospels book from the pulpit and holds it high as the worship leaders recess to the organ's triumphal music.

More than the other churches that we have examined, the Cathedral sets forth Lathrop's understanding of the *ordo*. The juxtapositions of the liturgy stand forth clearly. Though in a manner different from St. Stephen's, the congregation is no less attentive to the reading and interpreting of the Word. Through a variety of gestures, Scripture's sacramental character is emphasized. The book of Scripture itself—like its words—sets forth the risen Christ.

Nonetheless, this liturgical context is not without dangers of its own. The tension between Word and meal tends to resolve itself in the direction of the Eucharist when the sermon has not been prepared and delivered with the same care as the celebration of the sacrament. While the Cathedral, in contrast to much of pre-Vatican II Catholicism, is careful to emphasize the service of the Word, the celebration of the Eucharist still commands more ritual time and space. Scripture is well incorporated into the liturgy but does not always put the ritual actions under judgment. The liturgy allows for few rough edges.

ISSUES FOR MAINLINE PROTESTANTS

These examples, while drawn from outside the Protestant mainline, help to illustrate tensions within the Protestant mainline today: the traditional dominance of the Word, yet a new interest in sacraments; an emphasis on practical direction for the Christian life, yet a longing for transcendence; the rejection of traditional forms of prayer and worship, yet a sense that Christians now need a deeper wisdom than anything they can dredge up out of their own lives. These unresolved issues highlight questions that mainline Protestants will want to think through as they use Scripture in worship.

Who should read Scripture in worship? The minister alone? The congregation as a whole? (In unison or responsively?) Lay readers? Elders or deacons? What is communicated in each case? When mainline pastors feel obligated to include lay people in worship leadership, they frequently assign them the reading of Scripture. What is the message here? That the liturgy (as at the Cathedral) is the work of the whole people of God? Or that the reading of Scripture is less important than preaching or administration of the sacraments, both of which mainline pastors (and their Catholic counterparts) jealously guard?

Which portions of Scripture do we lift up in worship—and how many? At the Cathedral, special gestures attend the Gospels. At Southeast Christian, emphasis falls on certain portions of the Epistles. If we take Lathrop's principle of juxtaposition seriously, we will consider how we might carefully select Old Testament, Gospel, and Epistle readings that relate to each other yet stand in creative tension. Clearly, the reading of one short text will rarely suffice.

Similar questions relate to preaching. Even when a lectionary broadens a congregation's familiarity with Scripture, preachers still tend to select a narrow range of texts and themes for their sermons. (Some people claim that a minister has at most three or four sermons. He or she simply presents them in a variety of guises!) On the one hand, a focus on a few, key texts may be helpful. Because worship is also catechesis (education in the church's teachings), worship provides an incomparable opportunity to familiarize congregations with the most important parts of Scripture. On the other hand, I have also suggested reason to open ourselves to God's Word in texts that are more obscure. A broader selection of texts may enrich the congregation's understanding of central biblical stories and themes.

While a sermon will generally focus on one text, the selection of other readings can help the congregation and preacher to attend to that text more faithfully. When a New Testament passage refers or alludes to a particular portion of the Old Testament, we may wish to read both. If one is preaching on Jesus' Passion, it may be appropriate also to read one of Isaiah's suffering servant passages. If preaching on Paul's theology of justification, one might also read in Genesis about Abraham's faith in the promise that he receives from God.

How is the reading and interpreting of Scripture related to other sacramental actions? Where do they enhance Scripture's sacramental character? Where do they tend to obscure it? At Southeast Christian, the preaching tends to overshadow Scripture; at Evangel Christian Life Center, prayer is more important in worship than the reading and interpreting of Scripture. I have also noted the tendency of the Eucharist to overpower the service of the Word at the Cathedral of the Assumption. The centrality of Scripture stands forth most clearly at St. Stephen's, but (as in many Reformed congregations) it practically displaces the Eucharist.

Attention to the *ordo* cannot make up for thoughtless preaching. The power of Scripture is inevitably tied to a great degree to the power of preaching. If we are to open ourselves to the holy, the holy things must stand forth. Thus, preaching must assume a sacramental, poetic-like quality that communicates the privilege of exploring Scripture. Good preaching depends less on the preacher's personal style than on his or her ability to convey a love of the text and a personal, authentic faith. When the preacher is a person of integrity and truth, he or she will communicate something of the integrity and truth of the gospel.[33]

Yet, attention to the *ordo* ensures that the power of Scripture does not have to rest solely on the shoulders of the preacher. Despite the preacher's best intentions and preparations, interpretation of Scripture always involves a risk. One improvises on the text, seeking to set forth its compelling power.[34] At times, one may fail. Even then, Scripture can still speak powerfully, if worship has been crafted to lift up the tension points of the *ordo*.

At its best, the liturgy can help us to listen to Scripture in its own voice. Part of the wisdom of the Reformed tradition is its placement of a prayer of illumination prior to the reading of Scripture (note well: not right before the sermon, as happens so frequently in mainline Protestant worship today!). Through the Spirit, we listen together for God's Word as Scripture is read, and even before it is interpreted. We acknowledge liturgically that Scripture stands before us—and over us and against us. Scripture claims us in its own right, not just as it is incorporated into preaching or the sacraments.

A WORD BOTH CONCRETE AND FREE

Worship helps to guard the sacramental character of Scripture. In worship, Scripture never stands alone. Even those traditions that claim to be nothing but "Bible-based" and reject the language of "sacraments" have a variety of ways of evoking the presence of God in their midst, whether by prayer or song, preaching or the celebration of the sacraments, the declaration that one's salvation is certain or the distinctive way of life that a community of faith fosters. To speak of Scripture as a sacramental word is to say that a worshiping community expects to hear God speaking a living word to it through Scripture. The community awaits a "fitting word" for its life before God.[35]

The character of this fitting word is twofold: It is a word that is both concrete and free.[36] It is concrete because it is appropriate to a particular community in a particular time and place, with specific hopes and dreams, problems and failures; it is free because it challenges that community to entertain new ways of thinking about its faith.

The Christian community has always had ways liturgically of expressing the expectation that Scripture helps set forth a concrete word. While preaching is the most obvious medium for setting forth this fitting word, a similar expectation may accompany the incorporation of Scripture into other parts of worship. For a pentecostal church, Scripture may come most alive not in the reading prior to the sermon, but as it is incorporated into the language of prayer. For churches that focus on the Eucharist, Scripture may speak most powerfully as it in incorporated into the words of institution and the eucharistic prayers. What makes an interpretation fitting is never simply historical or literary accuracy. In worship, as in Scripture itself, earlier traditions are often interpreted with considerable freedom, but in the confidence that they will again speak God's Word to the community in the present.[37]

At the same time, the Christian community has always had ways of pointing to Scripture as a Word of God whose meaning is not wholly under human control. Scripture functions like an icon. Because it sets forth Christ, it is handled with reverence. Special care is given to reading Scripture aloud, or to praying for illumination, or to repeating Scripture's phrases, almost as though they were a mantra. Through gestures and rituals, people set Scripture apart, as though it were God's, not ours.

The interpretation of Scripture evidently involves a tension between human freedom and divine freedom. The community claims to find a divine Word for the present. Yet, that Word, as a divine Word, resists human efforts to reduce it to one "right" meaning. This tension again points to the sacramental character of Scripture. Following Karl Barth, we might say that we always hear the Word of God through Scripture, but that Scripture cannot be equated with the Word of God.[38]

Worship helps us to listen to Scripture, for the Word of God. The *ordo* does not prescribe Scripture's content in advance, yet it provides a way of listening for it. It holds forth to us the promise of experiencing God's grace, yet it never allows us to capture it once and for all. The way in which the *ordo* frames the use of Scripture suggests broad theological trajectories — the priority of God's grace (for we receive Scripture as God's good gift to us), the equality of all people before God and before one another (for we listen together for God's Word in Scripture), and God's call to justice (for

God's Word in Scripture demands that we reshape our lives). Yet, no particular ethical program is absolutely right for all time.[39] In worship, Scripture mediates an encounter with God, whose Word is both definite and free.

The notion of a fitting word ultimately raises the question of ethics (how we live the Christian life) and of politics (how we organize our life in community). It is not enough for the community of faith to describe the dynamics of the sacramental word. The community must finally take the risk of interpreting Scripture and reforming its life in accord with the Word that it hears.

7

THE LIFE OF THE CHURCH
AS COMMENTARY ON SCRIPTURE

In a time of church conflict—where battle lines run through denominations—North American Christians engage in their own version of the "culture wars." Scripture seems to be the weapon of choice:

> A fundamentalist Baptist preacher holds a Bible in his hand. As he proclaims his understanding of God's will on a controversial issue, his voice grows louder; his grasp, tighter. He soon begins waving his Bible angrily—up and down, back and forth—as though wielding a stick against his opponents.

> Several adults in a mainline Protestant church meet for an hour of discussion prior to worship. As they consider the church's current stance on a controversial issue, they argue heatedly with each other about the authority and interpretation of Scripture. The atmosphere grows tense, even nasty. Not once do they look at a biblical passage together.

When Scripture is nothing more than a weapon, it loses its capacity to speak as a sacramental word. No longer a source of life, Scripture becomes a flash point for a host of misunderstandings. Rather than mediating an encounter with the transcendent, it becomes a tool of human ambition and self-aggrandizement. It gives rise to rancor, rather than praise and thanksgiving.

When we wield Scripture as a weapon, we frequently do not even bother to open it. We use it to assert ourselves, rather than receiving it as a Word that stands over us, even against us. Scripture becomes a symbol of absolute authority that one group or another appropriates, in an effort to impose its will on others.

Scripture may be the church's book, but different parts of the church apparently read Scripture in profoundly different ways. Whether in relation to ethical debates about abortion or homosexuality, or theological debates about Christology or ecclesiology, North American denominations find themselves divided into competing camps, each of which claims to read and interpret Scripture rightly.

These ethical and theological issues strike to the heart of the church's faith and life. On some matters, we can celebrate diversity. Cultural and biographical differences enrich us. But on matters as fundamental as the nature of sexual fidelity or the significance of Christ as Lord and Savior, our differences are enervating. When "holy things" seem to be at stake, we do not happily agree to disagree. Rather, our differences threaten our life together. The dictates of personal conscience—our basic sense of right and wrong—collide with our commitment to live together in peace in the body of Christ.

Yet, the modern ecumenical movement has made us more aware of the scandal of church division. If the church is truly the body of Christ, it is one, and it must find ways to affirm and strengthen a life in common. Although church conflict may be a fact of life, we must not allow it the last word. In the face of division, the church is called to self-examination, confession of sin, and repentance.

Similarly, if Scripture is truly the source of the church's life, the fact of contradictory readings of Scripture challenges the church to rediscover Scripture's compelling power—its capacity to speak a Word that is larger than ourselves. Something is terribly wrong if we rest easy with the "Bible wars." Rather, we must examine our theology of the Word and correct its distortions. We must resist the reduction of Scripture to political ammunition.

Because Scripture is the church's book, a renewed sense of church unity may contribute to a renewed consensus about Scripture's basic message and the authority of that message. We therefore need to explore disciplines of prayer, discernment, and service that can transcend our differences. We need to listen again to the historic faith, confident that it offers us insight into the very issues that divide us. If we experience a sense of deeper community together, we may read Scripture with greater unanimity.

Conversely, a renewed sense of Scripture's capacity to mediate an encounter with Christ may contribute to a renewal of church unity. To the degree that Scripture comes alive—that it moves us to a new sense of awe and wonder, and offers us lenses for making sense of our lives—we find that our differences, as significant as they are, are finally less important than the common Word of grace that God speaks to us in Jesus Christ.

COMMUNITIES THAT BECOME
LIVING COMMENTARIES ON SCRIPTURE

For followers of Jesus Christ, attending to Scripture, practicing disciplines of reading Scripture, and listening to great commentary on Scripture are more than matters of intellectual curiosity. Rather, we think about Scripture because we wish to become "Scripture-shaped"—and, therefore, "Christ-shaped." In response to Scripture's compelling power, we wish to become living commentaries on Scripture. We wish to exhibit the reality of the risen Christ in our own lives. To use the words of Stephen Fowl and Gregory Jones, we wish to "perform," "enact," or "embody" Scripture, "in the hope that our own lives will be transformed into the likeness of Christ."[1]

Some individuals succeed better than others in this enactment of Scripture. They have skills of discernment—a kind of practical wisdom forged by Christian virtue. The lives of these "saints" can be exemplary for the entire community of faith.[2] They offer us steady reference points for molding our lives more fully and faithfully into the image of Christ.

Perhaps every congregation has such saints. They do not often wield a great deal of power in the church's decision making processes. Frequently, their advice is ignored. Yet, they have an uncommon ability to hear God's Word to the community as they read Scripture. A wise, elderly woman in a congregation of which I have recently been a part asks the hard questions that every congregation needs to hear. She is immensely loyal to the congregation, yet clear that she belongs to Jesus Christ alone. She inquires about everyone and everything—children, newcomers, the sick; why the congregation has money for certain causes and not others; what the love of Christ asks of us when we would rather have our own way; how we might live each day in joy and praise. She does not simply read Scripture; she embodies it.

Similarly, some communities have bequeathed us with especially compelling models of "life together." They have sought quite self-consciously to embody Scripture, to be living commentaries on it. The Rule of St. Benedict, for example, examines particular biblical passages not to explicate either their historical context or their literary construction, but to translate Scripture into a way of life in community. As Benedict writes in his prologue, those who enter the monastery should let the Scriptures stir them into action. "[G]uided by the Gospel, [let us] tread the path that [God] has cleared for us."[3]

The dynamics of great commentary are reflected in Benedictine use of the Rule. In opening the monks to the power of a Scripture-shaped life, the Rule assumed a Scripture-like character in its own right. It came to be treated as a holy text, second only to Scripture itself. Like Scripture, it was read daily. Like Scripture, it asserted a right to its own place architecturally. While Scripture found its home in the sanctuary and the church's worship, the Rule inspired the development of the chapter house, where the monks read the Rule (aloud, in community, in context, for memorization!) and conducted the monastery's business. Where the monks poured their artistic impulses into architecture, the chapter house came to rival the church in beauty and significance.[4]

In the Reformed tradition, Puritanism might be best understood as a self-conscious effort to realize Scripture as a way of life together. America became the new Canaan; the Puritans, the people of Israel.[5] The very location of the church in the middle of the Puritan town reflected not only its religious, but also its political significance.[6]

In recent years, Latin American base communities have presented us with yet another powerful effort to enact Scripture, to make it a way of life in community. The members of these communities have appealed to the Exodus, Mary's Magnificat, Jesus' ministry to the poor, and other biblical images to frame their self-understanding. Their life in community has centered on reading the Bible not simply as the church's traditions or hierarchy have dictated, but for themselves. They have been certain that the Bible speaks to their situation and offers them a program of ecclesial and political reform, even revolution.

Each of these communal commentaries on Scripture sets forth the power of Scripture to transform Christians into a different kind of people. Yet, we cannot simply take one program or another and apply it to our life in community today. The point of great commentary is not to replace Scripture, but to enable us to listen to Scripture more carefully for ourselves. We alone can enact Scripture for our time and place. Fowl and Jones note that "the form of Christ must be apprehended anew in each and every historical situation. As Bonhoeffer puts it, 'What can and must be said is not what is good once and for all, but the way in which Christ takes form among us here and now.'"[7]

As living commentaries on Scripture, we must therefore return to Scripture again and again. Every effort to hear its Word for our time and place may require us to revise and correct inherited notions of its meaning. We must enter "a lifelong process of learning to become a wise reader of Scripture capable of embodying that reading in life."[8]

A SACRAMENTAL WORD
FOR A DIVIDED CHURCH

Understanding our lives as commentary on Scripture might assist a divided church. Although a sacramental understanding of Scripture will not necessarily resolve the debates that cause us so much pain, it will challenge our tendency to reduce Scripture to mere information that we manipulate for one purpose or another. In a divided church, we too often get out of Scripture whatever we want. We have made up our minds even before we open the Bible. (It's no wonder, then, that we so often leave it closed!) When we read Scripture sacramentally, we may still find ourselves in deep disagreement with each other, but we may be able to understand that disagreement as itself a form of commentary on the mystery of God and God's ways.

Scripture as a sacramental word points us beyond our disputes because it sets forth Christ. Ancient words speak a new grace. We hear ourselves addressed by a living God, who invites us into relationship with him.

The Christ whom we encounter in Scripture is both free and concrete. Scripture testifies to a man who lived in a definite time and place. His life was conditioned by history, even as it reshaped history. Yet, this Jesus was also the Son of God, the firstborn of all creation, eternally present in God's work of framing the universe. He is the mystery of God, which remains greater than any of our efforts to understand it.

Touched by God's Spirit, we trust that Christ is among us here and now. In discerning how he is taking form among us, we believe that we are called to say and do something definite about the Christian life — about matters of ethics and politics, belief and practice. We may find that Christ speaks to us in new ways — ways that do not necessarily contradict our old understanding of Scripture but that correct it, deepen it, and enliven it. Every new situation challenges us to enact Scripture anew. "No particular community of believers can be sure of what a faithful interpretation of Scripture will entail . . . until it actually engages in the hard process of conversation, argument, discussion, prayer and practice."[9]

Disciplines of reading Scripture as the Word of God, which find their deepest expression in worship, set forth the mystery of this Christ who is beyond us, yet among us. They promise us a fitting word that speaks to the specifics of our time and place. Yet, these disciplines also remind us that this Word is never ours to use however we please; rather, this Word is God's gracious gift to us. We must acknowledge it as God's and patiently wait on God to offer it to us in God's own time.

This piety of the Word could assist a divided church. Rather than arming ourselves with Scripture to do battle against each other, we would first commit ourselves to living together *with* Scripture, as we immerse ourselves in its world—and *under* Scripture, as we allow it to shape our lives. The effects of this piety of the Word would be threefold. It would reshape the character of our life in community, including the way we deal with conflict; it would suggest a method of relating Scripture to the church's decision making, and it would define the content of the Word that we hear in Scripture. I wish to explore each of these points briefly.

THE CHARACTER OF THE COMMUNITY
THAT READS SCRIPTURE SACRAMENTALLY

A piety of the Word nurtures dispositions of reading Scripture thoughtfully and thankfully. Not only do we learn to come to Scripture with certain expectations of how it will speak to us, but we also learn what it means to be a community that gathers around the Word. Habits of reading Scripture in community nurture a way of life in community.[10]

A piety of the Word teaches us the *privilege* of reading Scripture. If Scripture is not simply facts and figures out of the past, if it is not simply a collection of aphorisms, if it truly sets forth a living word, then Scripture confronts us with the mysterious depths of life, human and divine. Scripture plumbs the heights and depths of the human condition before God. It promises us a life in God that surpasses any of our efforts to order life on our own. It offers us a relationship with the One who knows us better than we know ourselves. A sacramental reading of Scripture is never mere drudgery or duty, but evokes joy.

We might again reflect on the significance of the gestures that surround the use of Scripture in worship. Reading Scripture aloud reminds us that God wishes to address us. The spoken word is the word of relationship— of honesty and vulnerability. When we attend to the sound of Scripture, we care for Scripture. Reading it aloud, and hearing it read aloud, encourages us to attend to Scripture more closely and carefully. Similarly, gestures of honoring the book of Scripture as an icon of the risen Lord remind us that we are privileged to be able to hold Scripture and read it.

Other disciplines of reading Scripture reinforce this attitude. In memorizing Scripture, we attest to its privileged status—and to the fact that we are privileged to receive God's Word in it. Memorization is a gesture of care; we do not make the effort to memorize just anything.

Placing particular passages in a larger biblical context is another gesture of care. The privilege of reading Scripture is reflected in the respect that we demonstrate for the integrity of Scripture—and its particular literary units and themes.

These disciplines of reading Scripture remind us that the Word of God is both free and definite. In setting forth its freedom, in pointing to the mystery of Christ, Scripture evokes our awe and reverence. We understand these words to have priority over our own. To be sure, the words of Scripture are conditioned by the historical circumstances in which they were written. They are not words directly from God. In this sense, an understanding of Scripture as a sacramental word does not support classic theories of biblical inerrancy or verbal inspiration. Scripture points to the Christ who remains free; it does not pin him down.

Yet, we have the confidence that any of these words, resonating in the fuller biblical context, can help to set forth the reality of the living Christ. Through them, Christ becomes concrete for us here and now. They offer us a fitting word. Thus, God does not remain shrouded in darkness but speaks to us. In Scripture, we have an incomparable gift: a sacrament of the Christ who wishes to claim our lives, transform them, and use them to the glory of his kingdom.

A piety of the Word therefore teaches us *confidence* in reading Scripture. We will not come to Scripture concerned that it might refuse to yield us anything. We will not worry that we lack the right interpretive skills to unlock its meaning. We will not insist that every Christian first attend seminary or master the techniques of the historical-critical method before opening the Bible. Rather, we will trust that God wishes to set forth Christ to *us* in Scripture. We will read Scripture in the expectation that we will encounter God's own Son.

Disciplines of reading Scripture, and the use of Scripture in worship, help to support this confidence. As words that are read *in* community, Scripture will be understood to offer a Word *to* the community. As Christians gather around Scripture, they will listen together—not just to appreciate the beautiful sounds of poetic-like words, but to receive God's living Word for their lives here and now. The fact that this Word matters desperately for the life of the community will be reflected in the community's commitment to studying it and making it a part of its basic vocabulary. Christians will bother to memorize Scripture because they will expect it to guide and comfort them in times of crisis. They will receive Scripture as a Word that dwells in them as a source of life, a Word on which they can meditate, as they seek to chart life's course.

A piety of the Word also teaches us *humility*. We will come to Scripture not to justify ourselves, but to stand before the Holy One who is Lord of life and death. No individual, no particular community of faith, can exhaust the meaning of Scripture. Nor can any of us ever assume control of Scripture, as though it should simply confirm our personal intuitions or conform to our own purposes. The Word is free. Every effort to order it must finally reckon with other efforts that appear equally insightful and forceful. Next to a confidence that Scripture sets forth Christ for us will be a humility that acknowledges Scripture as setting forth the Word of *God*. Whatever we hear in it is limited by our partiality: by our distinct abilities to hear some things and not others, as well as by our sin.

As W. C. Smith writes, Bernard of Clairveaux was both confident that Scripture mediated Christ and humble about rightly apprehending and fulfilling it. Bernard risked interpreting Scripture—and he could be unhesitating in arguing for the rightness of his position. Yet, he also recognized that Scripture's meaning was not always clear. In striving for the best possible meaning, a reader enjoys great freedom, but the mystery of Scripture also gives him or her reason to be diffident.

> Bernard may remark that "there is no answer" to a question as to who is being addressed in a particular passage, and then add "unless perhaps" it be so-and-so; but he then continues, "I think it better to suppose" that it is. . . . Again: "If anyone thinks that this should be understood . . . in the sense that . . . , I do not dissent." His tentativeness appears regularly: "I do not think it would be wrong to say. . . ."[11]

Would that the church's current debates demonstrated more of this spirit! We need disciplines of reading Scripture, and of using Scripture in worship, to train us in humility. Hearing Scripture read aloud encourages us to nurture a humility in receiving Scripture passively through the ear before engaging it more actively through the eye. Reading Scripture in community humbles us as we become aware of perspectives other than our own. As we read particular biblical passages in their larger biblical context, we become aware of tensions in the text that defy quick resolution. In praying for the illumination of the Spirit, we acknowledge that we cannot make sense of Scripture on our own.

Humility in reading Scripture suggests the importance of *openness* to other interpretations. When we read Scripture sacramentally, we find that others' insights make our understanding of Scripture all the richer. For this reason, Scripture is truly meant to be read in community, especially in particular congregations.

A sense of humility before the Word will also teach us to expand our understanding of community.[12] We will learn to listen to other voices, including those that most challenge our own interpretations of Scripture. As we struggle to make sense of the different ways that Christians have read Scripture, we will be reminded again of the freedom of the Word. We will save ourselves from "interpretive arrogance."[13]

A sacramental understanding of Scripture need not imply that anything goes, that one reading of Scripture is just as good as another. Next to openness, we need an ability to engage in *moral discourse*.[14] The vitality of the church's faith depends not only on proposing interpretations of Scripture, but also on testing them. True conversation requires both an openness to other perspectives and a willingness to assess them. Through reasoned argument, the community will seek to determine which enactments of Scripture most faithfully demonstrate how Christ is concretely taking form among us.

Those who have unusual gifts of intelligence and scholarship have a special role in shaping this moral discourse. Biblical scholars help us to understand the original context of Scripture. Historians trace the development of biblical interpretation in the Christian tradition. Theologians order the diversity of the biblical materials into a coherent message. Ethicists propose the implications of that message for the way we live the Christian life.

But moral discourse will ultimately involve other parts of the community of faith as well. The process of discernment is more than a matter of intelligence. It is not reserved for an intellectual elite. Above all, it depends on skills of practical wisdom, an ability to see what is fitting in a particular situation. While the community's saints have this wisdom to a special degree, it is in the deliberations of the wider community of faith that it most clearly manifests itself. The Spirit that illumines Scripture is the Spirit that binds believers to each other. This community is most fundamentally the worshiping congregation, but it needs constantly to refer to the larger church catholic.

The Sacramental Word as a Resource for Dealing with Church Conflict

These attitudes toward Scripture define the nature of life together in Christian community. If people know the privilege of reading Scripture, they will not use it as a club to beat others. If they explore Scripture in confidence and humility, they will develop a capacity for patience with one another. They will agree on procedures for making decisions about the shape of life together, yet will also demonstrate a capacity to revise those decisions, in accord with a deeper understanding of God's Word.[15]

Such a community is best characterized as a "living conversation." On the one hand, the different points of view in this conversation can be mutually enriching. As Elizabeth Johnson notes, a diversity of interpretations of Scripture helps to protect our sense of the mystery of God. In rubbing up against each other, different names and symbols for God remind us that we can speak of God only by analogy. The effort to impose one idea, one point of view, or one name on God inevitably results both in idolatry—a mistaken confidence that we can know God and manipulate God for our own purposes—and in social oppression, with one group seeking to dominate another in the name of religion.[16] On the other hand, these differing points of view inevitably lead to moments of tension, even conflict. Any community of faith that seeks to listen to Scripture for God's Word will embody in its own life the tensions inherent to a Word that is both definite and free—where individuals try to say what they hear, while acknowledging the limitations of their hearing.

Karl Barth has reflected profoundly on these dynamics of diversity and conflict in the church. As Barth would remind us, the Word that we hear in Scripture is God's. We must therefore "subject ourselves to the right which does not dwell in us and is not manifested by us, but which is over me and us as the right of God above, and manifested to me and us only from God."[17] We must thankfully acknowledge God's Word to be a Word that rules over us all. It is the source of our unity.[18] An individual can never insist that his or her hearing of Scripture is absolutely right.

Barth argues, nonetheless, that each of us must represent the Word that we hear for ourselves, as best as we can. The Holy Spirit guides us in giving the command of God to each other. As Barth notes,

> It may well be the case . . . that one man has the task of interfering in respect of the conduct of another, that with the great or little authority and knowledge which he has in relation to the other he must warn him very concretely and particularly about this or that mode of behaviour or act, or visa-versa spur him to do it.[19]

Barth notes that we may well come into conflict with each other, as we speak the different words that God has given us. But he argues that this conflict will never become absolute if we remember that God's Word is finally larger than any of us. As Barth says, God's Word is "the command of absolute peace, and . . . we can engage in strife only for the sake of peace."[20] Where there is conflict, we will strive for fellowship. There is always a place "for right and friendliness and wholesomeness in [our] mutual relations."[21]

While conflict must not become absolute, Barth argues that we should not spare ourselves "relative conflict." Only as we grapple with each other's readings of Scripture will we discern what form Christ is taking among us here and now. The Second Helvetic Confession makes a similar point. God can use conflict "to the glory of his name, to illustrate the truth, and in order that those who are in the right might be manifest."[22] Relative conflict may be necessary, if the community is finally to determine which readings of Scripture are faithful.

Relative conflict need not result in paralysis or indecision.[23] Every community, if it is to remain a community, will have procedures for making decisions, and it may have to subject particular members of the community "to communal discipline if they are unwilling to be reconciled to the body's reading and performance of Scripture."[24] This process of community decision making begins in the congregation but is affected by that congregation's ties to other congregations, whether denominationally or by virtue of other kinds of relationship.

Yet, the process of discernment is frequently wearisome. Difficult questions may defy resolution. Interpretive conflict may prevail. Procedures for adjudicating disputes sometimes fail or simply stoke fires of discontent. Under these circumstances, communities of faith may need to develop a capacity to endure the tensions and differences that characterize their reading of Scripture—whether at the level of the congregation or in larger church bodies. Efforts to reach consensus may have to yield to forbearance.

This capacity to bear with each other's differences is what Bonhoeffer called "the ministry of bearing."[25] On the one hand, we need each other's different readings of Scripture. They broaden our vision; they help us to correct distortions in the lenses that we bring to the text. On the other hand, these differences may also cause us pain. Things that we care about most deeply—that we believe should be self-evident (such as the character of sexual fidelity, or the unique role of Christ as Lord and Savior)—will be in dispute, and the Word of God that we claim for ourselves will appear to contradict the Word of God that our brother or sister in Christ claims.

In mainline churches today, consensus seems elusive. We sometimes despair of hearing a common Word; we seem to be left only with different words, each of which is good only for the one who hears it. Each of us does what is "right in [our] own eyes" (Judg. 21:25, RSV). Or the Word that we hear together seems to contradict our personal sense of what is right and fitting—the call for compromise undermines our sense of personal integrity. The seeming contradiction between the unity of the church and its purity may weigh on each of us, regardless of where we stand. We need each other, yet find life together difficult, almost impossible.

As James Gustafson notes in relation to family life:

> The well-being of an individual member . . . does not necessarily serve the well-being of other members, or the family unit as a whole—its common good. The good of the parts are not always in equilibrium with each other, and the common good of the whole is not always in harmony with the legitimate ends and aspirations of the parts. . . . [T]here is interdependence without equilibrium.[26]

When the church listens to Scripture as a sacramental word, it too will sometimes find that "there is interdependence without equilibrium." We may not be able to resolve our differences. There is disequilibrium. Yet, as we remember that Scripture calls us into the life of Christ, we will refuse to allow such conflict to have the last word. We will seek ways for members of the church to share life together, despite their intractable differences. We are interdependent.

This capacity to live with difficult differences—in gratitude when they enrich our life together, and in love that is patient and kind when they prove painful, even destructive—may be the great commentary on Scripture that is required of the mainline churches of our day. Communities that would bear with each other's differences must live as faithfully as possible within the tension of a sacramental word that is both free and definite. While acknowledging that God's Word is finally larger than any effort to articulate it, they must risk articulating it as clearly and concretely as possible, despite the disagreements that may then erupt. Scripture may speak with particular power as we learn to appeal to it not only with conviction, but also with a spirit of gratitude, always open to the living Word, Christ the Lord.

IMPLICATIONS FOR THE COMMUNITY'S DECISION MAKING

A piety of the Word gives us resources for hanging in with each other when we disagree about basic questions of faith and practice. But it also offers us a way to use Scripture in the community's process of decision making. While this method will not resolve all our ethical and theological differences, it will help us guard against crass manipulations of the biblical text to suit our own purposes.

A brief consideration of the four disciplines that we have identified is suggestive. Reading Scripture *aloud,* attending to its importance as sound, lifts up its poetic, imaginative character. This hearing reorients us. It redirects our seeing. It summons us to a different way of interpreting the world. We will find in Scripture first of all not political ammunition, but a way of life in the presence of God. The poetic, imaginative word asks us to meditate on it. We will think "about the nature of things, about what is true, good, and beautiful . . . gaining critical distance from and so transcending the roles and relationships that otherwise narrowly define our perceptions and responses."[27]

In using Scripture in decision making, we will begin with this alternative vision of reality. We will not appeal to specific parts of Scripture—laws, stories, prophetic diatribes—as though they were authoritative in and of themselves. Rather, we will relate them to this larger understanding of what is fitting for the life of the community before God.[28] We will attend in particular to Scripture's images. We will allow Scripture to function first at the descriptive level, and only then at the prescriptive level. We will examine what Scripture tells us of who *God is*—and who therefore we are—before we ask it to tell us what *we should do.*[29]

The principle that Scripture is meant to be read *in community* will remind us that particular communities must consult wider communities as they relate Scripture to particular theological and ethical issues. Too much of the church's decision making is parochial. We consult only our own experience and look only at the needs and circumstances of our own communities—our own congregations, our own denominations. Or we get caught up in the excitement of the most recent theological fad. Too often, we fail to consult the larger Christian tradition or perspectives of the church universal. As one of my colleagues likes to point out, the marginalized voices to which we must attend include Augustine and Calvin, as well as liberation and feminist theologians![30]

Barth argued that we must listen with particular care to Scripture through the canon, the tradition's authoritative teachers (the church "fathers"), and the confessions of the Reformation. The broader confessional posture that these sources of authority represent should not be quickly or easily revised. The church's tradition has a certain priority in our decision making. Individuals or particular groups within the church do not have the authority to overthrow the church's wisdom. Even in the preparation of new church confessions, particular church bodies should seek to speak to the church universal, not simply to local or national interests.[31]

But Barth also acknowledged that "in all ages the will of God has been fulfilled outside the Church as well."[32] These "outsiders" include leaders of the wider social and cultural community. Calvin too spoke of welcoming truth wherever it appeared.[33] We need the insights of the arts and sciences as they bear both on the meaning of Scripture and on the church's understanding of particular social, ethical, and political issues.[34]

In consulting the insights of the world, congregations and denominations have the difficult task of relating them to the church's wisdom. At a minimum, however, we can insist that insights from the wider social and cultural community not be used to undermine the Christian community's piety of the Word. They must draw us into a richer appreciation and appropriation of Scripture's compelling power, not dismiss it.[35] Thus, the insights of communities that have helped to sustain Scripture's sacramental character will have a certain priority in our thinking. We will draw first on the wisdom of those Christian traditions—embodied in particular individuals, families, congregations, and theological traditions—that have taught us to honor Scripture as setting forth God's Word.

The discipline of reading Scripture *in context* will require us to attend to historical-critical studies. The living Word is grounded in the history of a particular people. The risen Christ is identical with the historical Jesus. The New Testament writings were directed to historical communities. Scripture reflects the language and cultural assumptions of a time and place different from our own. Historical criticism keeps us honest with the text.

As in using insights from the sciences, the church will use historical-critical studies to support the biblical context, not undermine it.[36] If the point is for Christians to be able to read Scripture more faithfully, they will not substitute the history behind Scripture for the text as it now stands and is used in the community of faith. On Sunday mornings, we read Scripture, not historical-critical commentaries on it.

Reading Scripture in biblical context ultimately requires theological work. The diverse materials of Scripture—a diversity that historical-critical studies help to point up—sometimes seem to contradict each other. How do we put together faith and works? Jesus the wandering sage, and Jesus the Old Testament prophet? The equality of women and men in the Spirit, and their different roles? Theologians can help us to order this diversity.[37] They can lift up broader themes that give Scripture a coherent meaning for our lives today. They can discourage us from appealing to isolated passages of Scripture to support positions to which we are already committed.

Finally, reading Scripture for *memorization* will remind Christians that they are called to immerse themselves in a different language, the language of the Bible. In seeking to relate Scripture to the church's decision making, we will not simply translate the biblical world into a secular vocabulary.[38] Christians need not reject the secular language of "rights," but their first language in worship and theology will be the biblical language of "God's righteousness." Similarly, Christians need not reject what is positive in the culture's emphasis on "individual autonomy," but they will never allow it to be absolute. They will, instead, remember their first language, the biblical language of "the body of Christ."

To ask the church to make the Bible's language its own does not yet answer the question of the content of that language—that is, what Scripture actually requires of us. But it does mean that we will rule out efforts to discard the language of Scripture, as though its poetic language obscures truths that secular philosophies can express more clearly. While we must be vigilant that biblical language not be reduced to one political cause or another, we must also reclaim the power of Scripture to give us a distinctive language for analyzing the social issues that we confront as Christians, and for articulating a response.

IMPLICATIONS FOR THE CHURCH'S THEOLOGY

To this point, I have focused on questions of *method*. But I believe that a piety of the Word also suggests a definite theological *content*. I believe that it implies not merely ways of *using* Scripture, but also ways of *understanding* God's will in Christ. Again, a piety of the Word may not provide specific answers to specific questions of faith and practice, but it may help to steer the church's process of decision making.

Theologian David Kelsey has argued that every effort to use Scripture theologically involves a "discrimen"—a pattern that imaginatively captures one's understanding of how God is at work in the world. This pattern enables one to sort out the value of various biblical materials. Kelsey shows how different theologians employ different discrimens and therefore weigh different parts of the Bible and different kinds of biblical materials in different ways.[39]

The sacramental understanding of Scripture that I am proposing suggests who this God is. It suggests a discrimen, or perhaps a set of discrimens. With Barth, I believe that these discrimens must be in accord with the church's canon, authoritative teachers, and confessions—as well as its worship! A sacramental word must point to a God of promise, to whom we respond in trust, and who sends us into service.

A sacramental understanding of Scripture reminds us of God's *promise* to be in relationship with us. God has not left himself shrouded in mystery. Rather, God wants us to know him. He accommodates himself to us in Christ, and in the Scriptures as they set forth Christ. The One who is beyond comprehension enters into our history and language.

Because God seeks relationship with us, he comes to us not to destroy us, but to draw us into his life. As Barth argues, prior to any other word, God says "Yes" to us.[40] We encounter Christ first of all not as God's demand on our lives—not as a perfect standard that exposes our imperfection, not as a lawgiver who punishes our transgressions—but as God's Word of loving promise. In Christ, God is not indifferent to us, but is concerned for every hair of our head. In Christ, God does not abandon us to ourselves, but comes to us to save us from ourselves.

A sacramental understanding of Scripture lifts up the Christ who offers new life to all whom he encounters. This Christ seeks to redeem the world. He challenges forces of death, evil, and chaos. He enters the human condition to fill it with God's grace. He suffers death, so that death might no longer have power over the world. He rises from the dead, so that we might rise to new life with him.

In response to God's word of promise, we live in *trust*. A sacramental understanding of Scripture suggests that God seeks our transformation. Not only does God come to us; God invites us into relationship with him. He calls us to put our confidence in him and his purposes. God wants to know us, so that we might know him. He offers us life, so that we might freely choose it for ourselves. He conquers powers of death, so that we too might resist them.

As a sacramental word, Scripture nourishes this trust. It reminds us of the generations of men and women who have found God and God's purposes to be trustworthy, despite all the evidence seemingly to the contrary. Scripture gives us a language for calling on God both in our times of thanksgiving and in our times of lament. Scripture impresses images and phrases of faith, hope, and love on our spirits, so that we might dwell on our understanding of God and God's ways—indeed, so that we might dwell *in* God, and God in us.

As a sacramental word, Scripture invites us to experience transformation in our relationships to each other. Because Scripture gathers us into Christ, we become Christ's body. We live in interdependence, both through and despite our differences.

This trust in God's promise issues finally in *service*. A sacramental understanding of Scripture suggests that God seeks our active engagement in his purposes. The precious gift that Scripture sets forth is not ours to use for our own purposes, but a gift that we receive, so that we might offer it to others. We commit ourselves to living in the way of the Christ whom we encounter in Scripture. We are servants of the Word, seeking to live out its possibilities not only for ourselves, but for the world.[41]

Because God has changed us, we wish to join in God's purposes of changing the whole of creation: to resist powers of death, wherever they appear, and to offer all people the gift of life in Christ. We seek to become a church that lives in trust, not fear, and that offers the world a taste of trusting, caring community in the midst of the world's broken promises and violence.

These three themes—promise, trust, and service—should frame our interpretation of particular biblical materials. When we read Old Testament laws, we will ask what, if anything, they tell us of God's *promise* to be in relationship to us. Do they point to God's gracious ordering of the universe? Do they reflect God's will to give us life? We will also consider whether, and in what respect, these laws have the capacity to deepen our sense of *trust* in God. Do they simply belong to a different culture? In what respect, if any, can they speak to us today? Finally, we will seek to determine whether fulfillment of these laws would issue in *service*. Do they set forth God's gracious presence to the world, or do they simply support the narrow, sinful interests of particular individuals or institutions? Do these laws invite others into relationship with the living God? Do they flesh out the contours of life in Christ?

A helpful theology of God's law is set forth especially well in the Westminster Larger Catechism, which understands the Ten Commandments to be embodied most fully in the life of Jesus, who asks us to love God with heart, soul, and mind (corresponding to the first table of the Ten Commandments, the first four commandments) and our neighbor as ourselves (the second table, the last six). Each commandment is best understood as not simply prohibiting specific acts, but as setting forth a broad trajectory of gracious possibilities that lead us to Christ. It gives definition and shape to Christ's love. Thus, the eighth commandment, "thou shalt not steal," sets forth a trajectory towards justice, as defined by Christ's love. We should do everything possible to guarantee the just distribution of goods by "giving and lending freely . . . moderation of our judgments, wills, and affections, concerning worldly goods . . . [and] an endeavor by all just and lawful means to procure, preserve, and further the wealth and outward state of others, as well as our own."[42]

Similarly, when we read particular biblical narratives, our interest will be not primarily in whether they simply say something wise about the human condition today, but in whether they draw us into God's promise of new life, deepen our trust in that promise, and stir us to set forth that promise to the world in acts of service. We will see the story of the Fall, for example, as not simply a parable for the human desire for forbidden knowledge, but as demonstrating the promise of God's continuing desire for relationship with us, despite our failure to trust in God.

Because these themes of promise, trust, and service are broad in scope, they do not by themselves immediately resolve any of the particular theological and ethical debates that overwhelm the church today. But they are trajectories along which we can faithfully search for answers.[43] When we think of Scripture as a sacramental word, we come to it in the confidence that we will hear God's Word. We also come in the confidence that this Word, though free, will speak to us consistently and coherently of God's promise in Christ.

METHODOLOGICAL AND THEOLOGICAL CONSIDERATIONS IN THE HOMOSEXUALITY DEBATE

A fuller exposition of these insights would require us to apply them to particular theological or ethical debates before the church. Here I simply wish to suggest in brief how an understanding of Scripture as a sacramental word might reframe the church's debate of homosexuality. Significantly, this debate presses all three dimensions of Scripture that I have discussed in this chapter: the character of life together when the church is in conflict, our method of applying Scripture to particular theological or ethical issues, and our understanding of the content of the gospel.

The intensity of the homosexuality debate challenges us to reflect on the character of *life together* in a time of church conflict. Scripture as a sacramental word asks us to live as a community of "interdependence without equilibrium." Because the debate in most mainline denominations has focused on the question of ordination, they have found themselves passing legislation and arguing judicial cases. Yet, no matter which side appears to be in the ascendancy, neither is presently able to resolve the issue once and for all.

Because the debate continues, the question becomes, What kind of community will we be as we debate these issues? Because power is at stake, people are tempted to employ excessive rhetoric and to control the manner in which debate legitimately proceeds (amount of time, number of speakers, manner of engaging opposing ideas). Polarization seems inevitable.

A sacramental understanding of Scripture reminds us of our unity in

Christ, even in the midst of the pain that we inevitably inflict on each other. We may not be able to win others to our point of view, but we must not forget that we need each other's passions and talents as we try to address other pressing issues before the church. The person whose position on homosexuality we may not be able to abide may be the very person whom we need to assist us in furthering God's kingdom in some other respect.

The homosexuality debate also challenges us to reconsider our *method* of relating Scripture to particular theological and ethical issues. As I have argued throughout this book, the character of the present debate about homosexuality reflects—and has perhaps contributed—to a more general undermining of Scripture's sacramental power. If we are to recover a sacramental understanding of Scripture, we must first attend to Scripture as a poetic-like word. The four disciplines that we have discussed are again suggestive. As evidenced in the discipline of reading Scripture *aloud*, our first concern will not be application of particular biblical pronouncements to particular ethical issues, but—as with poetry—a renewed capacity to discern an alternative vision of life.

A sacramental understanding of Scripture requires us to consult the full wisdom of the Christian church. We read in *community*. It is insufficient for us simply to adopt a "prophetic stance" against the tradition. The fact that the Christian tradition, until recently, has consistently condemned homosexual behavior should weigh heavily in our reasoning, as well as the fact that the wider Christian community in the world today continues to do so.

Nonetheless, those who oppose ordination of homosexual persons must resist the temptation to use these voices in a self-serving manner. The voices to which we must listen include those that challenge the tradition, even if they make us uncomfortable. We need to consult the best scientific evidence about the genetic and environmental factors that shape human sexuality. We need to hear from homosexual persons themselves, especially those Christians who strive to live faithfully.

A sacramental understanding of Scripture would encourage us to read particular passages on homosexuality in a larger, biblical *context*. We would not focus on a few isolated passages that appear to relate to homosexuality, but on larger theological themes. What does it mean to be human before God? What role does sexuality play, or not play, in defining us? How does sin distort sexuality? How do we repent of these distortions? What standards are required of church officers? The creation narrative, Paul's understanding of Jesus as the Second Adam, biblical themes of fidelity—as we plumb these materials, we may find that they may ultimately yield more clarity than the few, scattered passages on homosexual behavior as such.

A sacramental understanding of Scripture asks us to search our own distinctive biblical, theological *memory* as we reflect on these issues. We will not simply subscribe to one secular cause or another. We will be confident that words like grace, salvation, and sanctification speak uniquely of God's will for our lives, also in relation to questions of sexuality.

None of these criteria in and of themselves determine an answer to the specific questions before the church. They do, however, require that the debate become more explicitly theological.[44] The church will know that the quality of its debate has taken a turn for the better when the debate contributes to a deeper reading of Scripture, rather than leaving people cynically shaking their heads that one really can get whatever one wants out of the Bible.

Finally, the homosexuality debate challenges us to return to define more clearly the *content* of the gospel. At issue is the need not simply to frame sexuality issues theologically, but to articulate the kind of theology that guides us. A sacramental understanding of Scripture lifts up themes of promise, trust, and service. How is God at work in our lives? How do we respond in trust to God's ways? How do we share new life in Christ with others?

The homosexuality debate must not become a diversion from the full scope of the work that God has given the church. Any effort to resolve the debate must reflect the patience and love that the gospel engenders. Where the debate becomes panicked, where arguments appear forced, where people lose a sense of the larger ends of the Christian life, the church is challenged to pause—even to set the debate aside—until it can return to it out of a renewed confidence that God's ways will ultimately prevail.

Again, a fuller exposition of these matters would risk moving from these broad themes—promise, trust, service—to a particular answer to the homosexuality debate. Here I have simply wished to insist that these theological themes should principally undergird the debate, rather than a theology that draws primarily or even exclusively from secular notions of justice or law, on the one hand, or popular notions of love or toleration, on the other.[45]

WAITING ON THE TRANSFORMING POSSIBILITIES OF GOD'S WORD

When we become living commentaries on Scripture, we stand under Scripture, but we also stand next to Scripture. Not only the church's great confessions and works of art, but we ourselves become compelling witnesses to Christ. Our lives cannot take the place of Scripture, but they can interpret Scripture. They can even risk setting forth God's Word as it comes to us in Scripture. This life commentary is not insignificant, no matter how modest our influence on the world. As I have heard black preachers sometimes say, "We may be the only book that some people will read."

When we think of our lives individually and communally as commentary on Scripture, we remember that they are rarely simple, straightforward narratives. They are less like fact and prose, and more like pieces of art, poetry, or music. Each of us plumbs the depths of the human condition. We consist of complex juxtapositions of majority and minority opinions. We organize our lives into relatively coherent patterns, yet we are always being broken open to the new thing that God is doing among us.

These inner debates and tensions sometimes threaten to rend us apart as persons and communities. There is no guarantee that a sacramental reading of Scripture will forge bonds strong enough to sustain us through times of anguished debate and uncertainty. Scripture is a source of unity, but the potential for pain is all the greater when we find ourselves in honest disagreement about basic matters of belief and practice.

We live nonetheless in the hope that God's Word in Scripture will confront us anew, reshape us, and regenerate us, despite all our failures and hurts. In *Crime and Punishment,* Fyodor Dostoyevsky tells the story of Raskolnikov. Raskolnikov wishes to prove to himself that he is above the law—indeed, that he is a law to himself—and murders an old, despicable woman whom no one would ever miss. But his efforts to repress his deed merely intensify his inner anguish. He grows increasingly desperate. Finally, he confronts the one person whom he can trust, Sonya, who struggles with her own desperation in becoming a prostitute in order to save her destitute family.

When Raskolnikov demands that she read him the gospel, Sonya hesitates, as though afraid to betray her deepest hopes. Slowly, she picks up the book and begins reading the story of Jesus and Lazarus. Her voice trembles and almost breaks off. But then she regains her strength. She reads as if everything depends on it. Scripture speaks from the depths of her very being.

In those moments, no miraculous transformations take place. But at the end of the novel, Raskolnikov, now in prison, fingers the pages of Sonya's Bible, as though his life might yet become precious commentary on the gospel's promise of new life in Christ.[46] We, like Raskolnikov, are a host of contradictions. But God's Word does not let us go. It searches for the good soil in us, so that someday it may "bear fruit, thirty and sixty and a hundredfold" (Mark 4:20).

8

CONCLUSION:
A READING OF MATTHEW 4:1–11

One spring day, the Jehovah's Witnesses were going door to door in Skokie, a suburb—largely Jewish—of Chicago. They were making little progress, until they came to the home of a Jewish biblical scholar. When they told him, "We'd like to talk to you about the Bible," he responded, "Fine! What would you like to know?"

This scholar had quickly surmised that his visitors were not simply interested in a theoretical discussion. They were not going to talk to him about the right method of interpreting the Bible. Rather, they were going to try to persuade him to understand particular passages in light of a particular theology, and he wanted to beat them to the punch.

In this book, I have talked a great deal *about* the Bible. I have argued for recovering historic disciplines of reading Scripture, and for understanding Scripture as a poetic and sacramental word. But most of us do not wish to reflect abstractly on the character of the Bible. Nor are we interested in trying out just another method. Rather, we want to read the Bible itself, and to discern God's Word for our lives. The most pressing task, then, is not to talk about how to read the Bible, but to assume the risk of actually interpreting particular passages of Scripture and applying them to the controversial issues that currently beset the church and the wider culture.

Yet, as I have also argued, I fear that many of us are all too ready to apply Scripture to one issue or another and all too ready to devise new methods of interpretation that will justify a theological stance or a political cause to which we are already committed. If this book evades the hard work of developing particular theological or ethical positions on issues as contentious as homosexuality, it is both because I would need to write another book to do justice to the topic, and because I believe that we as mainline Protestants first need to develop the capacity to read Scripture in a different kind of way.

In sum, I do not understand myself to be offering just another method of interpretation that now needs to be applied, so that we might assess its value. Rather, I wish to nurture a *piety* that might accompany and shape our reading of Scripture. Only as we read aloud, in community, in context, and for memorization might we develop a new habits of reading Scripture. Only as we recover disciplines of reading Scripture as a sacramental word might we nurture a different set of dispositions toward Scripture, so that we might receive it as a living word, not merely as information or practical advice. If we would discover the Word that Scripture might hold for us today, each of us must now "take, and read" in this spirit of confidence and humility.

Nonetheless, it may be helpful to illustrate some of the riches that a piety of the Word might win from the Bible. I therefore conclude with a brief reading of a biblical narrative, in the hope that others too might be drawn to read Scripture in fresh ways.

THE DESERT SHALL BLOSSOM

Mark 1:12–13 briefly reports the temptation of Jesus. Matthew 4:1–11 offers a longer account, as does Luke 4:1–13. I am not interested here in accounting for the differences between these two longer accounts, such as the fact that they put the three temptations in a different order. While I will follow Matthew's order, I wish to reflect on some of the larger biblical themes that resonate in all three accounts.

Jesus is tempted in the wilderness. The wilderness was, of course, the place of Israel's temptation, as she fled Egypt and wandered toward the Promised Land. It was in the wilderness that Israel cried out for meat, worshiped the golden calf, and rebelled against Moses.

The wilderness is also the place of exile. At the beginning of time, Adam and Eve were driven out of the Garden of Eden to till ground that would bear them thorns and thistles. Toward the end of the Old Testament history, Israel is driven out of the Promised Land and crosses the wilderness to go into exile in Babylon.

Jesus is tempted for forty days, just as Moses spent forty days on Sinai, waiting for the law; just as Elijah needed forty days to reach Horeb, where God would speak out to him in a "still, small voice" (RSV). Israel herself wandered forty years in the wilderness, until Joshua led her across the Jordan River into the Promised Land.

Jesus grows hungry, just as Israel grew hungry in the wilderness, just as Adam and Eve desired the fruit that was forbidden. One of the most fundamental human questions is, Where will we get enough to eat? What will really satisfy our hunger?

Israel continually grumbled about her hunger in the wilderness: "If only we had died by the hand of the Lord in the land of Egypt, when we sat by the fleshpots and ate our fill of bread; for you have brought us out into this wilderness to kill this whole assembly with hunger" (Ex. 16:3). When God fed Israel bread from heaven, her complaining did not end: "If only we had meat to eat . . . there is nothing at all but this manna to look at" (Num. 11:4, 6). Adam and Eve, too, had plenty to eat, yet they wanted the one fruit that would truly satisfy them: "The woman saw that the tree was good for food, and that it was a delight to the eyes, and that the tree was to be desired" (Gen. 3:6).

Jesus, by contrast, does not make demands of God, does not rebel. He resists the devil's temptation to make bread out of stone and tells him, "It is written, 'One does not live by bread alone, but by every word that comes from the mouth of God'" (Matt. 4:4).

The devil then takes Jesus to the pinnacle of the temple and tells him to throw himself down. Quoting Psalm 91, the devil reminds Jesus that God "will command his angels concerning you . . . On their hands they will bear you up, so that you will not dash your foot against a stone" (Matt. 4:6).

This temptation relates to a second fundamental human question: Who will protect us? Who will take care of us? We too often answer that we can count only on ourselves. Even if we believe that God will protect us, we inevitably want God's protection on our own terms. We do not entirely trust God to act for our good.

Moses sent the spies into the Promised Land. They returned with reports of a land of milk and honey, whose inhabitants were giants: "The land that we have gone through as spies is a land that devours its inhabitants; and all the people that we saw in it are of great size" (Num. 13:32). Even though God promised to protect the people, they refused to go up. Fearful of defeat, they cried, "Let us . . . go back to Egypt" (Num. 14:4).

Then in the face of God's displeasure, they suddenly changed their minds: "Here we are. We will go up to the place that the Lord has promised, for we have sinned" (Num. 14:40). But God saw to it that they were routed, and that the time of wandering would extend another forty years. They had decided to go up not because they trusted God, but because they had decided that they could trust themselves.

Adam and Eve too wondered who would protect them, even though God had given them everything they needed. They ate the forbidden fruit, so that they might be like God, able to take care of themselves. Yet, when they saw their nakedness and realized just how vulnerable they really were, they were afraid.

The devil now wishes to sow doubt in Jesus' mind. Will God really protect him? But Jesus replied, "Again it is written, 'Do not put the Lord your God to the test'" (Matt. 4:7). Jesus trusts in God to demonstrate protection in his own good time.

Finally, the devil takes Jesus to a high mountain and shows him all the kingdoms of the world. Jesus can have their splendor if only he will fall down and worship the devil. This third temptation relates to a third fundamental question of human existence: Whom will we worship? To whom will we give our ultimate loyalty?

When Israel arrives at the foot of Sinai, she hears God's voice from the mountain, and falls down and worships (Exodus 19). But within a few days she has Aaron making a golden calf (Exodus 32). She forgets the living God, yet cannot forget her longing to have someone, something, to worship. Similarly, Adam and Eve did not trust in God alone. They heard the voice of the serpent and believed they could trust in it and in themselves.

Jesus, by contrast, tells the devil: "Away with you, Satan! for it is written, 'Worship the Lord your God, and serve only him'" (Matt. 4:10).

In each case, Jesus rejects the devil's temptations by saying, "It is written." Jesus appeals to Scripture, namely, three confessional statements in Deuteronomy (8:3, 6:16, 6:13). He claims to hear a Word of God in Scripture. Scripture sets forth to him a living word that he must proclaim against the devil's self-interested manipulation of Scripture. Jesus refuses to use the text like the devil to justify his own desires.

But we see that Scripture—especially key images, such as wilderness, hunger, temptation—infuse the whole story; the appeal to Scripture is not limited to Jesus' direct quotations of Deuteronomy. As Jesus walks into the wilderness, he is reenacting the history of Israel. He is walking where they walked; he is experiencing the temptations they experienced. Only his response is different. Whereas Israel rejected God's Word, Jesus faithfully embodies it.

I have also suggested that Jesus is reenacting the story of Adam and Eve. But if the story of the temptation of Jesus evidences significant parallels to the first temptation story, there are also key contrasts. The Garden of Eden was the peaceable kingdom, where creation was in harmony. In seeking to recapture a vision of the garden, Isaiah would describe it as a world in which the wolf dwells with the lamb, and the leopard with the kid (Isa. 11:6). The wilderness that Jesus enters is, by contrast, the place of wild beasts, of conflict between humans and creation, humans and God, and one human and another.

There are other contrasts, as well. Adam and Eve faced temptation in the midst of plenty; Jesus faces temptation in the face of a hostile, unyielding desert.

Yet, Jesus reverses the effects of the Fall. Adam and Eve (and Israel) disobeyed God's commandment; Jesus obeys God's Word. Adam and Eve were expelled from the garden; the story of Jesus is the story of "paradise regained" (to use the phrase of John Milton, the great English poet). Mark's account even suggests that in Jesus the wilderness becomes the peaceable kingdom. Jesus is "with the wild beasts" (Mark 1:13); there is no hint of fear.

The role of the angels is also reversed. God posted cherubim at the east of the garden, so that Adam and Eve could not return (Gen. 3:24); now angels minister to Jesus (Matt. 4:11 and Mark 1:13). Again, Jesus reverses the Fall.

The parallels to the first temptation story, and these great reversals, were captured by Paul when he called Jesus "the second man," the Second Adam (1 Cor. 15:45–47). In Adam, all died; in Jesus, all are made alive. Adam and Eve remind us of mortality and death; Jesus offers us eternal life (1 Cor. 15:21–22). The first Adam sought to be like God ("You will be like God" [Gen. 3:5]); the Second Adam "humbled himself and became obedient to the point of death—even death on a cross" (Phil. 2:8). The story of Adam and Eve ends in shame; Jesus offers us a story of unbending trust in God, even in the face of death on a cross. In Jesus, the words of Isaiah 35:1 find fulfillment: "The wilderness and the dry land shall be glad, the desert shall rejoice and blossom."

TEMPTATION AND BAPTISM

As those who have been baptized into the life of Jesus (Gal. 3:27–29), we too begin the trek out of the wilderness back into the garden. The baptismal rites of the early church dramatically traced this journey.[1] The process of preparing adults for baptism included a series of exorcisms. Candidates for baptism were understood to be gradually freeing themselves from their loyalty to the devil and his temptations. The most intense period of preparation took place in the forty days prior to Easter (resonating with the biblical images of forty). Significantly, the early church read the story of the temptation of Jesus on the first Sunday of Lent (which originally was the beginning of Lent).

In this symbolic universe, the church represented paradise—not because the church as a human institution was pure, but because it represented the body of Christ. As we noted in chapter 5, the very architecture of the church came to embody this symbolism. The depictions of plants and animals on the capitals of tree-like columns represented the lush vegetation of the Garden of Eden. Christians journeyed out of the West, the place of darkness and wilderness, toward the altar in the East, the place of light and resurrection—and the direction in which Eden lay, and from which Christ would return.

In the early church, baptisms took place during the Easter vigil service. Old and New Testament texts of deliverance and salvation, including the Exodus, were recited. After the proclamation of the Word, candidates for baptism were led to the baptismal pool, where they were stripped naked. Adam and Eve needed garments when they realized that they were naked; in stripping their garments, candidates for baptism symbolically reversed the process. They were casting off sin and returning to paradise. Adam and Eve had succumbed to the devil; now candidates for baptism renounced the devil and all his works. In some parts of the early church, candidates would even turn to the West and spit, as though spitting at the devil. They would then turn to the East, confess their faith (using the words of the Apostles' Creed), and vow their loyalty to Christ.

In entering the baptismal waters, candidates symbolically died to life in the first Adam and rose to new life in Christ—in contrast to Adam and Eve, who received life only to die. As they came out of the waters, candidates received new garments—not the animal skins that God had given Adam and Eve (as though their humanity had been distorted), but white robes, representing divine glory and incorruptibility (even as Jesus stood in dazzling white clothes on the mountain of transfiguration [see, for example, Matt. 17:1–8]).

The newly-baptized then joined the entire congregation in receiving the Eucharist. These new Christians could now understand themselves to be fully incorporated into the body of Christ. They had become members of a new community, a family of brothers and sisters in the faith.

A New Creation, a New Community

Baptism thus symbolized the restoration of creation, its redemption from the ravages of sin and evil. To be sure, worship could offer only a glimpse of this other reality. Yet, drawing on powerful, compelling biblical images, it offered Christians lenses that enabled them to see the deeper meaning of life. They could see hope, where others saw only despair. They had a confidence in God's purposes, even in a world of conflicting human interests.

The restoration of creation suggests a return to the order that God brought out of the chaos at the beginning of time (Genesis 1). The Spirit that hovers over the waters of creation is the same Spirit that comes upon Jesus in the form of a dove at the time of his baptism (see Matt. 3:13–17)—and that now comes upon every believer in his or her baptism. The God who separates night and day is the same God who now separates the children of light from the children of darkness (see 1 Thess. 5:5).

Leviticus, as we have seen, suggests that humans are called to participate in God's work of rightfully ordering reality. Things are to be separated out from each other; they have their proper place. Yet, the restoration of creation that we glimpse in the baptismal liturgy is not simply a return to Leviticus. The new community finds its proper ordering in Christ. Leviticus draws careful distinctions between male and female (see, for example, the special purification laws for women in Lev. 12, 15:19–30); yet, in Christ, "there is neither male nor female" (Gal. 3:28, RSV). What is important now is not purification of the unclean body, but participation in the body of Christ, with its different parts. To each part, the Spirit has given a particular gift—whether of preaching, teaching, healing, or something else—for building up the whole body (see 1 Corinthians 12).

These tensions within the biblical witness suggest the complexity of addressing the question of what is natural, whether we are speaking of sexuality, the relationship of men and women, or environmental protection. Nature is restored; yet, it is qualified by new life in Christ. Nonetheless, these are the tensions in which Christians are called to live and to discern God's Word for us today.

A PIETY OF CONFIDENCE AND HUMILITY

A piety of the Word that explores the sacramental, poetic-like qualities of Scripture keeps these tensions vital. We attend to the *resonance* of biblical images (how words like wilderness sound and "resound" throughout the canon); we draw on the wisdom of Christian *community* (even as embodied in the baptismal liturgies that we have inherited from the early church) in interpreting and applying these images; we allow these images to resonate throughout the *whole* of Scripture, as it sets forth the reality of the living Christ to whom we belong; and we make these images part of our deep *memory,* our language for thinking about the shape of the new order in Christ.

147

This piety of the Word reminds us again and again of God's promise (new life in Christ). It calls us to trust in God alone (to transfer our loyalty from the devil to Christ), and to serve God's purposes (to participate in the right ordering of creation and community).

Yet, this piety of the Word also reminds us that we may have to wait—as did the people of Israel, as did Raskolnikov, as did Alyosha—before we are able to hear the concrete Word that God would speak to us in our time and place. We may even find our waiting filled with pain and anguish, as different voices in the church raise conflicting claims to truth. At times, the Word of God may hardly seem clear or compelling.

When we live out of Scripture as a sacramental word, we may find that we are able to wait together, despite our differences. If we discover such a capacity, it will be because we wait on *God's* Word. We will live in confidence that God's Word in Scripture will become clear to us, for "the grass withers, the flower fades; but the word of our God will stand forever" (Isa. 40:8). But we wait not only in confidence. As we seek to hear that Word, we will also live in humility, "for now we see in a mirror, dimly, but then we will see face to face. Now I know only in part; then I will know fully, even as I have been fully known" (1 Cor. 13:12). A piety of the Word finally rests on the hope that God will continue to reveal what we barely begin to glimpse.

APPENDIX:
A BIBLIOGRAPHIC ESSAY

A principal goal of this book has been to reflect theologically on what it means to be the church in a time of diverse, even conflicting, readings of Scripture in the church. In particular, I have sought to investigate what the church might be doing to nurture a sense of Scripture's compelling power, such that Scripture might be experienced more as a source of life—what I have called a poetic, sacramental word—than as a set of right answers that one party wields against another.

A great deal of contemporary scholarship has touched on one aspect or another of these issues. In this bibliographic essay, I wish to identify and describe particular texts that have shaped my thinking. While my selection is necessarily limited, I believe that these texts are representative of the larger scholarly discussion. Moreover, they set forth key perspectives and questions to which the church must attend if it is to relate Scripture faithfully to its way of life in community.

It is noteworthy that recent literature on issues of Scripture and community represents a wide range of academic disciplines: Bible, theology, ethics, the history of Christianity, and the history of religions. Within each discipline, scholars have used a variety of approaches and have often crossed disciplinary boundaries.

It is also significant that this scholarship reflects a wide range of religious and theological commitments: Roman Catholic, mainline Protestant, evangelical Protestant, feminist, postliberal (influenced by such theologians as Hans Frei and George Lindbeck), and Jewish. Despite their differences, these thinkers share a sense of urgency about the importance of rediscovering the power of Scripture for our time.

BIBLICAL SCHOLARSHIP

Biblical scholars have offered a variety of perspectives on questions of Scripture and community. Some have sought to reconstruct the social context of early Christianity. Wayne Meeks describes his work in *The Origins of Christian Morality: The First Two Centuries* (1993) as a kind of ethnography. In examining Scripture and other early Christian writings, he identifies the rituals and root metaphors that gave the early Christian community a distinctive identity over against its culture.

From a feminist perspective, Elisabeth Schüssler Fiorenza's *In Memory of Her: A Feminist Theological Reconstruction of Christian Origins* (1983) remains a key text. Schüssler Fiorenza uses historical-critical methods to reconstruct a picture of the early Christian community as radically egalitarian and inclusive. This liberating core, embedded within and behind the text, becomes the lens through which she reads all of the biblical materials and removes their patriarchal overlay.

Other biblical scholars, such as Richard Hays, have focused on how the early Christian community interpreted Scripture. In *Echoes of Scripture in the Letters of Paul* (1989), Hays argues that the community's confidence in the reality and presence of the risen Lord enabled it to read Scripture as a Word for its own life. The hermeneutical center of Scripture was not so much Christological as ecclesiological.

While engaging in significant historical work, each of these scholars has also sought to make normative judgments for the life of the church (though Meeks's conclusions are more tentative than the others'). All three are concerned to define the character of Scripture in order to define the character of contemporary communities that would claim Scripture as their own.

Jon Levenson's *The Hebrew Bible, the Old Testament, and Historical Criticism* (1993; a collection of previously published essays) explores with particular clarity the hermeneutical questions that arise in this attempt to move from historical reconstruction to theological assertion. Levenson notes that historical critics have too often acted as though they had a purchase on the truth. They have tended, on the one hand, to overthrow traditional interpretations of Scripture and, on the other, to reduce Scripture to historical information.

Levenson insists that the work of the historical critic is not neutral; like every mode of interpretation, it reflects the ideological commitments of a particular tradition and community. He argues for an understanding of Scripture that allows for a plurality of interpretations. At the same time, he asks us to pay particular attention to the meanings assigned by traditional religious communities. Only because these communities have preserved and revered Scripture as God's Word do historical-critical scholars bother to study Scripture today.

In *The Death and Resurrection of the Beloved Son: The Transformation of Child Sacrifice in Judaism and Christianity* (1993), Levenson puts his methodological considerations to work. While drawing on historical-critical work to draw out the meaning of particular texts, his aims are ultimately theological; he wants to know what the text can tell us about God. Levenson notes that Jewish and Christian readings of Scripture's classic stories, such as the binding of Isaac, highlight different features. Neither reading is final; each is embodied in the particularities of a particular tradition and community. Yet, a consideration of each can contribute to a richer appreciation of the text.

Daniel Patte's *Ethics of Biblical Interpretation: A Reevaluation* (1995) makes similar points, though Patte, unlike Levenson, works from feminist and liberationist commitments. While not rejecting the historical-critical method, Patte argues that historical-critical scholarship reflects the power and privilege of academics; too often, they have failed to take seriously the perspectives of other communities of interpretation.

In different ways, Levenson and Patte ultimately raise the question of the relationship of biblical scholarship and theological reflection. Working out of a Jewish context, Levenson's theological interests are not systematic. He is sensitive not only to tensions in the text, but also to tensions between one interpretation of Scripture and another. Patte, too, does not attempt to resolve these tensions; rather, they are the basis for self-criticism and scholarly humility.

Others, however, have sought a more harmonious integration of historical-critical work with theological readings of Scripture. In *The Revelatory Word: Interpreting the New Testament as Sacred Scripture* (1991), Sandra Schneiders, a Roman Catholic, reviews a range of interpretive strategies, arguing that historical criticism helps to establish the world behind the text, literary criticism the world of the text, and hermeneutics the world before the text. Like Schüssler Fiorenza, she ultimately employs historical-critical methodologies in service of feminist theological commitments.

In *The Interpretation of the Bible in the Church* (1993), the Pontifical Biblical Commission also reviews different kinds of biblical criticism. Like Schneiders, the Commission concludes that historical-critical studies can contribute to, but not replace, theological readings of Scripture. Scripture has a revelatory, sacramental quality. In contrast to Schneiders, the Commission is critical of some feminist and liberationist approaches, arguing that they too often reject the inspired text for a hypothetical reconstruction of the history behind the text.

In such works as *Finally Comes the Poet: Daring Speech for Proclamation* (1989) and *Texts under Negotiation: The Bible and Postmodern Imagination* (1993), Walter Brueggemann, like Schneiders and the Commission, uses the historical-critical method, while acknowledging its limitations. For Brueggemann, the text is more than historical information; it offers us an alternative vision of reality. Through its poetic, metaphorical character, it calls us into a different way of being in the world. Shaped by a liberal Protestant heritage, Brueggemann ultimately sees Scripture as calling us to challenge the social and political forces that result in unjust use of power, economic disparity, and environmental devastation.

Richard Hays's recent *The Moral Vision of the New Testament: A Contemporary Introduction to New Testament Ethics* (1996) is perhaps the most persuasive effort in recent historical-critical biblical scholarship to develop a synthetic theology of Scripture (though focusing here on the New Testament). Hays argues that the poetic images of community, cross, and new creation offer a compelling vision of life before God. While his own theological and ethical commitments have been influenced by elements of evangelical Protestantism, Hays persuasively demonstrates that these images arise from the New Testament itself and reflect a theological coherence in Scripture deeper than some biblical scholars and theologians would readily acknowledge.

In relation to all these efforts to reappropriate Scripture's poetic, metaphorical power, one must mention the especially significant work of Everett Fox. In his translation of, and notes to, *The Five Books of Moses* (1995), Fox helps us to recapture a sense of the Hebrew in which the Hebrew Bible was written. Working from the insights of Martin Buber and Franz Rosenzweig, Fox attends carefully to the nuances of individual words, to the literary construction of particular books, and to the theological significance of the text. (For a guide to their principles of translation, see Martin Buber and Franz Rosenzweig, *Scripture and Translation*, trans. Lawrence Rosenwald [with Everett Fox] [1994].)

THEOLOGICAL APPROACHES

While much of the scholarly literature on Scripture and community has come from biblical scholars, it is not surprising that theologians have also been engaging these issues with renewed vigor. From one direction, the question has been the character of Scripture. What makes a particular set of writings *Scripture* for a community? Which of Scripture's materials are authoritative? What kind of authority do they carry, especially in relation to other norms (such as reason, experience, and tradition)?

From another direction, the question has been the character of the Christian community. What is the distinctive identity to which God calls the church? How does the church remain faithful to this identity, resisting the temptation to define itself in terms set by the surrounding culture? What makes the church *the church?* What kind of community must the church be in order to read Scripture rightly?

Some of the most creative thinkers in recent Christian theology have explored how these two sets of questions interrelate. Arguing that communities define themselves by narratives, these thinkers have asked what is the distinctive story of the Christian community in a post-Christian era.

Of particular significance has been the work of George Lindbeck. First in *The Nature of Doctrine: Religion and Theology in a Postliberal Age* (1984) and then in seminal articles, such as "Scripture, Consensus, and Community" (1988) and "Atonement and the Hermeneutics of Social Embodiment" (1996)," Lindbeck has asked theologians—and the church as a whole—to pay more attention to the basic biblical narrative. Scripture has the capacity to shape the church as a distinctive community. The text opens up a way of being in the world. Church doctrine and practice then help to relate this way of being to the particular cultural circumstances of particular communities of faith.

Garrett Green in *Imagining God: Theology and the Religious Imagination* (1989) pursues a similar line of thinking. He argues that Scripture engages the imagination. The biblical narrative functions like a paradigm; it frames our understanding of the world in terms of God's plans and purposes.

Ephraim Radner and George Sumner (eds.) and other contributors to *Reclaiming Faith: Essays on Orthodoxy in the Episcopal Church and the Baltimore Declaration* (1994) also argue that Scripture is important not so much as a collection of revealed truths, but as a narrative that sets forth the shape of life in Christ. Scripture uses the language of symbol and poetry to disclose both God's character and a way of life before God. Scripture reveals images of Jesus, to whom we are to conform our lives. It is addressed "to an imagination disciplined by participation in the catholic tradition."[1] It "provides us with a verbal icon of *koinonia*, an intricately complex, densely imagined, richly suggestive representation of the communion of God with his people, received from the memory of Israel and the apostolic communities to nourish the memory of the church in every generation."[2]

Other theologians, such as Stanley Hauerwas, have examined the implications of Scripture, understood as the church's distinctive narrative, for the church's social ethics. For Hauerwas, this narrative reaches its climax in the life of Christ and especially in Christ's way of nonviolence. This narrative shapes the church as a community of peace.

In *Unleashing the Scripture: Freeing the Bible from Captivity to America* (1993), Hauerwas also argues the converse: The character of the community shapes its reading of Scripture. Hauerwas argues that every interpretation of Scripture is a political act; it takes place in communities shaped by particular beliefs and practices. But not every community is able to read Scripture rightly. Only as the church finds the center of its life in the Eucharist, which sets forth Christ's peace, will it also be able to read Scripture as God's Word of peace.

In *Reading in Communion: Scripture and Ethics in Christian Life* (1991), Stephen Fowl and L. Gregory Jones expand on this way of understanding Scripture. On the one hand, Scripture shapes the community in distinctive ways. Scripture forms the community's character. It conforms the community of faith to the image of Christ. On the other hand, the character of the community shapes its reading of Scripture. Scripture is not simply a particular content, a "right" meaning, that one applies to life. Rather, the community, as it reads Scripture and seeks to embody it in its way of life, engages in a process of discerning how Christ is taking shape within the community here and now. If the community is to read Scripture rightly, it needs to be trained in such virtues as hospitality (especially to strangers) and practical wisdom.

Other theological approaches, such as Elizabeth Johnson's in *She Who Is: The Mystery of God in Feminist Theological Discourse* (1992), call into question Lindbeck's confidence that the basic biblical narrative as inherited (and as interpreted through the Christian tradition) has the capacity to disclose God's character to us. For Johnson, Scripture must first undergo a process of purification in which feminist theological commitments guide a historical-critical reconstruction of the character of the early Christian community. Nonetheless, Johnson resembles Lindbeck insofar as she sees questions of Scripture and community as interconnected. Scripture shapes the community in distinctive ways; conversely, only a certain kind of community can read Scripture rightly.

Similarly, David Wells's *No Place for Truth: Or Whatever Happened to Evangelical Theology?* (1993), despite its insistence that Scripture gives us objective truth, implicitly acknowledges that Scripture and community condition each other. Wells, however, is not interested in the feminist community, but in a community shaped by the church's great, historic confessional tradition. This kind of community will have the capacity to read Scripture as God's Word.

Of particular interest in this regard is Gordon Lathrop's work in *Holy Things: A Liturgical Theology* (1993), which approaches questions of Scripture and community through the liturgy. It is especially in worship, says Lathrop, that Scripture shapes us, even as we are shaped as a community that is able to read, hear, and embody Scripture. The interconnection between Scripture and community is not an abstract theological problem; rather, it lies at the heart of the church's worshiping life.

HISTORICAL APPROACHES

Recent historical studies have offered a third set of perspectives on Scripture and community. Some of this work has focused on the development and use of Scripture in the early church. Not only questions of canon, but the very character of reading and writing has received intensive study. In *Books and Readers in the Early Church: A History of Early Christian Texts* (1995), Harry Gamble explores the process of preparing, collecting, copying, and distributing the writings that became Scripture, as well as their use in early Christian worship and devotional practice.

Recently, a good deal of literature has also appeared on premodern ways of interpreting Scripture. While not among the most recent representatives of this interest, Jean Leclerq's *The Love of Learning and the Desire for God: A Study of Monastic Culture* (1982; first published in French in 1957) is still of particular usefulness. Leclerq notes how Scripture provided the monks poetic, metaphorical images for imagining—and seeking to embody in their own community—life with God. Scriptural language saturated the liturgy, as well as communal and personal devotional practice.

Ivan Illich's *In the Vineyard of the Text: A Commentary to Hugh's Didascalicon* (1993) explores the shift in consciousness that began to occur in the high Middle Ages. The monks of the early church understood Scripture as a sacramental word that, they believed, drew them into the very presence of God. With the rise of scholasticism, Scripture became, by contrast, a source of knowledge that was to be ordered rationally. Illich believes that this scholastic understanding of Scripture helped to give birth to the "bookish" culture that has long defined the character of written texts in Western culture—and that may now be endangered by the rise of a technology, information era. Illich challenges us to reflect on the very act of reading.

Reformation approaches to Scripture are helpfully summarized in Jaroslav Pelikan's *The Reformation of the Bible/The Bible of the Reformation* (1996).

155

Pelikan notes that the Reformers wanted to overthrow traditional readings of Scripture, so that God's Word might break forth with new power. In insisting that the church attend to the text itself, they rediscovered the poetic power of the original languages, and sought to set it forth in their translations, as well as in hymnody and the visual arts.

These historical studies invite us to reflect more carefully on the character of Scripture. What kind of literature is Scripture? What do its writings communicate—information, ideas, a relationship with the living God? What is asked of us, if we are to read Scripture as God's Word?

Patristic, medieval, and Reformation approaches, despite their differences, share an assumption that Scripture is, first of all, the church's book. If historical-critical approaches too often seem to reduce the text to historical information (or to manipulate it for one ideological purpose or another), a consideration of premodern exegesis reminds us that Scripture is, above all, a theological, liturgical, and devotional resource. (See, for example, poet Kathleen Norris in *The Cloister Walk* [1996]. Norris eloquently describes what contemporary Christians can learn from Benedictine disciplines of reading Scripture.)

Questions of the character of Scripture also lie at the heart of Wilfred Cantwell Smith's *What is Scripture?* (1993). Smith examines Scripture as a phenomenon that characterizes many of the world's great religions. He argues that a purely historical-critical reading of a religion's Scriptures will miss seeing what has been of greatest importance to most of their readers. Traditional religious communities have understood their Scriptures to mediate an encounter with the transcendent. They have found their Scriptures to set forth the ideal world. Their Scriptures seem to have the capacity to put the community in touch with the divine. In an era of historical consciousness, Smith challenges us to take seriously this transcendent dimension of Scripture.

KEY ISSUES

In response to the reality of conflicting readings of Scripture in the church, these biblical, theological, and historical studies suggest that the church needs to recover a deeper appreciation of Scripture's poetic, sacramental character. In addition, this literature suggests several key issues that invite additional reflection. As in chapter 1, I wish to take Johnson, Hauerwas, and Wells as representative of currents in the church today, though I will refer to several other authors as well.

First, why does an author (and why should the church) take Scripture to be authoritative in the first place? In an era of theological and biblical amnesia, the answer to this question is not obvious. In practice, much of the church seems to do just fine without Scripture. For some Christians, Scripture almost seems to get in the way of their being Christian. To them, appeals to personal experience or group identity seem more compelling.

Much of the contemporary scholarly literature that I have examined emphasizes that our reading of Scripture is shaped by the beliefs and practices of the communities to which we belong. What is at stake in this literature is not so much the authority of Scripture in and of itself, but these communal commitments. Schüssler Fiorenza and Johnson lift up the role of the community committed to the flourishing of women; Hauerwas, the community committed to Jesus' way of forgiveness, reconciliation, peace, and nonviolence; Wells, the community committed to the Reformation confessions. None of these authors believes that one can go to Scripture "cold" and read it rightly. One must first be disciplined in the community's way of life together.

Yet, as noted in chapter 1, this strong commitment to community also has the result of raising the question of why one should bother with Scripture in the first place. Each of these authors has a tendency to make Scripture instrumental to the ends of the particular community to which they have committed themselves. Scripture functions primarily to illustrate the character of this community. Scripture may help the community to become more aware of its identity, but the community and its way of life have priority. It sometimes appears as though each community simply finds in Scripture that to which it is already committed.

If these authors continue to turn to Scripture, it is because they understand Scripture to have a distinctive capacity to deepen the community's life. Schüssler Fiorenza wants to claim Scripture because, quoting feminist artist Judy Chicago, "our heritage is our power."[3] But Scripture also seems to have compelling power in itself. Despite her historical-critical interests, Schüssler Fiorenza speaks of Scripture's "numinous" power. For her, Scripture's patriarchal overlay has not completely obscured its revelatory power. For Johnson, similarly, Scripture (as purified by feminist critique) provides symbolic depth to feminist concerns.

Hauerwas turns to Scripture because it is the principal source of communal memory. Scripture continually corrects the community and reminds it of its true identity in Christ. For Wells, Scripture confronts us with the reality of a God who breaks into history and challenges us to hear a truth from beyond ourselves. Fowl and Jones speak of our need to read Scripture "against" ourselves. Other authors, as we have seen, lift up the poetic, metaphorical power of Scripture.

It appears that we cannot avoid a certain kind of circularity. We have to be a certain kind of community in order to read Scripture rightly; yet, it is Scripture that helps to shape us as this kind of community. The text is nothing in itself; rather, a set of writings becomes Scripture as a community reads them and finds them compelling.

This tension between Scripture and community leaves us with several questions. How do we take seriously the fact that we belong to a particular community of interpretation, while remaining open to the possibility that Scripture will radically challenge our communal commitments? What happens when we find ourselves committed to more than one community of interpretation? To what degree can a particular tradition and community allow Scripture to call its reading of Scripture into question? To what degree should our theology call into question the authority of particular biblical materials? Can we talk meaningfully today about Scripture setting forth a living Word of God? Is the language of "sacrament" retrievable for understanding the character of Scripture?

Second, what does an author (and what should the church) take to be authoritative in Scripture? Once we go to Scripture, we find ourselves confronted by a variety of materials. The theological task is to bring order to these diverse voices, so that the church might know more clearly the biblical witness to God, as well as the shape of its own life.

In *The Nature of Doctrine*, Lindbeck has helpfully described three types of theological reflection, each of which also represents a basic approach to the task of organizing Scripture. From the perspective of an experiential-expressivist approach, Scripture, rightly interpreted, helps to describe a more basic experience of God that is available to every human being. Experience precedes language. We then seek to capture experience in language and to structure reality by this language.

As noted in chapter 3, Schüssler Fiorenza and Johnson exemplify this approach. They reconstruct the character of the early Christian community in light of women's rediscovery of God in their lives. They argue that Scripture, when purified by feminist critique, provides a gestalt, an organizing picture or image, of the liberating God of Israel and Jesus.

Johnson is particularly interested in the role of religious symbols in reordering our thinking. She argues that these symbols arise out of an experience of the mystery of God in our own being. This mystery is prior to language, and our efforts to describe it always fall short. According to Johnson, Christian Scripture—like the sacred expressions of other religious traditions—provides symbols for guarding both the community's experience of God's mystery, and women's experience of their own value. In this sense, Scripture provides emancipatory speech.

Hauerwas and other postliberals (such as the contributors to the Radner and Sumner volume) represent a cultural-linguistic approach. Scripture provides a language that helps to shape Christian experience. Language precedes experience.

For Hauerwas, Scripture consists primarily of narratives that describe a way of life in community. These narratives help us to remember who God is and therefore who we really are. They give us material that we must "renarrate," such that we ourselves become part of the biblical narrative. As Fowl and Jones put it, we must learn to "embody" Scripture, to "perform" it.

Wells represents a cognitive-propositionalist approach. Scripture has objective truths that can be distilled into confessional propositions. Humans do not have an inherent experience of God that these truths help to articulate. Nor are these truths best described as "illustrations" of the character of the community. Rather, Scripture confronts us with the will of God. The question to us is simply whether or not we will obey.

Again, larger questions appear. How do we deal with scriptural materials that do not easily fit our interpretive scheme? Which of these schemes do unjustifiable violence to the text? What can we learn from Levenson's reflections on Orthodox Jewish readings of Scripture, which respect and even play up the tensions in the text? Do we need to rethink Christian efforts to harmonize Scripture according to one interpretive scheme or another? How do we learn to listen to Scripture as a whole?

Third, how does an author (and how should the church) deal with the fact of diverse readings of Scripture in the church? In a fragmented church, it is not surprising that different communities of interpretation read the same texts in fundamentally different ways. Conversely, the unity of the church depends on its ability to sort out legitimate from illegitimate readings of Scripture.

Much of the contemporary literature resists the notion that a passage of Scripture has one "right meaning." Levenson argues for the possibility of multiple senses of Scripture. Similarly, Wilfred Cantwell Smith argues that Scripture points to realities beyond itself and can never be reduced to one meaning. Scripture is poetic-like. It mediates a relationship to the transcendent. As Garrett Green argues, Scripture invites one into an act of imagination.

Yet, every author has criteria for sorting out a diversity of readings that builds up the community, from a diversity of readings that ultimately undermines it. At times, these criteria may relate to the locus of interpretive authority. Schneiders and the Pontifical Biblical Commission argue that the magisterium has an appropriate role to play in guarding the Catholic faith. While Schneiders and the Commission give a secondary authority to historical-critical scholarship, other scholars would make it primary.

At other times, however, these criteria are more explicitly theological. A particular understanding of God and God's will determines the parameters within which we may rightly read Scripture.

For Johnson, diverse readings of Scripture are valid to the degree that they ultimately contribute to the flourishing of women. On the one hand, Johnson celebrates diversity. Different readings of Scripture rub up against each other and remind us that God is greater than any of them. On the other hand, patriarchal readings of Scripture are to be rejected. They are not celebrated as part of this good diversity. They are not just one more valid expression of the biblical witness.

Hauerwas suggests that a diversity of readings must be grounded in the community's more basic confidence that the resurrected Christ is present to it, especially through the Eucharist. If we are a community transformed by the death and resurrection of Christ, we will welcome a diversity of readings; they will help us to explore the meaning of Scripture for the community today. But we will not simply celebrate them; rather, we will test them both against the tradition and against the virtues of the community: peacefulness, nonviolence, and forgiveness.

If, by contrast, we are united not by the biblical narrative but by nationalistic, Enlightenment assumptions, a diversity of readings will reflect an assumption that we are able to judge Scripture for ourselves, apart from life in Christian community. Our readings of Scripture will prove diverse and contradictory, and we will have no way to adjudicate them. Indeed, instead of the church, we will need the secular nation-state to exercise violent coercion and to restrain us from harming each other, even as it seeks to assert itself against other nations.

Wells's criteria for sorting out legitimate from illegitimate readings of Scripture are doctrinal. Wells seems to have little interest in affirming a diversity of readings; rather, he calls us to attend again to the basic character of God as the transcendent One who breaks into human history to offer us new life in Christ. Scripture has a right meaning that the church must assert.

Wells's dissonant note reminds us that questions remain. Can a poetic, sacramental word become binding on a community? Do theological criteria suffice to sort out diverse readings of Scripture, or does every community need some kind of magisterium, that is, authoritative teaching office, that adjudicates truth in light of what it takes to be the good of the community? To what degree can renewed attention to Scripture's compelling power unify the church? To what degree must the unity of the church precede a rediscovery of Scripture?

Fourth, how does an author (and how should the church) assess the value of the historical-critical method? Few lay people in mainline Protestant churches have been trained in the historical-critical methods their pastors take for granted. Yet, as I have argued, powerful cultural forces tend to reduce Scripture to historical information. The explosion of popular interest in the Jesus Seminar reflects both people's distance from Scripture and their desire to find a way back into it.

Much of the contemporary scholarly literature reflects on the possibilities and limitations of the historical-critical method. We have become more aware that the historical-critical method itself has a history. It reflects particular assumptions and interests; its practitioners speak out of a particular social location. Few scholars today would argue that historical-critical scholarship is a neutral enterprise.

Schüssler Fiorenza and Johnson put historical criticism into the service of their feminist commitments. Historical criticism enables them to reconstruct a picture of an egalitarian community, which the texts because of their patriarchal influences obscure.

Hauerwas and Wells, by contrast, have little interest in the historical-critical method. While acknowledging the usefulness of much historical-critical scholarship, Hauerwas makes clear that a right reading of Scripture ultimately depends on the character of the community, not on historical reconstruction. He argues that the effort to search for a historical Jesus (or for an objective meaning behind the text) simply betrays the fact that the community has no sense of the resurrected Christ in its midst. Rather than nurturing a faith that grows out of a living relationship with God, the community ends up placing its faith in a reconstructed text.

In emphasizing Scripture's poetic and imaginative qualities, much of the contemporary scholarly literature has criticized historical-critical efforts to find the one "right meaning" of scriptural texts (for example, the meaning that the author intended). Writers such as Levenson, and Fowl and Jones, also criticize the way feminist and liberationist authors have used historical criticism to reconstruct a normative history behind the text that they then turn against the text.

Yet, the most persuasive of this critical literature has refused to abandon historical criticism; rather, it has insisted that historical-critical scholarship can help the church to listen to Scripture more carefully. Historical-critical approaches help us to guard against our temptation to force Scripture into interpretive schemes that overlook real tensions and contradictions in the biblical materials. Levenson's work provides a helpful example of historical-critical work that opens up a richer, more theological reading of the text, without appropriating the historical-critical method for one ideological cause or another.

Yet, questions remain. Does reliance on historical criticism make Scripture less accessible to lay readers? What happens when historical-critical findings contradict traditional readings of the text? Does historical-critical scholarship inevitably make scholars into a new magisterium? Or does it provide common ground across ideological differences, perhaps more so than Levenson would acknowledge?

CONFLICTING READINGS OF SCRIPTURE

These questions may provide a helpful framework for analyzing other scholarly literature on Scripture and community. It is clear that issues of diversity and unity will continue to dominate the life of the church in years to come. Conflicting readings of Scripture have always been part of the church's experience; the question is how we will come to terms with them in our time. I believe that a poetic, sacramental understanding of Scripture will remind us of the richness of the biblical materials, while calling us to know the One whom Scripture ultimately sets forth: Jesus Christ.

NOTES

Introduction

1. The term *Christendom* is used in recent literature to describe a society shaped largely by Christian values. See, for example, Loren B. Mead, *The Once and Future Church: Reinventing the Congregation for a New Mission Frontier* (Washington, D.C.: The Alban Institute, 1991).

2. See Peter L. Berger, *The Heretical Imperative: Contemporary Possibilities of Religious Affirmation* (New York: Anchor, 1980).

Chapter 1: Church and Scripture in Crisis

1. Stanley Hauerwas, *Unleashing the Scripture: Freeing the Bible from Captivity to America* (Nashville: Abingdon, 1993), 15.

2. Ibid., 29–38.

3. Several years ago, Martin Marty of the *Christian Century* solicited readers' best jokes about fundamentalists. First place went to the joke about an historical-critical scholar who was invited to speak at conservative Bob Jones University. The scholar told his audience that the Red Sea was really the Sea of Reeds, and that the Israelites had not passed through divided waters, but through a marsh. When he asked for questions, there was stunned silence, until a hand went up in the back of the room and a student declared, "Praise the Lord! Yet another miracle! God drowned the Egyptians in two inches of water!"

The point is telling. Liberal Protestants who employ the historical-critical method to demythologize the miraculous elements of the text have a way of sneaking faith commitments back into the text, such that we end up with "yet another miracle," for example, God's activity on behalf of the poor and oppressed.

4. Helpful critiques are included in Carl E. Braaten and Robert W. Jenson, eds., *Reclaiming the Bible for the Church* (Grand Rapids: Eerdmans, 1995); Stephen E.

Fowl and L. Gregory Jones, *Reading in Communion: Scripture and Ethics in Christian Life* (Grand Rapids: Eerdmans, 1991); Roy A. Harrisville and Walter Sundberg, *The Bible in Modern Culture: Theology and Historical-Critical Method from Spinoza to Käsemann* (Grand Rapids: Eerdmans, 1995); and Jon D. Levenson, *The Hebrew Bible, the Old Testament, and Historical Criticism* (Louisville, Ky.: Westminster John Knox, 1993).

5. These themes are nicely developed in the volume by Fowl and Jones.

6. Hauerwas, 61.

7. Ibid., 67.

8. Ibid., 103.

9. Elizabeth A. Johnson, *She Who Is: The Mystery of God in Feminine Discourse* (New York: Crossroad, 1992), 103, 148.

10. Ibid., 70, 72.

11. Ibid., 33–40.

12. David F. Wells, *No Place for Truth: Or Whatever Happened to Evangelical Theology?* (Grand Rapids: Eerdmans, 1993), 27–282.

13. Ibid., 98–99.

14. Fowl and Jones, 99.

15. Both together and apart, Stanley Hauerwas and William Willimon have authored the best-known examples of this literature. See, for example, Stanley Hauerwas and William H. Willimon, *Resident Aliens: Life in the Christian Colony* (Nashville: Abingdon, 1989). Other recent critiques of the theological impoverishment of the Protestant mainline include Leander E. Keck, *The Church Confident* (Nashville: Abingdon, 1993); Loren B. Mead, *The Once and Future Church: Reinventing the Congregation for a New Mission Frontier* (Washington, D.C.: The Alban Institute, 1991); and George A. Sumner and Ephraim Radner, eds., *Reclaiming Faith: Essays on Orthodoxy in the Episcopal Church and the Baltimore Declaration* (Grand Rapids: Eerdmans, 1993).

Avery Dulles, *The Craft of Theology: From Symbol to System* (New York: Crossroad, 1992) has raised similar questions about American Catholicism, and David F. Wells, *No Place for Truth: Or Whatever Happened to Evangelical Theology?* (Grand Rapids: Eerdmans, 1993), about evangelicals.

Recent sociological perspectives focusing on the theological crisis of the church include Benton Johnson, Dean R. Hoge, and Donald A. Luidens, "Mainline Churches: The Real Reasons for Decline," *First Things* (March 1993): 13–18. For historical perspectives on the Presbyterian Church (U.S.A.) that come to similar conclusions, see Milton J Coalter, John M. Mulder, and Louis B. Weeks, *The Reforming Tradition: Presbyterians and Mainstream Protestantism* (Louisville, Ky.: Westminster John Knox, 1992).

16. George Lindbeck, "Scripture, Consensus, and Community," *This World* 23 (fall 1988): 5.

17. Ibid.

18. I'm referring, of course, to the famous scene in the *Confessions* (Book

VIII, Chap. 12) where Augustine, in great inner distress about his sinfulness and inability to trust wholly in God, has a conversion experience. "Suddenly a voice reaches my ears from a nearby house. It is the voice of a boy or a girl (I don't know which) and in a kind of singsong the words are constantly repeated: 'Take it and read it.'" Augustine snatches up Scripture and reads in silence the passage on which his eyes first fall: "Not in rioting and drunkenness, not in chambering and wantonness, not in strife and envying: but put ye on the Lord Jesus Christ, and make not provision for the flesh in concupiscence" (Rom. 13:13–14). *The Confessions of St. Augustine,* trans. Rex Warner (New York: New American Library, 1963), 182–83.

19. Chapter II.

20. Chapter I.5.

21. See Robert W. Jenson, "Hermeneutics and the Life of the Church," in *Reclaiming the Bible,* ed. Braaten and Jenson, 89–105.

22. Carl E. Braaten, "The Il/legitimacy of Lutheranism in America?," *Lutheran Forum* 28 (February 1994): 44.

23. Ibid.

24. Lindbeck, for example, has argued that a rediscovery of classic hermeneutics would contribute to a rediscovery of Scripture's power to shape the church. See Lindbeck, "Scripture, Consensus, and Community," 19–24.

25. Chapter XIX.

26. Franz Rosenzweig, "Scripture and Luther," in Martin Buber and Franz Rosenzweig, *Scripture and Translation,* trans. Lawrence Rosenwald with Everett Fox (Bloomington, Ind.: Indiana University Press, 1994), 56.

27. See Levenson, *The Hebrew Bible.* Levenson argues, however, that historical criticism can play this role only if it interacts positively with literary and theological approaches to Scripture, rather than undermining them.

28. See Michael Fishbane, "Martin Buber's *Moses,*" in *The Garments of Torah: Essays in Biblical Hermeneutics* (Bloomington, Ind.: Indiana University Press, 1989), 95, as quoted in Everett Fox, "The Book in Its Contexts," in Buber and Rosenzweig, *Scripture and Translation,* xxvi.

Chapter 2: Whatever Happened to the Compelling Power of Scripture?

1. Fyodor Dostoyevsky, *The Brothers Karamazov,* trans. David Magarshack (New York: Viking Penguin, 1958), 422–27.

2. G. G. Coulton, *The Medieval Village* (Cambridge: Cambridge University Press, 1925), 257.

3. Dietrich Bonhoeffer, *Letters and Papers from Prison,* enl. ed., ed. Eberhard Bethge (New York: MacMillan, 1971), 300.

4. James D. Smart, *The Strange Silence of the Bible in the Church: A Study in Hermeneutics* (Philadelphia: Westminster, 1970).

5. In personal conversation, June 1995.

6. George Lindbeck, "Scripture, Consensus, and Community," *This World* 23 (fall 1988): 17.

7. My thanks to the Rev. K. C. Ptomey, Westminster Presbyterian Church (Nashville, Tennessee) for first telling me this story.

8. As noted by Thomas Reeves in a review of George Barna, *The Index of Leading Spiritual Indicators* (Dallas: Word Publishing, 1996). See *First Things* (February 1997): 55.

9. "Biblical Authority and Interpretation: A Resource Document Received by the 194th General Assembly (1982) of the United Presbyterian Church in the United States of America" (Louisville, Ky.: Office of the General Assembly, Presbyterian Church [U.S.A], 1992), 32.

10. Ibid.

11. Ibid., 31.

12. Ibid., 33.

13. For these and following statistics, see "The Bible: The February 1995 Presbyterian Panel" (Louisville, Ky.: Research Services, Presbyterian Church [U.S.A.], 1995). One must remember, however, that people do not always report their actions accurately. Researchers have found that people consistently underestimate how much alcohol they consume. One suspects that they tend to overestimate how much Scripture they read.

14. Wilfred Cantwell Smith, *What Is Scripture? A Comparative Approach* (Philadelphia: Fortress, 1993), 240.

15. Ibid., 239.

16. See, for example, Martin Heidegger, *Poetry, Language, Thought,* trans. Albert Hofstadter (New York: Harper and Row, 1971).

17. Charles Taylor, *Sources of the Self: The Making of the Modern Identity* (Cambridge: Harvard University Press, 1989).

18. As quoted in Claude Welch, *Protestant Thought in the Nineteenth Century,* vol. 1 (New Haven, Conn.: Yale University Press, 1972), 50.

19. See, for example, Elisabeth Schüssler Fiorenza, *In Memory of Her: A Feminist Theological Reconstruction of Christian Origins* (New York: Crossroad, 1983).

20. For a penetrating analysis of this dilemma, see Jon D. Levenson, *The Hebrew Bible, the Old Testament, and Historical Criticism* (Louisville, Ky.: Westminster John Knox, 1993), 106–10.

21. Smith, 241.

22. See Stanley Hauerwas, *Unleashing the Scripture: Freeing the Bible from Captivity to America* (Nashville: Abingdon, 1993).

23. Ivan Illich, *In the Vineyard of the Text: A Commentary to Hugh's Didascalicon* (Chicago: University of Chicago Press, 1993), 1–6.

24. The following analysis draws extensively from Neil Postman, *Technopoly: The Surrender of Culture to Technology* (New York: Knopf, 1992).

25. For provocative insights into the Simpson trial, and for more general insights into the media's production of cultural symbols, see Susan Bordo, *Twilight Zones: The Hidden Life of Cultural Images from Plato to O. J.* (Berkeley, Calif.: University of California Press, 1997), 66–106.

26. Illich, 118.

27. See Dieter E. Zimmer, "Viel zu früh fürs Schlusskapitel," *Die Zeit* (September 30, 1994): 60. While Zimmer focuses on West Germany and Switzerland, his observations seem to confirm what one also observes in American bookstores.

28. Carl E. Braaten, "The Il/legitimacy of Lutheranism in America?," *Lutheran Forum* 28 (February 1994): 44.

29. Lindbeck, 17.

30. David F. Wells, *No Place for Truth: Or Whatever Happened to Evangelical Theology?* (Grand Rapids: Eerdmans, 1993), 173.

31. Form letter from Paul Eschelman, Director, The Jesus Film Project, October 1997.

32. "Out of the Tombs: Discussion Guide" (New York: American Bible Society, 1991), 1.

33. Wells, 176.

34. See Randall Balmer, *Mine Eyes Have Seen the Glory: A Journey into the Evangelical Subculture in America,* exp. ed. (New York: Oxford University Press, 1993), 207.

35. Free sampler for the Gospel of Matthew, *The Word in Life Study Bible* (Nashville: Thomas Nelson, Inc., 1993), iv.

36. Leander Keck, *The Church Confident* (Nashville: Abingdon, 1993), 53.

37. For an incisive review of the role that ideological factors can play in Bible translation, see Gail R. O'Day, "Probing an Inclusive Scripture," *Christian Century* (July 3–10, 1996): 692–94.

38. M. Robert Mulholland, Jr., *Shaped by the Word: The Power of Scripture in Spiritual Formation* (Nashville: The Upper Room, 1985).

Chapter 3: Scripture as Sacramental Word

1. Kathleen Norris, "Incarnational Language," *Christian Century* 114 (July 30–August 6, 1997): 699.

2. Kathleen Norris, "Drawing on Metaphor," *Christian Century* (September 24–October 1, 1997): 842.

3. Helen Vendler, "The Language of Life," *New York Times Book Review* (June 18, 1995): 14.

4. "Untergang," 5th version, in Franz Fühmann, *Vor Feuerschlünden: Erfahrung mit Georg Trakls Gedicht* (Rostock: VEB Hinstorff Verlag, 1984), 12, 285–86. My translation.

5. For this account of Fühmann's encounter with Trakl's poetry, see Fühmann, 11–32.

6. The two approaches that I describe, the "orthodox" and the "progressivist," draw on James Davison Hunter, *Culture Wars: The Struggle to Define America* (New York: Basic Books, 1991). See, especially, pp. 43–45, 77–86, and 120–27. While reflecting on the larger cultural situation, his reflections also help us to make sense of conflicts in the church today.

7. We have already seen an example of this approach in our discussion of David Wells in chapter 1. For Wells, the church's confessional heritage helps to distill the truths of Scripture.

8. In chapter 1, this approach was exemplified by Elizabeth Johnson.

9. See, for example, John Paul II, *Crossing the Threshold of Hope,* ed. Vittorio Messori, trans. Jenny McPhee and Martha McPhee (New York: Knopf, 1994), 41. John Paul II asserts that we can never exhaust the mystery of Christ as Scripture reveals him to us.

10. The Catechism of the Anglican *Book of Common Prayer* defines a sacrament as "an outward and visible sign of an inward and spiritual grace." Augustine called it a "visible form of invisible grace." See the entry under "sacrament" in *The Oxford Dictionary of the Christian Church,* 2nd ed., ed. F. L. Cross and E. A. Livingstone (New York: Oxford University Press, 1983), 1218–19.

11. Wilfred Cantwell Smith, *What is Scripture? A Comparative Approach* (Philadelphia: Fortress, 1993), 232, 240.

12. Ibid., 240.

13. Ibid., 14. Smith acknowledges the late Dr. Kendall Folkert as the source of this observation.

14. Alister E. McGrath, *A Life of John Calvin* (Oxford: Blackwell, 1990), 132.

15. "The Second Helvetic Confession" in Arthur C. Cochrane, *Reformed Confessions of the 16th Century* (Philadelphia: Westminster, 1966), as reprinted in *The Book of Confessions* (Louisville, Ky.: Office of the General Assembly of the Presbyterian Church [U.S.A.], 1991).

16. Ironically, as my former colleague the Rev. Dr. Joseph Small has noted, the polity of the Presbyterian Church (U.S.A.) today reserves the administration of baptism and the Eucharist to ordained ministers, while allowing anyone to read Scripture in worship and preach!

17. For the influence of medieval mysticism (and especially Bernard of Clairveaux) on Calvin, see Dennis E. Tamburello, *Union with Christ: John Calvin and the Mysticism of St. Bernard* (Louisville, Ky.: Westminster John Knox, 1994).

18. Michael Fishbane, *The Garments of Torah: Essays in Biblical Hermeneutics* (Bloomington, Ind.: Indiana University Press, 1989), 124.

19. Ibid., 24.

20. Ivan Illich, *In the Vineyard of the Text: A Commentary to Hugh's Didascalicon* (Chicago: University of Chicago Press, 1993), 19, 54. See also Jean Leclerq, *The Love of Learning and the Desire for God: A Study of Monastic Culture,* trans. Catherine Misrahi (New York: Fordham University Press, 1982), 71–86.

21. Smith, 32.

22. Ibid.

23. Dogmatic Constitution on Divine Revelation, *Dei Verbum*, paragraph 21, in Walter M. Abbott, S. J., ed., *The Documents of Vatican II* (New York: America, 1966), 125.

24. See, for example, Kathleen Norris, *The Cloister Walk* (New York: Riverhead Books, 1996), 31–46.

25. See Smith, 228–29.

26. Ibid., 232.

27. John Calvin, *Institutes of the Christian Religion* 1.6.1, ed. John T. McNeill, trans. Ford Lewis Battles (Philadelphia: Westminster, 1960), 70.

28. Fühmann, 20–22.

29. See Garrett Green, *Imagining God: Theology and the Religious Imagination* (San Francisco: Harper and Row, 1989), 105–25. Green speaks of Scripture as paradigm and gestalt. See also Walter Brueggemann, *Texts under Negotiation: The Bible and Postmodern Imagination* (Minneapolis: Fortress, 1993).

30. See, for example, Nicholas Lash, "Performing the Scriptures," in *Theology on the Way to Emmaus* (London: SCM Press, 1986); and Michael G. Cartwright, "The Practice and Performance of Scripture: Grounding Christian Ethics in a Communal Hermeneutic," *The Annual of the Society of Christian Ethics* (1988): 31–53.

31. Compare Thomas Levenson's comments about music in Thomas Levenson, "How Not to Make a Stradivarius," *American Scholar* (summer 1994): 377–78.

32. Fühmann, 29.

33. Levenson, 376–77.

34. See Stanley Hauerwas's protest against fundamentalism and historical criticism in Stanley Hauerwas, *Unleashing the Scripture: Freeing the Bible from Captivity to America* (Nashville: Abingdon, 1993).

35. I am thankful to the Rev. Dr. Joseph Small, Coordinator of the Office of Theology and Worship, Presbyterian Church (U.S.A.), for this analogy.

36. George Lindbeck, *The Nature of Doctrine: Religion and Theology in a Postliberal Age* (Philadelphia: Westminster, 1984).

37. George Lindbeck, "Scripture, Consensus, and Community," *This World* (fall 1988): 21.

38. For an outstanding analysis, see Brian A. Gerrish, *Grace and Gratitude: The Eucharistic Theology of John Calvin* (Minneapolis: Fortress, 1993).

39. See the reflections on Bonhoeffer in Stephen E. Fowl and L. Gregory Jones, *Reading in Communion: Scripture and Ethics in Christian Life* (Grand Rapids: Eerdmans, 1991), 156.

40. See Leclerq, 73.

41. I am thankful to the Rev. Dean Thompson of the First Presbyterian Church in Charleston, West Virginia, for making this point to me.

42. See H. Richard Niebuhr, *The Purpose of the Church and Its Ministry* (New York: Harper and Row, 1956), 43–45.

43. See Karl Barth, *Church Dogmatics* i/2, ed. G. W. Bromiley and T. F. Torrance, trans. G. T. Thomason and Harold Knight (Edinburgh: T. and T. Clark, 1956), 597–98.

44. Compare the comments in Werner Georg Kümmel, *Introduction to the New Testament,* rev. ed., trans. Howard Clark Kee (Nashville: Abingdon, 1975), 507–10.

45. The Vulgate, however, placed 1 and 2 Maccabees between Malachi and the New Testament.

46. Though, of course, Romans — the first in the sequence — has also played an especially significant role in Christian theology.

47. Calvin, for example, prepared, and wrote a commentary on, a harmony of Matthew, Mark, and Luke.

48. For the tension between liberation and service/servitude in the Hebrew Bible/Old Testament, see Jon D. Levenson, *The Hebrew Bible, the Old Testament, and Historical Criticism* (Louisville, Ky.: Westminster John Knox, 1993), 146–50.

49. See Barth, 478–85.

50. Ibid., 506, 513.

51. This interest in typology appears in the New Testament itself. See, for example, Galatians 4:22–31, in which Isaac is a prefiguration of those who live in Christian freedom, while Ishmael represents those who persecute them.

52. As Augustine argued, "These hidden meanings of inspired Scripture we track down as best as we can, with varying degrees of success; and yet we all hold confidently to the firm belief that these historical events and the narrative of them have always some foreshadowing of things to come, and are always to be interpreted with reference to Christ and his Church." Augustine, *The City of God,* ed. David Knowles, trans. Henry Bettenson (New York: Penguin, 1972), 652. As a result, Augustine feels that he has to find Christ everywhere in the Old Testament. Even the door in the side of the ark becomes a prophetic type of the wound made by the spear in Jesus' side!

53. See the comments on monastic exegesis in Leclerq, 81.

54. See Richard B. Hays, *Echoes of Scripture in the Letters of Paul* (New Haven, Conn.: Yale University Press, 1989), 165.

55. See Michael Fishbane, *Biblical Interpretation in Ancient Israel* (Oxford: Clarendon, 1985); James Sanders, *Community and Canon: A Guide to Canonical Criticism* (Philadelphia: Fortress, 1984); and James Sanders, *From Sacred Story to Sacred Text: Canon as Paradigm* (Philadelphia: Fortress, 1987).

56. Franz Rosenzweig, "Scripture and Luther," in Martin Buber and Franz Rosenzweig, *Scripture and Translation,* trans. Lawrence Rosenwald with Everett Fox (Bloomington, Ind.: Indiana University Press, 1994), 50.

57. Ibid., 64.

58. See the notes to Leviticus in *The Five Books of Moses: Genesis, Exodus, Leviticus, Numbers, and Deuteronomy,* trans. Everett Fox (New York: Schocken, 1995).

59. See Mary Douglas, *Purity and Danger* (London and Henly: Routledge and Kegan Paul, 1966), 53, as cited in Jon D. Levenson, *Creation and the Persistence of Evil: The Jewish Drama of Divine Omnipotence* (San Francisco: Harper and Row, 1988), 118–19.

Chapter 4: A Piety of the Word

1. Stanley Hauerwas, *Unleashing the Scripture: Freeing the Bible from Captivity to America* (Nashville: Abingdon, 1993), 15.

2. See Harry Y. Gamble, *Books and Readers in the Early Church: A History of Early Christian Texts* (New Haven, Conn.: Yale University Press, 1995), 203–4.

3. Wolfgang Braunfels, *Monasteries of Western Europe: The Architecture of the Orders* (New York: Thames and Hudson, 1971), 110.

4. *The Rule of St. Benedict,* trans. Anthony C. Meisel and M. L. del Mastro (Garden City, N.Y.: Image Books, 1975), 85 (chap. 45).

5. Joan Chittister, *The Rule of Saint Benedict: Insights for the Ages* (New York: Crossroad, 1992), 129.

6. *Rule,* 80 (chap. 38).

7. Ibid., 79–80.

8. Chittister, 115.

9. "Torah," of course, refers not only to the Hebrew Scriptures, but also to the Talmud. For an outstanding study of the significance of Torah study as a communal experience, see Samuel Heilman, *The People of the Book* (Chicago: University of Chicago Press, 1983).

10. See, for example, Michael Fishbane, *Biblical Interpretation in Ancient Israel* (Oxford: Clarendon, 1985); and Richard B. Hays, *Echoes of Scripture in the Letters of Paul* (New Haven, Conn.: Yale University Press, 1989).

11. See Gerald L. Bruns, *Hermeneutics Ancient and Modern* (New Haven, Conn.: Yale University Press, 1992), 139–40, as quoted in Jaroslav Pelikan, *The Reformation of the Bible/The Bible of the Reformation* (New Haven, Conn.: Yale University Press, 1996), 28–29.

12. See Avery Dulles, *The Craft of Theology: From Symbol to System* (New York: Crossroad, 1992), 12–13, 105–7.

13. For this reason, Calvin's understanding of Scripture is not exhausted by his comments directly on the matter in Book I of the *Institutes* but is informed by his comments on the church in Book IV. See chapter 1.

14. Everett Fox, "The Book in Its Contexts," in Martin Buber and Franz Rosenzweig, *Scripture and Translation,* trans. Lawrence Rosenwald with Everett Fox (Bloomington, Ind.: Indiana University Press, 1994), xxvi.

15. Throughout this period, various Christian writings were still making their way into circulation; none had yet acquired the status of Scripture. See Gamble, 214.

16. See Gamble, 217. See also my article "Shaping a Congregation through Lectio Continua," *Reformed Liturgy and Music* 30 (November 1, 1996): 3–6.

17. See James Sanders, *Torah and Canon* (Philadelphia: Fortress, 1972). It is also interesting to note that the Jewish canon ends with verses in Chronicles that foresee the rebuilding of the temple—the people are once again on the edge of the "Promised Land."

18. For trenchant observations on these matters, see Eugene H. Peterson, *Working the Angles: The Shape of Pastoral Integrity* (Grand Rapids: Eerdmans, 1987), 87–145.

19. The Christian tradition has also made this point liturgically. It is the Gospels book that is especially revered in worship, not other collections of biblical books.

20. Jon D. Levenson, *The Hebrew Bible, the Old Testament, and Historical Criticism* (Louisville, Ky.: Westminster John Knox, 1993), 155.

21. Jean Leclerq, *The Love of Learning and the Desire for God: A Study of Monastic Culture,* trans. Catherine Misrahi (New York: Fordham University Press, 1982), 77.

22. Ibid., 73–74.

23. Indeed, Calvin preached and wrote commentaries on nearly all of Scripture. The most notable exception was Revelation. Like Luther, Calvin was concerned about the way the Radical Reformers appealed to Revelation to justify violent revolution.

24. Ivan Illich, *In the Vineyard of the Text: A Commentary to Hugh's Didascalicon* (Chicago: University of Chicago Press, 1993), 54–57.

25. See Illich, 35–42; and Leclerq, 77.

26. Hughes Oliphant Old, "What Is Reformed Spirituality? Played Over Again Lightly," *Seventh Colloquium on Calvin Studies* (January 1994): 63.

27. My thanks to the Rev. Dr. Joseph D. Small of the Presbyterian Church (U.S.A.) for bringing this story to my attention.

28. For trenchant observations, see Neil Postman, *Technopoly: The Surrender of Culture to Technology* (New York: Knopf, 1992); and Kathleen Norris, "Words and the Word," *Christian Century* (April 16, 1997): 381. See also chapter 2.

29. *Bible for Today's Family: New Testament* (New York: American Bible Society, 1991). Interestingly, in a later edition (*Holy Bible: Contemporary English Version,* [New York: American Bible Society, 1995]), these verses have been retranslated. Jesus is now laid on a bed of hay.

30. As quoted in Pelikan, 43.

31. As quoted in Franz Rosenzweig, "Scripture and Luther," in Buber and Rosenzweig, 49.

32. Personal conversation, June 1995.

33. *TANAKH: The Holy Scriptures* (Philadelphia: Jewish Publication Society, 1985).

34. Edward Hirsch, "In the Beginning: A New Translation of the Hebrew Bible Offers a Text for the Ear as Well as the Eye," *Religious Studies News* 11 (February 1996): 1 (reprinted with permission from the *New York Times,* 1995).

35. Interestingly, when I attended McCormick Theological Seminary, there was an annual Scripture-reading contest.

36. Sabine Rückert, "Die Welt in sechs Punkten," *Die Zeit,* October 14, 1994. My translation.

37. Richard Robert Osmer, *A Teachable Spirit: Recovering the Teaching Office in the Church* (Louisville, Ky.: Westminster John Knox, 1990). For Calvin's emphasis on showing ourselves "teachable toward [God's] minister," see John Calvin, *Institutes of the Christian Religion* 4.3.1, ed. John T. McNeill, trans. Ford Lewis Battles (Philadelphia: Westminster, 1960), 1053–54.

38. For a particularly eloquent statement of this point, see Stephen E. Fowl and L. Gregory Jones, *Reading in Communion: Scripture and Ethics in Christian Life* (Grand Rapids: Eerdmans, 1991), 156.

39. See Karl Barth, *Church Dogmatics* i/2, ed. G. W. Bromiley and T. F. Torrance, trans. G. T. Thomason and Harold Knight (Edinburgh: T. and T. Clark, 1956), 603–20.

40. See Jon D. Levenson, *The Death and Resurrection of the Beloved Son* (New Haven, Conn.: Yale University Press, 1993), 124.

41. See Phyllis Trible, *God and the Rhetoric of Sexuality* (Philadelphia: Fortress, 1978), 144–65.

42. A startling example of this problem occurs in the Revised Common Lectionary for the 7th Sunday of Easter: Revelation 22:12–14, 16–17, 20–21. Those verses that are excluded disparage "the dogs and sorcerers and fornicators and murderers and idolaters" (vs. 15). Apparently, we are to hear only of the blessed!

The omission of verses 18–19 is even more remarkable: "I warn everyone who hears the words of the prophecy of this book: if anyone adds to them, God will add to that person the plagues described in this book; if anyone takes away from the words of the book of this prophecy, God will take away that person's share in the tree of life and in the holy city, which are described in this book."

43. For an excellent analysis, see Edward Farley, "Preaching the Bible and Preaching the Gospel," *Theology Today* 52 (April 1995): 90–103.

44. The Rev. Paul Nazarian (First Presbyterian Church, Monroe, Louisiana) has adopted the practice of memorizing weekly the Scripture passage on which he is going to preach. He then recites the passage by memory in worship. Nazarian had told me that this exercise not only gets him more deeply into the passage as he prepares his sermon but also encourages members of the congregation to listen more intently to the words of Scripture.

45. See the author's "Biblical Poet and Prophet: Gerrard Winstanley's Use of Scripture in *The Law of Freedom,*" *Journal of Religious History* 17 (winter 1987): 269–82. For a good explication of this point in relation to Puritan literature more

generally, see John R. Knott, *The Sword of the Spirit: Puritan Responses to the Bible* (Chicago: University of Chicago Press, 1980).

46. Kathleen Norris, *The Cloister Walk* (New York: Riverhead Books, 1996), 38.

47. Ibid., 33.

Chapter 5: Commentary on Scripture

1. According to a recent report of the United Bible Societies, "More copies of the Bible are still being printed than any other book." See Edmund Doogue, "1996 Publication Figures Show that the Bible Is Still Number One," *Ecumenical News International,* April 2, 1997.

2. Wilfred Cantwell Smith, *What Is Scripture? A Comparative Approach* (Philadelphia: Fortress, 1993), 204–5. See also p. 94.

3. Jaroslav Pelikan, *Reformation of Church and Dogma (1300–1700),* vol. 4 of *The Christian Tradition: A History of the Development of Doctrine* (Chicago: University of Chicago Press, 1984), 307–8.

4. The RSV, for example, refers to "a long robe with sleeves."

5. Note, for example, the statement in the *Book of Order* of the Presbyterian Church (U.S.A.): "Confessional standards are subordinate to the Scriptures" (G-2.0200). Reformed confessions make the same point when they insist that the Word of God takes precedence over the decisions of church councils. See, for example, the Scots Confession, chapter XX.

6. Or, as the case may be, to each day.

7. Smith, 109.

8. See Willa Cather, *Death Comes for the Archbishop* (New York: Vintage Books, 1971), 18, 131. A Protestant might assume that Father Latour's well-worn book that he uses for devotions is a Bible, but it is in fact a breviary.

9. Jaroslav Pelikan, *The Reformation of the Bible/The Bible of the Reformation* (New Haven, Conn.: Yale University Press, 1996), 28–29.

10. As quoted in Jon D. Levenson, *The Hebrew Bible, the Old Testament, and Historical Criticism* (Louisville, Ky.: Westminster John Knox, 1993), 156.

11. Ibid., 157.

12. One might think, for example, of the "Hallelujah Chorus." It sets forth Scripture, yet evokes reverence in and of itself, as symbolized by the audience's act of rising when it is performed. See also Pelikan, *The Reformation of the Bible,* for a number of examples.

13. See Pelikan, *The Reformation of the Bible,* 65–69.

14. A Protestant parallel to the Orthodox and Catholic practice of processing with Scripture in worship is found in the Scottish Presbyterian tradition, where the beadle brings the book of Scripture to the front of the sanctuary at the beginning of worship, plops it on the lectern, opens it, and reads the call to worship.

15. See Louis Bouyer's classic study *Liturgy and Architecture* (Notre Dame, Ind.: University of Notre Dame Press, 1967), 34.

16. Ibid., 68.

17. Ibid., 66.

18. One wonders whether the lines painted on the arches over the choir represent marble or jewels, such as one would expect to find in the New Jerusalem. See Revelation 21:19–20.

19. Bouyer, 74.

20. See Wolfgang Braunfels, *Monasteries of Western Europe: The Architecture of the Orders* (New York: Thames and Hudson, 1971), 130–40. See also André Biéler, *Architecture in Worship: The Christian Place of Worship,* trans. Odette and Donald Elliot (Philadelphia: Westminster, 1965), 47. These "hall churches" may have also reflected the aspirations of a growing urban middle class. See Hans Müller, *Dome—Kirchen—Klöster: Kunstwerke aus zehn Jahrhunderten,* 2nd ed. (Berlin: VEB Tourist Verlag, 1986), 10.

21. The phrase "Scripture-shaped community" is Richard Hays's. See Richard B. Hays, "Scripture-Shaped Community: The Problem of Method in New Testament Ethics," *Interpretation* 64 (January 1990): 42–55. The power of art and music to effect conversion is well represented in Hugh T. Kerr and John Mulder, *Conversions* (Grand Rapids: Eerdmans, 1985).

22. See chapter 3 for a more extensive development of these themes.

23. This relationship between Scripture and Christ is well articulated in the Confession of 1967, 9.03, 9.27. See *The Book of Confessions* (Louisville, Ky.: Office of the General Assembly, Presbyterian Church [U.S.A.], 1991).

24. This point is developed more fully in chapter 7.

Chapter 6: The Search for a Fitting Word

1. Charles Dickens, *David Copperfield* (New York: Bantam Books, 1981), 13–14 (chap. 2).

2. Fyodor Dostoyevsky, *The Brothers Karamazov* (New York: Viking Penguin, 1958), 341–45.

3. Louis Bouyer, *Liturgy and Architecture* (Notre Dame, Ind.: University of Notre Dame Press, 1967), 19.

4. As quoted in Gordon W. Lathrop, *Holy Things: A Liturgical Theology* (Minneapolis: Fortress, 1993), 45.

5. See Harry Y. Gamble, *Books and Readers in the Early Church: A History of Early Christian Texts* (New Haven, Conn.: Yale University Press, 1995), 82–143.

6. Lathrop, 1–2.

7. Thomas Hoyt, Jr., "Testimony," in Dorothy C. Bass, ed., *Practicing Our Faith: A Way of Life for a Searching People* (San Francisco: Jossey-Bass, 1997), 98. See also Thomas G. Long, *The Witness of Preaching* (Louisville, Ky.: Westminster John Knox, 1989), 44–45.

8. Theology and Worship Ministry Unit, *Book of Common Worship* (Louisville, Ky.: Westminster John Knox, 1993).

9. As the *Book of Common Worship* notes, "The principle of continuous reading provides a responsible alternative to the use of the *Common Lectionary* in liturgical reading of the Bible and in preaching in worship." See also my article "Shaping a Congregation through Lectio Continua," *Reformed Liturgy and Music* 30 (November 1, 1996), 3–6.

10. *Book of Common Worship,* 36.

11. Ibid., 37.

12. See note 5.

13. Lathrop, 47.

14. Ibid., 46–47.

15. By "myth," I believe that Lathrop is trying to get at the sacramental, poetic-like dimension of Scripture that I have been describing. I myself prefer not to use the word *myth,* because it may imply to some readers that Scripture functions only on a metaphorical level. As I have tried to make clear, I believe that particular passages of Scripture may be literally true, but that they always retain a capacity in association with other biblical passages to point to God's active presence among us.

16. Ibid., 27.

17. Ibid., 15–20. James Sanders makes similar points in his discussion of the development of the canon. See James Sanders, *Community and Canon: A Guide to Canonical Criticism* (Philadelphia: Fortress, 1984); and James Sanders, *From Sacred Story to Sacred Text: Canon as Paradigm* (Philadelphia: Fortress, 1987).

18. Lathrop, 19.

19. Ibid., 210.

20. Ibid., 18.

21. Ibid., 19.

22. Ibid., 176.

23. Ibid., 20.

24. Ibid., 51.

25. Ibid., 50.

26. Ibid.

27. John Calvin, *Institutes of the Christian Religion* 4.1.12, ed. John T. McNeill, trans. Ford Lewis Battles (Philadelphia: Westminster, 1960), 1025–26.

28. See Lathrop, 169.

29. I am thankful to the Rev. Tommy Sikes (Madison, Mississippi) for these reflections.

30. Alexander Schmemann, *The Eucharist: Sacrament of the Kingdom* (Crestwood, N.Y.: St. Vladimir's Seminary Press, 1987), 68.

I am also thankful to the Rev. Ronald Byars of Birmingham, Michigan, for his reflections on the way weekly celebration of the Eucharist has redefined his understanding of preaching.

31. Note that Calvin's two marks of the church are "the Word of God purely preached and heard, and the sacraments administered according to Christ's insti-

tution." Calvin, 4.1.9 (p. 1023). See also Calvin, 4.3.1–3 (pp. 1053–56), 4.14.1–11 (pp. 1276–87), 1.17.1–4 (pp. 1359–64).

32. Karl Barth, *Church Dogmatics* i/2, ed. G. W. Bromiley and T. F. Torrance, trans. G. T. Thomason and Harold Knight (Edinburgh: T. & T. Clark, 1956), 651.

33. See Theology and Worship Ministry Unit, *A Proposal for Considering the Theology and Practice of Ordination in the Presbyterian Church (U.S.A.)* (Louisville, Ky.: Theology and Worship Ministry Unit, Presbyterian Church [U.S.A.], 1992), 73–74.

34. See chapter 3 and especially the quote by Thomas Levenson.

35. For a helpful discussion of fittingness and discernment in the interpretation of Scripture, see Allen Verhey, "Scripture and Ethics: Practices, Performances, and Prescriptions," in Lisa Sowle Cahill and James F. Childress, eds., *Christian Ethics: Problems and Prospects* (Cleveland: Pilgrim Press, 1996), 33.

36. This tension is, of course, central to Barth's theology. See, for example, Barth, i/2, 661–740.

37. See Richard B. Hays, *Echoes of Scripture in the Letters of Paul* (New Haven, Conn.: Yale University Press, 1989), 160–61.

38. Barth calls Scripture the Word of God, but only "derivatively and indirectly." Scripture is God's Word when it bears witness to God's revelation. See Karl Barth, *Church Dogmatics* i/1, ed. G. W. Bromiley and T. F. Torrance, trans. G. W. Bromiley (Edinburgh: T. and T. Clark, 1956), 108–20.

39. Lathrop, 209–16.

Chapter 7: The Life of the Church
as Commentary on Scripture

1. Stephen E. Fowl and L. Gregory Jones, *Reading in Communion: Scripture and Ethics in Christian Life* (Grand Rapids: Eerdmans, 1991), 63.

2. Ibid., 63, 78.

3. *The Rule of St. Benedict,* trans. Anthony C. Meisel and M. L. del Mastro (Garden City, N.Y.: Image Books, 1975), 44 (prologue).

4. See Wolfgang Braunfels, *Monasteries of Western Europe: The Architecture of the Orders* (New York: Thames and Hudson, 1971), 98–101, 140.

5. For a masterful study, see Sacvan Bercovitch, *The Puritan Origins of the American Self* (New Haven, Conn.: Yale University Press), 1975.

6. See D. W. Meinig, *Continental America, 1800–1867,* vol. 2 of *The Shaping of America: A Geographical Perspective on 500 Years of History* (New Haven, Conn.: Yale University Press, 1993), 265–66.

7. Fowl and Jones, 153.

8. Ibid., 29.

9. Ibid., 20.

10. My approach in this section has been greatly informed by Allen Verhey, "Scripture and Ethics: Practices, Performances, and Prescriptions," in Lisa Sowle

Cahill and James F. Childress, eds., *Christian Ethics: Problems and Prospects* (Cleveland: Pilgrim Press, 1996), 18–44.

11. Wilfred Cantwell Smith, *What Is Scripture? A Comparative Approach* (Philadelphia: Fortress, 1993), 32.

12. See Fowl and Jones, 110, 123. See also Pontifical Biblical Commission, *The Interpretation of the Bible in the Church,* trans. John Kilgallen and Brendan Byrne (Boston: St. Paul Books and Media, 1993), 103.

13. Fowl and Jones, 110.

14. See James M. Gustafson, "The Church: A Community of Moral Discourse," in *The Church as Moral Decision-Maker* (Philadelphia: Pilgrim Press, 1970), 83–95.

15. Hence, the Reformed motto "Ecclesia reformata, semper reformanda," that is, "The Church reformed, always reforming" (according to the Word of God and the call of the Spirit). See the *Book of Order* (Louisville, Ky.: Office of the General Assembly, Presbyterian Church [U.S.A.], 1996), G-2.0200.

16. Elizabeth A. Johnson, *She Who Is: The Mystery of God in Feminine Discourse* (New York: Crossroad, 1992), 10, 32, 34, 68.

17. Karl Barth, *Church Dogmatics* iv/1, ed. G. W. Bromiley and T. F. Torrance, trans. G. W. Bromiley (Edinburgh: T. and T. Clark, 1956), 451.

18. Ibid. See also Pontifical Bible Commission, 132.

19. Karl Barth, *Church Dogmatics* iii/4, ed. G. W. Bromiley and T. F. Torrance, trans. A. T. MacKay et al. (Edinburgh: T. and T. Clark, 1961), 9.

20. Karl Barth, *Church Dogmatics* ii/2, ed. G. W. Bromiley and T. F. Torrance, trans. G. W. Bromiley et al. (Edinburgh: T. and T. Clark, 1957), 717.

21. Ibid.

22. Chapter XVII.

23. For very helpful reflections on this topic, see Franklin I. Gamwell, *The Meaning of Religious Freedom: Modern Politics and the Democratic Resolution* (Albany, N.Y.: State University of New York Press, 1995), 163–71.

24. Fowl and Jones, 114.

25. Dietrich Bonhoeffer, *Life Together,* trans. John W. Doberstein (New York: Harper and Row, 1954), 100–103.

26. James M. Gustafson, *A Sense of the Divine: The Natural Environment from a Theocentric Perspective* (Cleveland: Pilgrim Press, 1994), 66–67.

27. Timothy Sedgwick, "The Ascetics of Ethics," 9, unpublished manuscript delivered at the annual meeting of the Society of Christian Ethics (January 10–12, 1997). Sedgwick notes that this kind of meditation is grounded in biblical images.

28. See Verhey, 33.

29. James Sanders makes this point eloquently in his writings. See James Sanders, *Community and Canon: A Guide to Canonical Criticism* (Philadelphia: Fortress, 1984); and James Sanders, *From Sacred Story to Sacred Text: Canon as Paradigm* (Philadelphia: Fortress, 1987).

30. My thanks again to the Rev. Dr. Joseph Small.

31. Karl Barth, *Church Dogmatics* i/2, ed. G. W. Bromiley and T. F. Torrance, trans. G. T. Thomason and Harold Knight (Edinburgh: T. & T. Clark, 1956), 586–89.

32. Barth, ii/2, 569.

33. See John Calvin, *Institutes of the Christian Religion* 2.2.15, 16, ed. John T. McNeill, trans. Ford Lewis Battles (Philadelphia: Westminster, 1960), 273–75.

34. This position has been made with particular power in our time by James Gustafson. See, for example, James M. Gustafson, *Intersections: Science, Theology, and Ethics* (Cleveland: Pilgrim Press, 1996).

35. See Jon D. Levenson, "Historical Criticism and the Fate of the Enlightenment Project," in *The Hebrew Bible, the Old Testament, and Historical Criticism* (Louisville, Ky.: Westminster John Knox, 1993), 106–26 (especially, p. 123); and Richard B. Hays, "Salvation by Trust? Reading the Bible Faithfully," *Christian Century* (February 26, 1997): 218–23.

36. See Levenson; and Hays.

37. See William C. Placher, "Why Bother with Theology?," *Christian Century* (February 2–9, 1994): 104–8.

38. This theme has been articulated most powerfully by Stanley Hauerwas and John Howard Yoder. See, for example, Stanley Hauerwas, *The Peaceable Kingdom: A Primer in Christian Ethics* (Notre Dame, Ind.: University of Notre Dame Press, 1983); and John Howard Yoder, *The Politics of Jesus* (Grand Rapids: Eerdmans, 1972).

39. See David Kelsey, *The Uses of Scripture in Recent Theology* (Philadelphia: Fortress, 1975). See also Richard B. Hays, *The Moral Vision of the New Testament: A Contemporary Introduction to New Testament Ethics* (San Francisco: Harper Collins, 1996) for an illuminating discussion of discrimens. Hays appeals to the images of community, cross, and new creation to synthesize the New Testament materials.

40. See, for example, Karl Barth, *The Humanity of God* (Richmond: John Knox, 1960), 59–61.

41. For thoughtful reflections on ministers as servants of the Word, see Brian A. Gerrish, "Tradition in the Modern World: The Reformed Habit of Mind," 20–21, unpublished manuscript.

42. Westminster Larger Catechism, Question 141.

43. For an insightful exploration of Barth's appeal to biblical trajectories in his theological ethics, see Nigel Biggar, *The Hastening that Waits: Karl Barth's Ethics* (Oxford: Clarendon, 1993), 97–122.

44. See my article "Sexuality, Mortality and the Presbyterian Debate," *Christian Century* (March 5, 1997): 246–49.

45. It is important to note, however, that secular notions of justice and rights have been deeply informed by the Christian tradition. For one illuminating discussion, see Charles Taylor, *Sources of the Self: The Making of Modern Identity* (Cambridge: Harvard University Press, 1989).

46. Fyodor Dostoyevsky, *Crime and Punishment,* trans. David Magarshack (New York: Penguin, 1966), 340–43, 558–59.

Conclusion: A Reading of Matthew 4:1–11

1. My observations about the early church are drawn largely from the magisterial study of Josef A. Jungmann, *The Early Liturgy: To the Time of Gregory the Great* (Notre Dame, Ind.: University of Notre Dame Press, 1959), 74–86.

Appendix: A Bibliographic Essay

1. Ellen F. Davis, "Holy Preaching: Ethical Interpretation and the Practical Imagination," in George A. Sumner and Ephraim Radner, eds., *Reclaiming Faith: Essays on Orthodoxy in the Episcopal Church and the Baltimore Declaration* (Grand Rapids: Eerdmans, 1993), 201.

2. David S. Yeago, "Memory and Communion: Ecumenical Theology and the Search for a Generous Orthodoxy," in Sumner and Radner, 259.

3. Elisabeth Schüssler Fiorenza, *In Memory of Her: A Feminist Theological Reconstruction of Christian Origins* (New York: Crossroad, 1983), xx.

INDEX

Calvin, John *(contd.)*
and his understanding of Scripture as
spectacles, 46
and his understanding of Scripture as
the church's book, 4, 13–14, 132,
133, 171 n.13
and his understanding of the Eucharist,
51
and his understanding of the significance of all of Scripture, 68, 172
n.23
and memorization of Scripture, 68
canon
and simultaneity of all its parts,
67
as a coherent narrative, 66
arrangement of, 53, 66
significance of, 52–53
canon within the canon, 53–54, 67
Cathedral of the Assumption, 114–15,
116, 117
Chariots of Fire, 52
church, early. *See* baptismal rites of early
church; and Scripture: early church's
use of
Confession of 1967 (C67), xviii, 84
confessions. *See* Scripture: and the confessions
Contemporary English Version, 70–
71
Coulton, G. G., 20
Cranach, Lukas, 88

Dei Verbum. *See* Dogmatic Constitution
on Divine Revelation
Descartes, René, 28
Dickens, Charles, 98
disciplines of reading Scripture. *See*
reading memorization of Scripture;
reading Scripture aloud; reading
Scripture in community; and reading
Scripture in context
discrimens, 134, 179 n.39
Dogmatic Constitution on Divine Revela-
tion, 45
Dostoyevsky, Fyodor, 19–20, 98, 140
Dürer, Albrecht, 88

Eastern Orthodoxy. *See* Scripture: Eastern
Orthodox use of
Evangel Life Center. *See* Scripture: pente-
costal use of

feminist theology, 19, 132, 154
and its commitment to a community of
mutuality, 6, 7
and its use of historical criticism, 8,
161
as critiquing Scripture's patriarchal traditions, 28, 54
as claiming Scripture's symbolic depth,
8
See also Johnson, Elizabeth; and
Schüssler Fiorenza, Elisabeth

Fishbane, Michael, 44–45
Fowl, Stephen
and his understanding of a right reading
of Scripture, 122, 123, 154
and his understanding of historical criticism, 161
and his understanding of reading Scripture against ourselves, 10, 157–58
Fox, Everett, 71, 152
Frei, Hans, 149
Fühmann, Franz, 40–41, 46, 47

Gamble, Harry, 155
Geneva Bible, 63
German Bible, 54, 70, 88 (*see also*
Luther, Martin)
Green, Garrett, 153, 159
Gustafson, James, 131

Hauerwas, Stanley, 58
and his understanding of issues of biblical authority and interpretation, 157,
159–61
and his understanding of Scripture as illustrative of the community's character, 6–7, 9, 10, 50, 153–54
and his understanding of Scripture as
the community's book, 2, 3
Hays, Richard, 150, 152
Heidegger, Martin, 27–28

WHY SCRIPTURE MATTERS

'The Last Things'
in a Process Perspective

NORMAN PITTENGER

'The Last Things'
in a Process Perspective

London EPWORTH PRESS

Set in 11/12 pt Imprint
and printed in Great Britain
by W & J Mackay & Co Ltd
Chatham Kent
SBN 7162 0149 6

Contents

Preface

The purpose of this book ought to be clear from its title. It is an attempt to sketch briefly, mostly by way of suggestion, what significance may be discovered, for men and women living today, in the traditional scheme of the 'last things'— death, judgement, heaven, and hell. It admits frankly that this scheme, as it has come down to us, is incredible, however valuable and helpful, not to say apparently 'true', it was for many who have gone before us in the path of Christian discipleship. But it tries to point out certain indispensable realities in human, above all in Christian, life which that outworn scheme somehow managed to present to those who accepted it.

I should like to emphasize that at best this is a 'sketch'; and that it is 'mostly by way of suggestion'. I should be the last to assume that I have said everything that might be or ought to be said on the subject, and I am very conscious of serious omissions as well as of many shortcomings. In extenuation, however, I plead that in the compass allowed me—for these chapters were originally lectures—nobody can say everything. What I have done is to select, according to my best judgement, what seemed of crucial importance and hence could not be omitted. And that is all that I *can* say, as an excuse for this book's inadequacy to the theme with which it attempts to deal.

It remains to thank the authorities of the several divinity schools in the United States which were kind enough to ask me to lecture in February 1970. The principals, deans, and other officials, as well as the theological students and others who heard the lectures, will know how deeply indebted I am to them all. The lectures, practically in their present form, were delivered at the Episcopal Theological School, Cambridge, and the Boston Theological Institute.

Two further chapters (on The Centrality of Love and After the 'Death of God') have been added, since they deal with related subjects. The second of these (Chapter Eight) originally appeared in *The Church Quarterly* for April 1969; I am indebted to the Editor for permission to reprint it here.

NORMAN PITTENGER

King's College
Cambridge

*To my students
in New York and
in Cambridge
1935–70*

ONE

The Traditional Scheme

It is frequently said, in criticisms or comments on the various new movements in Christian theology these days, that the one area to which they give little or no attention is the one that has to do with what are called in text-books of doctrine 'the last things'. For example, one of the charges against *Honest to God*, almost as soon as it appeared, was that John Robinson had said nothing in that book about 'future life'—although the critic must have forgotten that not many years before the bishop had written, while still a theological teacher, a treatise entitled *In the End God* which is a considered and very interesting and suggestive discussion of exactly that subject as well as of the related aspects of 'the last things'.

Although, in this particular instance, the charge was misdirected, it is true, I think, that the detailed and careful consideration of 'the last things' has been infrequent in the 'new theology'. Much is said about the eschatological perspective, much is written about the way in which the 'coming Kingdom' impinges on the present world, and much is asserted about the need to take the eschatology of the Bible seriously. Here, however, eschatology does not signify what the theological text-books include under that phrase. The term is used, perhaps more properly, to denote the special Jewish insistence on 'the end', 'the good time coming', the Kingdom either in its final appearance (with some) or in its 'anticipated' or 'realized' form (with others).

Whatever may be the case with the new theologians who are influenced by 'secularization', by 'the death of God', or the existentialist conceptuality provided by Heidegger—and here John Macquarrie is an exception, since his *Principles of Christian Theology* does include a consideration of the subject—not many theologians who prefer to approach the re-conception of Christian theology with the use of 'process thought' have published extended studies of 'the last things'; or, if they have, I have not come across them. Schubert Ogden is the notable exception, in what I regard as his excellent essay on 'The Hope of Faith', included in *The Reality of God*. By and large, though, the subject is not one that appeals to such thinkers.

I should wish to associate myself entirely with the process theologians. And it seems to me a useful enterprise to undertake in these chapters a consideration of 'the last things', although in short compass and in the light of my own obvious incompetence I can only open up the discussion and make what may be a few helpful suggestions. Certainly I do not claim that I shall do more than raise questions, suggest a few possible answers, and urge readers to pursue the matter for themselves. But of the importance of the subject I have not the slightest doubt; and as you will see, this is not because I wish to cling in some obscurantist way to something that has been traditionally sacred, but because I am convinced that death, judgement, heaven, and hell—'the four last things'—are subjects with which we *must* concern ourselves, however different from our ancestors may be the way in which we wish to understand what those terms denote.

So much, then, by way of preface to the lectures. I now turn to a fairly straightforward and, I hope, accurate sketch of what the tradition in Christian theology, found in those textbooks to which I have referred, does in fact have to say on these matters. Since I myself was taught this scheme, many years ago, I shall outline what I *was* taught, under the heading used in those days, of 'Christian Eschatology: Death, Judgement, the Intermediate State, Heaven, and Hell'. You will see that a fifth term has been added here—'the intermediate state'; this is because my own instruction was received in an Anglican theological school of tractarian background and of Anglo-Catholic sympathies. Hence the common Catholic and Orthodox view that 'something happens between' death for every man, and arrival in heaven, so to say, was included in the picture. Had I been educated, theologically, in a more Protestant divinity faculty that term would not have been found, of course. But 'the intermediate state' was certainly an element in the general picture for most Christians, indeed it still is and increasingly so among Protestants too; hence I shall include it in my outline-sketch.

What were the sources of this teaching? The present study is too brief to permit any proper analysis, but we may say that Christian eschatology, understood in this sense, is the product of a marriage of ideas found in Jewish thought, including the inter-testamental period, and the hellenistic soul-body portrayal of man. The story is exceedingly complicated; it would be a great service if some scholar or group of scholars would investigate it, in the light of our modern knowledge of Jewish and early Christian ideas, as well as with attention to the diversity of the thought about man found in the Graeco-Roman world.

Things are not quite so simple as an earlier generation of historians and theologians took them to be. There are questions like the possible development of a more 'spiritual' view of resurrection of the body, among Pharisaic thinkers in the period immediately before and contemporaneous with the beginning of the Christian era; the uncertainty about the supposed fate of the non-Jewish peoples when Judaism began to talk of God's Kingdom 'coming on earth', however transfigured the earth may be, and with this the nature of that Kingdom and the degree to which and the way in which it *was* coming; exactly how early Christian thinkers brought together the Jewish notion of resurrection and the hellenistic idea of immortality—for it is apparent that they resolved the obvious contradictions in a far from simple manner. But, generally

3

speaking, we can say that the doctrine of the last things was gradually worked out from taking with utmost seriousness, and even with a stark literal understanding, much in the later Old Testament documents, as well as what the teaching of Jesus, then of St Paul and St John and the rest of the New Testament, was supposed to have said. Here was a disclosure, in so many words (and I would emphasize that it *was* thought to be 'in words', that is, in propositions stated in or deducible from that teaching), of man's destiny. Along with this, the philosophical notions about soul, about immortality, about a realm above and beyond the hurly-burly of this world, present in the tradition of Greek philosophy and variations on that philosophy in the early Christian era, had become so much part of the atmosphere of thought that inevitably these two affected Christian thinkers.

The marriage of this Jewish-Christian eschatological picture and the Greek philosophical view was not easily accomplished, nor was that marriage without its difficulties—it was hardly a quiet and successful relationship. But such as it was, it slowly matured; and the end-product was the sort of thing which finally was worked out in, say, St Thomas Aquinas and other medieval theologians, on the one hand, and in Calvin's *Institution of the Christian Religion*, on the other. And so far as the Bible had its unquestioned place in the enterprise, it was used as if the teaching found in it, especially in the gospels and the Johannine-Pauline literature, were a revelation in actual words of what death, judgement, heaven, and hell (and, where this was accepted, purgatory or paradise or the 'intermediate state') really were. As in so many places in Christian theology, the 'proof-texts' were found for what the Church wished to say, through its theologians.

It is a nice question, of course, whether a good deal of the teaching was based on these texts, or whether the texts were discovered, after careful searching, to bolster up ideas that had slowly gained acceptance. But this situation is not peculiar to 'the last things'; it has been found fairly generally in the whole

Christian theological enterprise. In any event, so far as the Bible was used, it was used in a way like that followed today by fundamentalists: the words were taken at their face-value, even if that 'face-value' seems a little odd and not always *obviously* what it is assumed to be. When there were contradictions in those materials, a reconciliation was effected, or at least attempted, through the use of the 'different levels of interpretation', where the historical meaning, the moral meaning, the theological meaning, and the highly mystical meaning could be distinguished and an appropriate distribution made in the discussion of this or that biblical text.

But what was the resulting teaching?

First of all, that human life in our span of years and so far as man's history is concerned is, like the created world itself, derivative from a realm of heavenly existence which abides eternal over against the transient, mortal, and uncertain span of our years. Of this fact, death stands as the great sign. Every man dies. This is the inescapable fact which no one can deny. But not *all* of him dies, for man himself is compounded of soul *and* body; and while the body dies, the soul cannot die. By its very nature it is immortal.

You must remember that I am not attempting here to make critical comments on the scheme; rather I am trying to present it as it was generally, and commonly, held and taught. If I were to make those critical comments, I should be obliged to say something at this point about the way in which this notion of the soul's immortality is very doubtfully found in the Scriptures and how it is an importation into Christian thinking from elsewhere. But that is not the point. For the generality of Christian theologians, the soul was taken to be immortal, so that when the human body came to die, the soul was 'released' from its bodily dwelling-place and enabled (shall we put it this way?) 'to go elsewhere'. The Book of Common Prayer, before recent revisions, talked in just this fashion; and, in doing so, it was typical of the common Christian teaching.

Death was the most important thing that happened to man

5

and all of his life before death was to be seen as a preparation for that event. The importance of death was not only in its being the end of this mortal life; it was also in its being the moment when, in a 'particular judgement', the future destiny of the one who died was fixed. There was no possibility of repentance *after* death; as we must note, there was either the definite sending to eternal damnation of the evil man or the preparation of the good man for a final heavenly state (in circles that did not accept some doctrine of an 'intermediate state', there was instead a sort of 'waiting' until the final consummation)—but the moment of death, with its judgement of this and that individual, was absolutely final in its determination of the direction that was thereafter to be taken.

But if the soul was immortal, and human destiny determined at that particular judgement by a God who, although he was indeed merciful, was also just and would treat each man according to that man's merits—whether simply his own merits or in the light of 'the merits of Christ' in which by repentance for sin he took refuge—what happened to the body? Obviously the body corrupted in the grave. Yet there was the teaching about the resurrection of the *body*, so somehow this must be included in the final destiny of each man. Hence it was taught that at a later time, when God began to wind things up as we might put it, there would be a resurrection of all bodies. Precisely how this could occur was not known, but in some appropriate fashion these bodies would be raised from their graves, reconstituted in some equally appropriate fashion, re-united with 'their' souls—and then there would be a final judgement, in which the soul-and-body together would face the Grand Assize, to receive the statement of the great Judge as to its eventual fate.

There was a good deal of puzzlement here. *How* would these bodies be raised? What would they be like? How, in some transformed condition, were they to be permitted to enter into heaven, to be in the presence of God for ever? What about the bodies of those whose destiny had been determined, at their death, to be not heaven but hell? This sort of question was much discussed—St Augustine, for example, was troubled about the bodies of the very young or the very old or those who had been maimed or crippled. The general picture is clear, however. Bodies would be raised, quite literally. Soul and body would be re-united, as the hymns put it and as art portrayed it. Graves would be opened, bodies would emerge in their re-constituted form, and man as the union of soul and body would face the judgement of God.

Some very few would be, so to say, exempted from at least part of this. In the Catholic theology in which I was brought up, the saints were somehow to be granted the *immediate* vision of God, at the point of their death. What happened to *their* bodies was not entirely clear, although in Roman Catholic circles it was believed (and in quite recent times it has been made an indisputable dogma) that the body of the Blessed Mother of our Lord had not in fact died at all but had been received into heaven, thus anticipating the general resurrection which was to be a part of the more general human lot. Those saints, already in heaven, were constantly interceding for men and women on earth. With God himself, they were in bliss; but because they had shared and hence knew our mortal lot, they could be trusted not to forget their human brethren and they continually prayed for those left behind.

On the other hand, the souls which were not thus in heaven already were in a state either of preparation for heaven (among Protestants, this of course was denied—but exactly 'where' those souls might be was left an open question, although some have described the 'state' as being a sort of 'cold freeze' until the day of final judgement), or, having completed their preparation, were now awaiting the day when they would be re-united with their bodies and so enabled to enjoy the heavenly bliss which was promised them. They could be helped by the prayers of their brethren who were still 'in the flesh', we were taught; or at least, *I* was. Prayers for the dead were an important part of Christian devotion, since through them those who were in the intermediate state would be furthered on their way towards the perfection which God intended for them.

It was, of course, a natural and very human thing to wish to remember, and indeed to demand the right to remember, those whom we 'have loved long since, and lost awhile'. But it was also an act of piety to do so. In Protestant communions, the practice of prayers for the dead had been given up, along with acceptance of the notion of an intermediate state of some sort. But even there, as recent liturgical forms show, the human desire sooner or later had to be satisfied; and in some fashion, perhaps by *comprecation* (that is, praying for the departed by associating them with prayers for ourselves), the realization of this 'communion' had to be made available. In Catholic circles, especially in the west, such prayers were taken to be a way in which somehow the purification or purgation of the departed soul might be accomplished more effectively, even if the idea of the intermediate state as 'punishment' was not held.

Furthermore the most solemn and sacred of all acts of Christian worship, the Eucharist, could be 'applied' to those who were dead. How often have I heard, and how often after ordination have I said: 'Of your charity, pray for the *soul* of X, that God may grant it a place of light and refreshment and peace.' Thus the 'intention' of the celebration could be *for* the departed, either one by one or, on All Souls' Day, for them all.

So far I have spoken of the way in which death and judgement were presented, with, perhaps, too extended a reference to the idea of the intermediate state. Now we come to heaven, the goal or end of those who in that state were being purified and prepared for heavenly joy. Heaven, of course, was said to be the vision of God, so far as 'immortal mortals' could see him; it was the place, in a spiritual sense of course, where the blessed dwelt in profound fellowship one with another in God himself. Responsible theological teachers did not take at their face value the pictures of heaven which were found in hymnody, nor did they regard the somewhat extraordinary set of images in Revelation as being an exact representation—indeed, these images, laden with Jewish eschatological conceptions of the nature of the Kingdom of God when there should be 'a new heaven and a new earth' were sometimes felt to be slightly embarrassing. But there was a reality behind *all* the pictures and images—and that reality was life in God, with all the saints, where suffering and pain would be no more and where all the anguish of this mortal life would be absent entirely, being replaced by sheer joy such as that of the angels themselves.

Some of the greatest theologians had been prepared to say that *one* of the joys possessed by the blessed in heaven would be to witness the suffering of the damned in hell. This unpleasant idea was refined in these responsible thinkers to mean that the blessed would rejoice to see God's justice vindicated, rather than delight in the actual sufferings of those who through their own choice had shown themselves utterly unworthy of heavenly bliss. But hell was a real possibility. In certain of the theologies the fires of hell were taken almost literally, but in most of them the everlasting pains endured there were summed up in phrases like 'deprivation of God'— and hence of abiding happiness—or the pain of recognizing the evil done in this life with its inevitable consequences. A few more recent writers had interpreted hell in a less terrible fashion; they had even turned it into a kind of purgatory in which the anguish was a necessary means of purification—for such thinkers hell was not everlasting or eternal (whichever you choose) but temporary; in the end God would win all men to himself. Such universalism was not regarded as orthodox, however, no matter how much more it might seem to be in accordance with the supposedly Christian conviction that God is love.

I quite realize that the sketch which I have just given can be faulted as being too brief and too selective; it can also be called an unfair parody of what was in fact taught. To this I can only reply that this *is* what I myself was taught, first, as part of instruction given in my parish as a child and later, with many refinements and qualifications, in lectures in theology as an ordinand—although I should add that my teacher was himself, quite obviously, very ill at ease about the scheme, left it to the very end of his course, and even then touched upon it gingerly. In fact he engaged in a process of gentle 'de-mythologizing', although that word had not been invented in that time. Certainly the two or three 'standard texts' which we were supposed to master *did* talk in that way, however, although at least one of them left it open to the reader to make his own interpretation of what the scheme, presented as *the* orthodox view, set forth in such precise detail.

It is hardly necessary to say that this scheme does not commend itself to most of us today. Obviously there are many who still accept it, or something like it; to deny that would be nonsense. But, by and large, it has been given up in that form or in any close approximation to that form. This has been for various reasons. A new approach to the Bible has been one of them. A view of revelation as found, not in propositions, but in events of history and their meaning has been another. A third has been a conviction that much in the scheme stands in stark contradiction to the belief in God as love—especially in the bits about hell and endless suffering. Still another has been the feeling that nobody could ever have the knowledge to enable him to draw so exact and precise a map of 'the future life', as it has been called. And a fifth reason is that the portrayal of 'the last things' in these terms, indeed the emphasis on some destiny for man out of this world which makes what goes on *in* this world merely preparatory for heaven or a way of avoiding hell, is thought by a great many people to entail a neglect of their duty here and now to live in Christian love and to find in that their deepest satisfaction, whatever may await them when this life is ended.

But however we may analyse the reaction, reaction there has been. Thus in a large number of sermons, in much religious instruction, and in the emphasis found in theological teaching, death, judgement, heaven, and hell have little if any place. I can recall, in recent years, only one sermon that I have heard on death, one on judgement, and none whatever on either heaven or hell. Nor do I think my experience very unusual, for it has included many parish churches, college chapels, and the chapels of theological schools. Furthermore, a glance through the syllabuses of a number of theological colleges has disclosed that they include but the briefest mention of the traditional scheme. And an admittedly hurried examination of several texts intended for use in courses of instruction before confirmation or in 'religious studies' in schools for adolescents has made it plain that this whole set of ideas is either entirely absent or is so 'muted' (to put it so) that it plays no really significant part in what children or confirmands learn as they are introduced to the Christian faith and its theological implications.

I do not wish to dwell on this, however; surely the change in atmosphere and attitude must be familiar to most of us. What I do wish to say is that we still find in our liturgical forms, even in some (if not all) of the revised ones, the relics of the traditional scheme, and that our hymns still suggest many if not every one of the ideas that I have so briefly, and some will think unfairly, sketched for you. Perhaps this is one reason why there is so often an air of unreality about our worship, when such liturgical forms and such hymns are used, as they must be. For these reflect, however dimly, a scheme which is no longer *taught*, as part of the faith, or in fact believed.

But what chiefly I wish to suggest is that while I for one welcome the disappearance or 'muting' of the traditional teaching about the last things, I also think that they did point to important truths about human life as well as about Christian faith. This does not mean that I desire a return to the former state of affairs; it does mean, on the other hand, that it may very well be incumbent upon us to attend to these matters, to see what 'values'—if I may use that not too happy word—the old scheme somehow preserved, and then to consider whether or not those values may be stated in some other fashion—that is, in a fashion which will not be quite so out-rageous as I, with many others, think the scheme I was taught really was.

In other words, I have the feeling that we have a job to do. This is why I very much regret that the so-called 'new theologians' have not written much, if anything, on the subject, for I believe that they could have helped us considerably and that their failure to do so has left us impoverished. There is a familiar saying about 'throwing out the baby with the bath-water'. In a way that saying applies here. We certainly do *not* want the old 'bath-water'; but maybe the 'baby' has something still to say to us. I apologize for this very strained image; but I am confident that you will take my point. What, then, did the older scheme have to say, in terms of enduring values or meaning, which we should *not* reject when quite rightly we reject the scheme itself?

In the remainder of the book I shall attempt this task, but in a very preliminary and suggestive way. First, however, I must indicate the particular approach which I shall take and the materials and method that I wish to use. That will occupy our attention in the next chapter. Then I shall say something about death, judgement, heaven, hell, and the so-called inter-mediate state. A later chapter will consider what may be said about the Christian hope in its relationship to 'personal ex-istence' after death.

In closing the present chapter, let me say, very briefly, what seem to me some of the obvious values in that older scheme which most of us have by now given up. Such a statement will perhaps provide some preparation for the more detailed dis-cussion in the following pages.

First, then, the fact that death was so stressed in the scheme made it very clear that this event in every human life is of enormous importance. That we shall die is the one inevitable thing to which we must adjust ourselves. But death is not simply the inescapable end of each man's life; it is also the plain demonstration of his mortality, a mortality which both conditions and characterizes everything that he is and does up to the moment when he is pronounced dead. Doubtless it is absurd to dwell on death as such; it is equally absurd to attempt to deny it, to cover it up, to pretend that it is not there —one thinks of the pathetic way in which contemporary funeral customs so often try to disguise what as a matter of obvious truth a funeral is all about. Such fashions are pathetic; they are also silly. So is the evasion of the use of the word itself, with the substitution of such phrases as 'passed on', 'has left us', 'has gone away'. People *die* and we should honestly and courageously accept that this happens. And as I have said, this dying stands as the sign over every bit of human life. We are mortal men, who during a certain relatively short period have responsibilities, know joy and sorrow, contribute to the race of which we are part. Anything else that we may wish to say about ourselves cannot be a denial of that mortality.

Again, the stress on judgement in the old scheme made apparent the place of decision in human life and at the same time the responsibility that comes with decision. It faced men with the one-way movement of history, in which what has happened has indeed happened; it cannot be *undone*, no matter what may be *done with it*. We are what our decisions have made us, even when we grant that the area in which those decisions were taken may have been restricted. Having made the decisions we have made and having become what we are in consequence of those decisions (although obviously other factors have entered in as well), we cannot evade or avoid appraisal in terms of them. *Who* appraises is not the issue here; but *that* there is appraisal is plain enough. The traditional scheme made it impossible to escape from this.

When the scheme included, as it did in my case at least, the intermediate state, this was by way of showing that nobody was good enough, loving enough, faithful enough, to be counted perfect, save (as the scheme claimed) for those few who were called 'saints' in a quite special sense of that word—not the New Testament sense, incidentally. Furthermore, in its own odd way it stressed the love of God, who provided opportunity for 'growth in his love and service', as a prayer puts it, and whose justice was therefore mitigated by his mercy. When this belief was coupled with the notion of a last judgement which would not occur until God 'had accomplished the number of his elect', in words from still another prayer, it said something about the corporate nature of human life, the equally corporate nature of whatever destiny men have, and the need for patient waiting until our fellowmen have found their capacity for fulfilment along with us. Prayers for the dead again indicated the social nature of human life, our belonging together, and our helping one another as we move on towards our goal, whatever that may be.

Heaven stood for the sheer joy which may be known when men are in such a relationship with God, in company with their fellows, as will mark their own realization or actualization, through the gracious influence of love at work in and even beyond this mortal life. At its best, it did not invite those who believed in it to a selfish satisfaction but spoke of 'social joys', in widest sharing, in and under and with God himself.

Hell is the difficult aspect of the scheme, for all too often it succeeded in introducing the element of terror or fear into human existence. 'The fear of the Lord' frequently became sheer terror in the face of possible unending pain. Hence there was always the danger, and often the horrible reality, of men and women trying 'to be good', as the phrase goes, lest they find themselves in 'the fires of hell'. That, certainly, was not only a poor way to persuade people to 'be good', but was also an invitation not to be good at all, in any genuine sense—only to be 'prudent' in the worst meaning of that word. And yet there was something else. That was the utter horror of lovelessness, the desperate state of life in which no response is made to God's solicitations and invitations. And there was the stark recognition that evil *is* evil. A good God might have ways of dealing with evil, but that it was evil could not be denied. So Thomas Hardy's words were seen to be true:

If way to the better there be
It exacts a full look at the worst.

The reality of death as a fact: the inescapable element of decision and the consequences in searching appraisal: the social or communal nature of human existence, coupled with the honest recognition that *no* man is in and of himself a perfect agent of the purpose of God and the love of God: the joy of fulfilment with one's brethren in the imperishable reality of God: and the terrible character of evil—these were values which the older scheme somehow affirmed and expressed.

This does not mean that we should attempt to resurrect that scheme. It is far too late in the day to do that, I should claim. Nor does it mean that the scheme as it stood was a very satisfactory or even worthy mode of expressing the values which I have noted. On the other hand, it suggests—if it does nothing more than that—a necessity on our part to find ways which will provide for an expression, an affirmation, of those values in our own terms and in our own way. If we can achieve something like that, we shall also have maintained a certain continuity with our fathers in the faith. I believe that this last is not unimportant for us; indeed I believe that it is of the highest importance. My reason for believing this is that true *radicalism* in theology, as elsewhere, consists in penetration *to the roots*; which is to say, in getting at what utterly unacceptable ideas, as we see them, were attempting to say. It may well be that then we shall feel obliged to reject that which they *were* trying to say; on the other hand it may be that we shall discover that this which they were trying to say is significant, perhaps even essential, in the total Christian stance of faith. In respect to the impossible and incredible scheme which I learned as a young man, I believe this to be the case. For God's sake, quite literally; for man's sake, quite surely, let us give up the *scheme*—but let us see to it that we do not lose altogether the insight or intuition which was behind it and which was expressed, sometimes in ghastly and ridiculous fashion, in its several elements.

TWO

An Approach to a New Perspective

In closing the last chapter I spoke of the values which had been represented in the outworn traditional scheme of the last things. I suggested that true radicalism in theology meant an effort to get to the roots, to see what was deeply intended in patterns, pictures, and propositions that to us are not credible. And I mentioned the importance of maintaining such continuity as is possible, in this and in other respects, with our ancestors in the Christian fellowship. In a word, I was urging a theological variation of Leonard Hodgson's by now well-known point about Biblical enquiry. What must the case really be, so far as we today can grasp it, if people who thought and wrote and naturally accepted such and such ideas put things in the way in which they did put them? Hodgson was suggesting that after all the preliminary scholarly work has been done, this is the question which the interpreter of Scripture must ask. And I am suggesting that after we have discovered, so far as may be, how this or that theological idea came to be, on what grounds and with what intention it was asserted, we have then to ask a similar question.

I realize that some of those who call themselves 'radical theologians' will regard such a procedure as quite absurd. They will disclaim any responsibility for maintaining continuity with the past of the Christian fellowship and will urge that we must start afresh, with no *impedimenta* from the past. It must be observed that such theologians usually do not fulfil that implied intention, for they still insist on their loyalty to Jesus, at least, even if their way of being loyal to Him is as various as, say, William Hamilton's talk about Jesus as being 'the place where we stand' or Paul van Buren's sense that somehow association with Jesus provides a 'contagious freedom'. What is more, when some of these thinkers say that they are 'giving up' God, it is to be noted that at the very same moment they seem anxious to preserve, in some fashion or other, what the faith in God meant and supplied to those who did, as a matter of fact, deeply believe in Him. Their presentation of that significant and presumably enduring 'reality' is not very impressive, in some instances anyway; but the intention is there.

Thus I would conclude that *in principle* what I have been urging is not so obscurantist, reactionary, or nostalgic as it might appear. But I wish also to remark that what such critics often imply is a very unhistorical notion of how any faith, and *a fortiori* Christian faith, does work as a matter of historical development. They are not really radicals at all, when they suggest the necessity of starting entirely fresh, and demand that there be no commitments of any kind to the religious traditions of the past. For religious faiths do not grow that way, nor do they come into being in that way in the first place. Such entirely revolutionary ideas rest upon a failure to see that the Jewish prophets, for example, were related to, and in many ways dependent upon, the tradition which they received, and were enormously affected by the fact of their participation in the life of the people of Israel. Jesus Himself, claimed by some of them as the great revolutionary, was first and last a *Jew*, thinking in Jewish terms, talking in Jewish ways, dependent for His teaching upon the Jewish tradition. He was *not* a revolutionary in the sense intended; He was a genuine radical in the sense that I have suggested. Nor is this process limited to Judaism and Christianity. It is the way in which religions and faiths of all types have historically developed.

Of course some complete revolutionary may propose his own esoteric religious ideas or proclaim his own peculiar faith.

The men I am criticizing evidently do not much like such ideas or faiths, which they are likely to denounce as 'mysticism' or as erratic affirmations of eccentric individuals. But even if they did take a more favourable attitude, the fact would remain that the positive religions, as they used to be called in studies of religious phenomenonology—that is, the faiths or religions which grasp large numbers of people, make an impact on the world, and show a capacity to persist in some community form —are social in nature; grow out of a past which is not entirely rejected even when the great prophets, teachers, reformers, and renovators come along; and always, or almost always, take towards their supposed origins and their historical development a respectful if (thank heaven) not an uncritical stance.

And the same is true in what used to be called 'secular' areas, although that word has now become so ambiguous in meaning that one hesitates to use it. In philosophical development, A. N. Whitehead said, all western thought is 'a series of footnotes' to Plato's dialogues. Something like that is indeed the case; and only a very ignorant person would be prepared to deny the continuities, with genuine differences and, one hopes, genuine advances, in the total philosophical enterprise. Similarly, in scientific thought, where once again we are indebted to Whitehead, among others, for making clear to us the way in which such thought, along with the procedures it uses and the attitudes it takes, represents a genuine process of development and not sheer novelty entirely unrelated to the past. In social theory and its implementation in social structures, of which Marxism may serve for an example, we may observe the same sort of movement. Karl Marx himself was keenly conscious of this, as a study of *Das Kapital* will show; and, what is even more significant, his doctrine of the dialectic in history is a clear illustration of what I have been urging. Novelty, yes; but continuity, too. The *talk* may be about 'revolution', about the 'qualitative leap', but what happens is a development of social, economic, and political ordering out of the past, while the 'qualitative leap', as Marx himself remarked, comes from the accumulation of a quite enormous number of quantitative changes. It is not *sheer* novelty, although it is new; it is not *unthinking* continuity, although it is related to the past and builds upon, while it also greatly modifies, that which the past has done.

By my references to 'process' in the preceding remarks I have indicated that I stand within a certain philosophical school. Thus I begin my admission or confession of the approach, the materials, and the methods which I believe to be necessary in the indispensable job of re-conceiving the last things, along with re-conceiving the totality of the Christian theological tradition. First, then, a processive view of the world and everything in it; and along with that, what might be styled, perhaps daringly, a processive view of what-it-is or who-it-is that the term *God* points towards.

It is hardly necessary to state here what process thought has to say; and, in any event, I can refer those who do not know about it to a recent small book of my own, entitled *Process Thought and Christian Faith* (Macmillan, New York, and Nisbet, London, 1968), in which I attempted to give a brief sketch of that conceptuality with special reference to its availability for the enterprise of Christian re-conception. Perhaps sufficient will have been said if I point out that process thought is based upon wide generalizations made from those experiences of fact, and those facts of experience, which demonstrate to us the dynamic, active, on-going 'creative advance' of the world; and which, in recognizing and accepting the patent reality of such a world, sees man as part of it sharing in that movement, and a principle of ordering and direction, which may properly be called *God*, explaining why and how the advance goes on as it does.

God, so understood, is not only the chief causative principle, although He is not by any means the *only* such principle (since there is freedom of decision throughout the world-order); He is also the supreme affective reality, because what happens in the world, by precisely such free decision and its results, makes a difference to and (if we may put it so) contributes to the divine principle in providing further opportunities for advance as well as in enriching the experience of the divine itself or himself.

The world is a processive order; it is also a social one, in which everything in it affects everything else, from the lowest structures and forces up to man himself—and, says process thought, to God too. There is a mutual prehension by one occasion of other occasions, to the remotest point in space and time. That prehension may be positive or negative—a grasping and being grasped that accepts or rejects what is offered and being offered. Since God, on such a view, is not the great 'exception to all metaphysical principles to save them from collapse', in Whitehead's by now famous declaration, but is 'their chief exemplification', He too is in a real sense processive. But He is *chief* exemplification, not simply another one of the same sort as all others known to us. He is in some genuine fashion *eminent*. He is, as Charles Hartshorne would put it, 'the supremely worshipful', who is un-surpassed by anything which is not Himself; yet in His own life He may surpass, in richness of experience and capacity for adaptation and provision of new opportunity for advance, that which He has been. Hence God is supremely temporal rather than eternal in the common acceptation of the word, which usually is taken to mean utterly 'time-less'.

God works in the world by providing 'initial aims' for each occasion or event or occurrence or 'entity' (which was Whitehead's word); His 'power' is in His persuasion, in His 'lure' (which is also Whitehead's word), not in coercive force. In a word, 'his nature and his name is love'. Both Whitehead himself and his distinguished American exponent (who also makes his own distinctive contribution to process thought) Charles Hartshorne are very clear about this. It is these two who have been the fathers of this conceptuality, so far as English-speaking countries are concerned, although many others have assisted, some of them (like Teilhard de Chardin) from a quite different starting-point.

Whitehead once wrote that Christianity, unlike Buddhism, is a faith—based on certain historical events taken to be, in his own term used elsewhere, 'important' or crucial or disclosing —seeking a metaphysic. The fact is the total impact of the person of Christ, in whom Christianity finds 'the disclosure in act of what Plato discerned in theory'. And what is this? It is, again in his own words, that 'the divine nature and agency in the world' are precisely such love, such persuasion, such tenderness. Nor was this asserted without regard for the patent presence of evil, both in man himself and in those recalcitrant, negative, retarding, occasions, with their consequences, which anybody with his eyes open must admit. Hence, in its wholeness, the availability of process thought for use in Christian thinking: Christ as the disclosure of 'what God is up to' in the world.

But I have used the term 'metaphysic' and this can provoke an instant reaction from those who think that the day of metaphysics or of ontological statement is over. Here I should respond that *it all depends*. If by metaphysics or ontology one means either the construction of grandiose schemes in which some super-terrestrial being is set up as controlling the world, having once got it going, reducing the world to irrelevance or meaninglessness in comparison to his subsistence as absolute or *esse a se subsistens*, in Aquinas's phrase; or some privileged knowledge of the *what* of things behind all appearances, such as gives us a precise acquaintance with Kant's *ding an sich*, the realm of the noumenal as above, beyond, and unrelated (save by logical connection) to the phenomenal—if either of these be what metaphysics means, then its day is indeed past.

On the other hand, if by metaphysics one means exactly what I suggested earlier—the making of wide generalizations on the basis of particular experiences, the constant reference back of those generalizations to further areas of experience, and the resultant 'vision' of how things 'are' and how 'they go'—

then metaphysics is by no means finished. Even those who denounce metaphysics in the former sense are eminently metaphysical in the latter. One has only to read such 'anti-metaphysical' writers as the earlier positivists, whether Comteian or in the Vienna Circle with its English disciples known as 'logical positivists', to see how true this is. They indeed do have a metaphysic, in my second sense; but, if I may venture to say so, it is a very *bad* metaphysic since it is not recognized as such and hence has not been exposed by these thinkers to severe and searching criticism. The same is the case with the 'anti-metaphysical' theologians. Harvey Cox's *The Secular City* simply reeks of metaphysics, in that second sense; so does R. Gregor Smith's *Secular Christianity*—and admittedly Thomas Altizer's books are highly metaphysical in statement and intention, while William Hamilton for all his eschewing of metaphysics presupposes throughout his 'death of God' writing exactly the same sort of thing.

Thus I am not ashamed of the metaphysical emphasis in process thought, once it is seen what kind of metaphysics the process philosophers are talking about. Here there is no setting-up of a super-terrestrial, sheerly supra-natural, being called 'God'; since, in Whitehead's words, 'God is in this world or he is nowhere'. Here there is no claim to privileged access to the *ding an sich*, for any such dichotomy between noumenal and phenomenal is absurd—*what a thing is* is known in, and consists of, *what a thing does*; or, in Christian terms, we know God in terms of His activity in the world, working towards communities or societies of shared good in spite of the recalcitrance, the back-waters, the negativities, or compendiously 'the evil', with which he has to deal. And when the Dutch philosopher C. A. van Peursen in his exciting article called 'Man and Reality' (*Student World*, LVI, 1963) and others who think like him contrast the *ontological* and the *functional* and insist that metaphysics *must* mean the former attitude, they do not see that there is a sense in which this need not be said at all. How things go—their functioning—may be, and I believe it is, *what they are.* Thus, again in Christian terms, God *is* love precisely because He *acts lovingly*; and any statement of a formally abstract sort, such as the one I have just made—'God *is* love', etc.—is precisely what I have now called it: a formally abstract statement made on the basis of what are taken to be concrete events or occasions, and with validity only insofar as it affirms exactly such an understanding of the functioning which is observed, experienced, and hence must be talked about.

But I have said enough about all this. My main point is simply that I find process thought, with its view of God, eminently available for Christian use. Particularly, I find the view of God both as providing the 'initial aim' and also as being the 'supreme affect' most suggestive and helpful. In respect to the deep significance seeking expression through the traditional teaching about the last things, I find this conceptuality so suggestive and so helpful that it will provide a framework within which I shall try to urge a way of securing for ourselves those meanings or values or existentially significant affirmations.

The mention of 'existentialism' here, while I intended it in a slightly different way, brings us to the second point which I wish to make. This has to do with the interpretation of Scripture. More especially, it has to do with the enterprise known as 'de-mythologization', in relation to what the father of that enterprise calls *existenzialinterpretation* of the biblical material and most importantly of the material that has to do with the *kerygma* or the Christian gospel to which faith is a response.

I think that the word '*de*-mythologizing', in its English form, does not do justice to what Bultmann really intends; and it is a puzzle to me why he has accepted this term as a satisfactory English description of the enterprise which in German is styled *entmythologisierung*. Admittedly the English term does translate the German, but at the same time the '*de-*' suggests to the English reader almost exactly the opposite of Bultmann's intention. For what he wishes to do is not to discard the mythological material—mistaken science, talk about the divine in this-world idiom, highly fanciful material about descent and ascent of a supernatural divine being who pre-existed this world, etc., etc.—but to get at what it is *really* saying. I think that the term *in*-mythologizing would serve better, since the whole programme is concerned to get 'inside' the myth and there discover the *kerygma* or gospel which the myth clothes and states in a form natural at one time but impossible, because incredible, today. It is not necessary for me to recount *why* Bultmann finds this incredibility in the form; suffice it to say that he is not committed to any particular scientific world-view, although Jaspers and others have charged him with this, but is simply stating that the contemporary man does not as a matter of fact think or talk in terms of such a form. Hence, if the gospel is to speak to him with its demand for decision, it must be freed from those thought-patterns so that its essential *drive* may be made clear to him, a drive or proclamation in action which the ancient forms today succeed in covering up or making absurd.

I ought here to admit that I should wish to go beyond Bultmann; I agree with Fritz Buri and his American exponent Schubert Ogden that we need also to *in-kerygmatize*, if I may put it so, the gospel proclamation itself. But this does not suggest that there *is* no gospel and that Jesus Christ is not central to Christian faith. What is involved here is exactly what the ancient 'Fathers', or some of them, affirmed when they spoke of the possibility of salvation for those who had never heard about and hence could not or did not respond to the specific historic event of Jesus Christ. The work of the Eternal Word of God, present in men spermatically, as Justin Martyr for example put it, offered this possibility of salvation, so that the historical accident of having lived *after* Jesus or having heard about Him was not the necessary condition of the salvation which God purposed for His human children. These 'Fathers' spoke of the specific activity of God in Jesus Christ as being indeed the fulfilment, completion, and adequate expression, *vis-à-vis* men, of the Eternal Word of God, but they did not regard salvation as available *only* through Jesus; even in the Fourth Gospel, it would seem to be the writer's intention to have the *Word* speak, rather than the historical Jesus in isolation from that Word 'who was in the beginning with God', 'by whom all things were made', 'who was the light of every man', and who in Jesus Christ was decisively 'made flesh and dwelt among us'.

In the sort of language which Bultmann and Buri would employ, the possibility of authentic existence before God, in which men live in faith and with love, is granted to every man by virtue of his being human. This Bultmann would deny; this Buri would affirm. I should agree with Buri and I should say that the point of the Christian gospel is to 're-present', as Ogden puts it, that possibility; to 're-present' it in starkly human terms, under human conditions, in Jesus as what I like to style 'the classic instance' of what God is always 'up to', rather than the totally other or the sheer anomaly, as so many (including Bultmann, presumably) would wish to regard him.

What is important for our present purposes in Bultmann's enterprise, however, is the insistence on getting at what the biblical material is saying without our being obliged at the same time to accept for ourselves the form in which it is said. It is exactly this method which I wish to employ as we continue in succeeding chapters to discuss the truth found in the last things. Or once again, in Leonard Hodgson's way of phrasing it, we are trying to find what the state of things really is, how things really go, in a fashion which makes sense to us, when we grant that men and women who lived at *that* time, under *those* conditions, with *those* presuppositions, spoke about the matter in *that* way.

Furthermore, this kind of approach will free us from supposing that because this or that particular description of man's destiny is found stated in this or that particular way in Holy Scripture, we are obliged to accept it as necessarily 'the case'. This applies, I should claim, not only to Old Testament material and the literature of the New Testament apart from the gospels. It also applies to Jesus' own teaching. He was a Jew, He thought and spoke like a Jew; this is part of His being 'very man', as Chalcedon said He was. Hence with His own statements, so far as they are His own, such a 'proportionate interpretation', in a fine phrase from Bishop Westcott, is required quite as much as it is required for other pieces of biblical teaching.

I also wish to stress the importance for us, in this enterprise, of the social and psychosomatic understanding of man which has been so wonderfully recovered in recent years. The biblical perspective in regard to 'corporate personality' is now restored in quite 'secular' circles; to be a person *means* to be intimately and essentially related with other men. 'No man is an island entire unto himself'; and to come to know our personal humanity is to see it in its rich relationship with other persons. Atomistic views of man will no longer serve, not because we dislike them but because they are not accurate statements of a truth which is known to us in our deepest human existence. And with this stress on 'the body corporate' goes also an emphasis on man's corporeal nature. We are not 'souls' inhabiting 'bodies'; we are psychosomatic organisms, more or less integrated entities in which bodily existence is characterized by the capacity to think, to feel, to will. Here again it is not because we prefer this view; it is because, so far as we can understand ourselves and what human existence is like, we see it to be true. We owe much here to the depth psychologists and equally to those who in medical work have shown the relationship of mental processes to bodily ones. Man is an organic unity, however adequately or inadequately this is actualized in a given person's experience.

Furthermore, we belong to and with our environment. The *mit-welt* of which Heidegger speaks is not confined to our fellow-men; it includes the realm of nature as well, since we are 'organic to nature', as Pringle-Pattison insisted many years ago. The evolutionary perspective makes this apparent; our animal origin demonstrates it. This is why we cannot follow certain existentialist writers in speaking about human history as if it were being played out against a background of irrelevant natural recurrence. Nature itself, the whole world of stuff or matter, is *there* and we are somehow part of it. We ought not to attempt to separate human experience and history from nature, but rather to see that nature itself is historical—by which I mean that it is processive, with movement and change, even if on the macrocosmic scale this does not seem obvious to us. The sort of philosophical conceptuality which I urged upon you earlier is from one point of view merely an affirmation of exactly that kind of historical view of the whole world-process. But for our present purpose, it is enough to say that when we are thinking about the last things, our thought must include much more than human existence and human personality in its body-mind totality, even in its social relationships. The realm of nature itself must be in the picture.

I am not competent to speak about what may be contributed to us by the depth-psychologies which I have just mentioned. Harry Williams has written a useful little book on *The Last Things* in which he does just this; and I refer you to that book as well as to other essays, by him and by such writers as the late David Roberts, for some development of this theme. But insofar as this psychology talks of man's deep emotional drives, his purposive activity, his striving for realization of selfhood, his need to love and to be able to receive love, and with these the twistings and distortings which may be uncovered in him— insofar as it does this, it helps us see something of what true fulfilment is about and has much to say concerning such actualization of man, with man's consequent 'satisfaction' and the joy which it provides, about which in an entirely different idiom the heavenly city was a picture. At the same time, the horror of hell, as real deprivation on the part of those who were loveless, because they could not love nor accept love, finds its parallel in the state of lovelessness and hence of utter despair, concerning which this psychology has so much to say.

My final point has been implied in everything that has so far been advanced. This is the practical consequences in actual and concrete human living which may be found in coming to some awareness of what the last things were trying to say. God, as chief causative principle and as supreme affect, is 'in this world or he is nowhere'; biblical material, and in relation to it Christian liturgical and hymnological imagery, with the theological articulation of this, intend to make affirmations which are to be found *in* the pictures and forms and myths— and these we must seek to make meaningful and valid for ourselves in our present existence; man is an 'embodied' and a social occasion or series (or 'routing') of occasions, organic to the world of nature, and can only truly *live* as he lives in due recognition of these facts and sees them as integral to himself. Each of these points, which we have so far discussed, along with whatever of value is to be found in the psychological analysis to which I have just referred, speaks directly to us as and where and when we *are*.

In other words, the talk about the last things is not only, if it is at all, talk about something that happens in an imagined future state, once we have died the death which each man must die. It is talk about us as we now live, in this world and with this world's responsibilities as well as its privileges. From one point of view, it might be said that futuristic references are by way of being *aberglaube*—'over-beliefs' which may or may not be necessary consequences of what is said about the here-and-now as Christian faith interprets it.

I do not wish to deny those futuristic references, as I have called them. In a later chapter I shall have something to say about them, although I shall emphasize that they belong to the realm which our ancestors used to describe as 'a religious hope' rather than to the realm of verifiable experience or the realm of concrete Christian existence as we are called to share it. I do wish to stress, however, the reference to concrete and actual existence *now*.

Many years ago, when James Pike and I were commissioned

to prepare, for the Authors' Committee of the Division of Christian Education of the Episcopal Church, a book which would state in fairly simple fashion the 'faith of the Church' (so the book was entitled when finally it appeared, after much revision and re-writing), we talked with Bishop Angus Dun of Washington about the project. The two authors, with the whole membership of the committee charged with preparing the book, visited Bishop Dun and spent with him an entire day. We discussed the plan of the volume, the subjects to be included, and other such topics. I shall never forget Bishop Dun's repeated insistence that in approaching each topic, we must see to it that the main emphasis was always on what he called, as I remember it, 'what this means for living as a Christian today'. The particular topic upon which he first made this comment was the doctrine of creation; and he said that the only way in which this could properly be approached was by being as clear as we could about what it means to a man 'to be a creature, living in a created world' with all that this implies, entails, and suggests.

I do not wish to father on Bishop Dun what I am trying to suggest in these pages, but I think that the point which he made at that time is highly relevant to what we are attempting to do here. What did the last things *mean* to men and women who accepted the scheme quite literally or with this or that reservation or re-interpretation? What is the deepest *meaning* in that scheme, which because it is somehow integral to the Christian faith we must seek to guarantee and preserve in our re-conception and re-statement of that faith? What does this *mean* for you and for me, for any Christian? And finally what can it *be made to mean*, without cheating or falsification, for every man and woman who wants to come to that profound self-understanding which is the other side of (and utterly integral to) the understanding of God *vis-à-vis* man?

So in the next chapter we shall begin by thinking about death.

THREE

Death

Many years ago a visiting preacher at the General Theological Seminary—I *think* it was Allan Whittemore, then superior of the Order of the Holy Cross—began his sermon with some words which startled the congregation into almost shocked attention. The words were these, as I remember them: 'Everyone of you within sound of my voice will, within not too many years, be a corpse'. The sermon which followed was the one sermon about death and its meaning that I have ever heard preached; I noted that one sermon earlier.

I confess that I have entirely forgotten what the preacher said after his striking first sentence. But that sentence I have never forgotten, nor can I; since it made me face, for the first time and with utter seriousness, the absolutely inescapable fact that *I* was going to die. Of course I had always known that *men* died, and in a sense I was well aware of my own death as one of those men. What that sentence did, however, was to make me starkly conscious of the fact that not only do *men* die but that I, in my concrete actual human existence, faced death too. In a way, it was a realization of what Martin Luther meant when he said that every man dies *alone*—in his particularity, in what Whitehead called, in another connection, his 'solitariness'. That is, it was I, Norman Pittenger, then a young man and a somewhat eager theological student, looking forward to a long and I hoped successful span of years, who was brought face to face with the inevitability of my own entirely personal death.

Now the fact that each of us dies alone, in his 'solitariness', as this or that particular person, does not for a moment signify that we do not belong to the human race, exist in relationship with our fellowmen, and find the meaning of our lives not in isolation but in solidarity with others. Far from doing that, it emphasizes our belonging, relationship, and solidarity, since it makes plain that in this mortal existence of ours, before that 'moment of truth'—not the *only* such moment, but a determinative one in so many ways—which is our own death, we can find our deepest satisfactions and our best fulfilment only in companionship and in the giving-and-receiving which is love. Once we know that we are to die, each for himself and each by himself, we are brought to value all the more highly and treasure all the more carefully that companionship and that giving-and-receiving which is life in loving. Every moment of our existence before death is now coloured by the realization, however dim it may be at any given moment, that *now* is the time 'the accepted time', if I may use here St Paul's phrase in a very different context—when we must find ourselves in others and become what nowadays we have learned to style a man 'for others'.

Death is not simply a biological fact. Obviously it *is* that, since as a matter of human biology men do and must die. As Heidegger has said, death is indeed human life in its finality; and, in a very profound sense, all of our existence is 'towards death', precisely as a biological fact which we must accept. Yet it is not *this* sense, the straightforward biological reality, which gives to the fact of our dying both its high significance and its peculiar poignancy. What does that is the related and equally inescapable truth that death is also 'the finality of human life'. By this I mean that it is the qualifying of human life in such a way that we know ourselves to be mortal men who have no claim to anything else and who must honestly and bravely face the truth of their mortality. If they do not do so, they are less than men. Someone has said that a distinguishing factor, as between human life and animal life, is that while the animals die, as do we, they do not know that they are going to die, whereas we die, as do they, but we know that we are going to do so.

Not only does each man die, and because he is going to die recognize himself as mortal, but all men, each for himself and as himself, are also to die. Thus it is not only *I* who know myself to be mortal; every other man, and all men together constituting the human race, are able only to understand himself and themselves, when the mortality which I am stressing is accepted for what it is.

If we agree, as surely we must, that the one inescapable and inevitable fact about every man and about the whole race of men is this death, we should also agree that it is in no sense morbid to face up to it and endeavour to come to terms with it. On the contrary, it is the measure of our humanity that we live daily as those who know that they are going to die, and hence are mortal, and that we can, as it were, adjust ourselves to that stupendous fact.

Indeed, at no time in his history has man been content to consider death 'a mere incident', however much he has been tempted to do so and however many times he has sought to cover up the fact in one way or another. Or, if this statement seems too extreme, at least we can affirm confidently that those who have thought longest and deepest about human life have never been able to dismiss death in a cavalier manner. They have seen it, rather, as a tremendous event which is to be regarded seriously and respectfully, often fearfully; and, if they have been 'religious' in any sense, they would add that they must approach death and regard its importance faithfully, too. In recent years, more especially, we have learned to take death with high seriousness, not only because there has been so much of it through war and famine and other ills but also because our literature, whether in poetry or novel or drama, has been so conscious of the fact and so insistent on bringing it to our attention. In this there has been a return to the attitude of an earlier day, although with marked differences because of loss of faith or enfeebling of it. The easy dismissal of death, or the assertion that 'for those who believe, there is no death', is taken to be, what it often is, an easy evasion of the dread reality itself—escapism, childish refusal to face facts, and above all (in our special interest) unwillingness to accept our human mortality.

Death is *there*, then. The question is, how can we come to terms with it?

Death is not there alone; it is there, as I have argued, with a finality about it. For if it is true, on the one hand, that death is the end of human existence for each and every one of us, it is on the other equally true (to repeat the words I have already used) that death is human life in its finality. That is, it is the distinctive event which colours, conditions, and qualifies every moment of our existence. And as I have also said a few moments ago, man is the only animal, so far as we know, who is aware of his mortality and who may therefore meditate on the fact that he dies. He who has never pondered this truth, and, in this sense, if in no other, 'prepared for death', is by that token less than a true man. His life is less than authentic; it is properly to be described, by the phrase that Heidegger uses, 'inauthentic'—that is, false, based on wrong understanding, cheapened and superficial. Such a man is living under an illusion because he is out of touch with 'things as they are' in human existence.

One of the most familiar ways in which people seek to evade both death *as* finality and the finality *of* death is through the notion of the 'immortal soul' which 'survives' the fact of our biological death. The ideas associated with that notion are specifically Greek in origin, so far as our culture and our Christian theological development are concerned. We are well aware of this ancestry. The classical statement of the notion is to be found, of course, in the speeches which Plato records from Socrates, or which he has put into the mouth of Socrates, in the dialogues which tell of the last days and death of that great and noble man.

The rational principle in man is individuated; it inhabits a corporeal 'house' for this present time. But since it is one and simple it is indestructible. It participates, in some mode, in the eternal realm of forms, although it is not identified with that realm. When a man's body dies and suffers corruption, the soul is not affected by this occurrence; it 'escapes' from the body which is dying and returns to its true abode. Thus no matter what may happen to the body, man's soul is immortal and since it is *this* which constitutes his distinctive human quality, death is an important and tragic incident, certainly to those who loved and cared for the one who dies, but it is not a final incident—there is more to come, so to say.

The old American song,

> *John Brown's body lies a-mouldering in the grave,*
> *His* soul *goes marching on* . . .'

puts the idea succinctly and popularly.

A great many Christians have thought that this was the teaching of the Christian faith on the subject. They have confused 'immortality of the soul' with whatever may be intended by the biblical phrase 'resurrection of the body'; while theologians have attempted, as we have already observed, when I described the older scheme which comprised the last things, to bring the two conceptions together in a fashion which will retain each of them and yet relate them so that a consistent pattern may be provided. But of course the two conceptions cannot be brought together in that way; and the internal conflicts, the lack of balance, and the arbitrary way in which the two have been associated, demonstrate this plainly enough. We shall have something to say about 'the resurrection of the body' at a later point. For the present, my argument is simply that the talk about 'immortality of the soul' has served to provide for a great many Christian people what they wrongly took to be the right and proper Christian way of escaping the stark reality of total death.

Years ago, in my course in Apologetics in the General Seminary, I put what I take to be the truth of the matter in the

following words: 'We all die; and all of us dies.' Perhaps that
was too glib a phrase; and I know that, when my students
repeated it to their friends, and later in their ministry to their
parishioners, my intention was misunderstood by the auditors.
Yet I remain convinced that what I was seeking to say in that
phrase is the truth. And it is the truth which traditional talk
about the last things has served to emphasize, however uncomfortable it may be and however men may have sought to
evade it. All of us *do* die; that we know. And all *of us* does die—
that is the point which I am now making.

In the Old Testament we find that even the Jews could not
quite easily find their way to accept this. *Sheol* was certainly
not much of an existence; in that dim realm, 'the dead praise
not thee, O Lord', we read. And for a Jew a 'state' in which
God could not be praised was hardly a condition of genuine
life. But apart from the teaching about *sheol*, borrowed or
inherited from more primitive modes of religious thought, the
Jew at least was prepared to recognize the full reality of death.
Until the time of the Maccabees, Jewish faith was not dependent upon nor did it presuppose a kind of 'immortality' or
'resurrection', call it what you will, which alone made it possible to commit oneself wholly to Jahweh and to the doing of
his holy will. And I should say that this plain fact of Old Testament faith stands as a judgement upon any effort in more
recent times to insist that *unless* 'immortality' or 'resurrection'
—again call it what you will—is in the picture, there can be no
deep and genuine faith at all. Christians may wish to say something more, but they simply must not suppose that God, faith
in Him, commitment to Him, service of Him, *and* a denial of
the reality and inescapability of death go together. Above all,
they must not suppose that it is integral to faith in God, with
its consequences, to believe that all *of us* (in the special sense I
have given that phrase) does not die.

While this is the fact, the very reality of our mortality has
emphasized our responsibility for what we do and thus what
we are during the time which we have. 'We shall not pass this

way again'; yet while we are *in via*, as St Augustine puts it, we have both our duty to fulfil and our contribution, such as it may be, to make to the ongoing creative advance of the cosmos. That contribution may be very slight, to all appearances, but it is *ours* to make—and unless *we* make it, it will not be made. This statement introduces us to other ideas, about which something must be said in another context. Among these is the point that with the 'perishing of occasions', as Whitehead has described *one* side of the process, there is also the reception into God and hence both the preservation and use, of whatever good has been achieved within the process itself, to the end that the advance may continue, that further good may be actualized, and that the purpose of God (which is just that actualization of good, through love which is shared in the widest conceivable degree) may be realized in more places and times and in more ways. That is the *other* side of the 'perishing of occasions' which includes our own perishing through the inevitability of the death which awaits us.

In St Paul's letter to the Romans there is a celebrated and much discussed passage: I quote it in the version found in the New English Bible: 'It was through one man that sin entered the world, and through sin death, and thus death pervaded the whole human race, inasmuch as all men have sinned.' Or, in the Revised Standard Version: 'Therefore as sin came into the world through one man and death through sin, and so death spread to all men because all men sinned' (Romans 5:12). The meaning of this passage has been a matter of dispute among New Testament experts, although it is quite obvious that if it does nothing more it asserts that the Apostle believed that there was some connection between the fact of death and the reality of human sin. But whether he intended to tell his readers that death, as a biological fact, is the consequence of one man's sin (namely, Adam's) becoming contagious and hence affecting all men, is by no means entirely certain. Some think he intended to say just this; others seem to believe that St Paul is working up towards his plainly stated conviction that

sin in itself *is* death—shall we say, death as loss of God whose
service is not only, as the collect tells us, 'perfect freedom', but
also true *life* as men are intended by God to live it.

If the latter be the correct interpretation, then 'the sting' in
death, as a biological happening which all of us must experience, is to be found in man's sin which is his alienation or
separation from God. It is not that because Adam, or anybody
else, or the whole race of men, have sinned that they come to
die; rather, it is that in facing death, as they must, they know
themselves to be in a fashion *already* dead, because to live as
'the enemy of God' is really to be a dead man, however 'alive'
one's physical body might be.

Whatever St Paul was trying to communicate about his own
belief, there has been a strain in the Christian tradition which
has taken the first of the two meanings and has talked as if
death were the punishment inflicted on man for his failure to
obey God's commands. Had Adam not sinned, it has been
said, man would have been immortal, although what this
might entail has not been worked out in any great detail. The
second of the two possible meanings has been stressed by
another strain in the Christian tradition, with more probability
so far as our human experience can guide us. And it is this
aspect which seems to me to be of significance for us as we see
what the scheme which included death among the last things
has to say to *us*.

At this point it would be desirable to spend considerable
time in discussing the meaning of the word 'sin' itself, but we
shall not do that. I take it that we shall agree that 'sin' does *not*
denote the various particular acts of this or that man which in
some ways contravene God's purpose—the sort of acts with
which codes and commandments and sets of rules or laws
concern themselves. These are manifestations of something
more basic—and that more basic 'something' is what we are
getting at when we speak about 'sin'. I should define this in
two ways; or rather, in one definition with two aspects.

First, sin is a condition or state or situation in human

existence in which men find themselves impotent before the requirements which they see, however dimly, are laid upon them simply by virtue of their being men. It is a 'grace-less' state, as one might put it; because it is a state in which there is failure in harmonizing the ideal and the actual, failure in integration of the self—always, mind you, the self in its relation with others, for we know of no other human selfhood—and failure to move towards the actualization of the possibilities which are present as the 'initial aim' of our lives is made into the 'subjective aim' (in Whiteheadian language) whose realization constitutes our 'becoming' in manhood.

That is one aspect of the meaning of sin—it is the humanly understood side. The other aspect is introduced when we are aware, as we ought to be, that God's purpose for man, as Paul Lehmann has so admirably told us, is 'to make and keep us human'. That condition or state or situation in which we are *not* realizing our subjective aim and find ourselves impotent in the face of the requirements which it makes upon us may be summed up simply by saying that although we are made to become men, we do not actually get very far along the path, knowing ourselves to be both incompetent and impotent, however grand may be our projects and however optimistic may be our hopes. God's purpose for us, his will, is nothing other than that we should become ourselves as he initially aims us to become—and I have put it in this somewhat clumsy way because I wish to stress the *aim* which is integral to human nature.

Sin, the noun in the singular, is a religiously freighted term whose purpose is to point to *that* state: our failure to become what we are created to become and hence our failure to 'obey' God's command which is precisely that we shall become what we are created to become. With that definition in mind, we may (if we wish—and moral theologians *have* wished) go on to speak of the particular acts, in thought or word or deed, in which this situation manifests itself. But as every sensitive person ought to know and as every counsellor (and every priest who has 'heard confessions') does know, man's root problem is not in these particular acts. They are symptomatic of something much more serious and those who think that by dealing with symptoms they have cured a disease are only deluding themselves and harming the patient. The disease, if the word may be permitted, is the situation or state or condition which I have described and it is *that* which requires attention. One central element in the Christian gospel is the affirmation that in a very real way God deals with that situation—this is the meaning of what we call redemption or salvation or atonement.

For the moment, however, that is not our concern. Our concern is that the fact of human death, as an inescapable biological event which is also the qualification of our humanity as mortal, brings vividly before us something else. It makes us realize, with a startling clarity and with sometimes terrible anguish, that *at our best* we are mortal failures. I quite realize that this may seem an exaggerated, even an emotive, way of stating it; but I am quite sure that any honest man or woman, conscious of his mortality, is also conscious of the fact that he is not what he might have been, that he cannot shift the blame to somebody else's shoulders (however many extenuating circumstances he may feel justified in adducing), and that, in at least one sense, the sense I have indicated above, he *is* a mortal failure. 'I am an unprofitable servant, for I have done only what was commanded of me'—yes, but more than that, 'I am a *very* unprofitable servant, for I have not even done, nor been competent and willing to do, that which was commanded of me.'

This at once introduces us to the responsibility which is ours, as men, to become what we are intended to become. Such responsibility is not imposed upon us from without, by some alien agent or a *deus ex machina*; it is the law of our being or, in much better language, the law for our becoming. If it were thrust on us from outside, it might be only a threat with penalty attached. Because it is integral to our very 'routing', to ourselves as a series of occasions constituting our personality-in-the-making, it is a lure or an enticement or solicitation. But our failure involves penalties, none the less. The penalties are not imposed from outside, either, as if by an alien agent or a *deus ex machina*. They are the ineluctable working-out, in our own existence, of decisions which have been made by us in whatever freedom we possessed. And those decisions, as Robert Frost once wrote of 'The Road Not Taken', 'have made the difference'.

God is love: every Christian would agree with that Johannine affirmation, based as it is on the certainty that God *acts lovingly*: 'Herein is love, not that *we* loved God, but that he loved us, and sent his Son that we might live through him.' I wish to gather together what so far has been said and relate it to this basic Christian affirmation of God as love, 'pure unbounded love', and nothing but that sheer love-in-action.

We die, physically. All of us dies. Death, as giving our existence its specific quality, shows us to be mortal, along with all our fellow-men. This mortality includes the responsibility that we shall become what we were created to be, which is authentic or true men, fully and completely human. Our failure to become what is initially our aim, and subjectively our intentional aim as well, means that we are, in at least one sense, precisely *that*—viz., 'failures'—although God may, and Christians at least believe that He does, deal with that situation if we permit Him to do so. These things the fact of death makes clear.

This is what we have been saying so far in this chapter. But now, as I have said, we turn to what I might call, as I heard a young man put it, 'this love business which Christians talk about'. How, it must be asked, does *that* come into the picture? My own reply would be that it comes in at every point and in every way. Far from being an addition, it is the very heart of the matter. For as God *is* love, so that the affirmation of His love is no afterthought or addendum to a series of propositions about His omnipotence, omniscience, omnipresence, transcendence, etc.; in similar manner in respect to human nature and activity, to human becoming, to human existence as such,

love is no addendum, no afterthought, no extra, but the central
reality itself. This needs development, however. The mere
statement of it will not suffice.

Man is intended to be a lover. It is for this purpose that he
comes into existence and it is for this purpose that he lives.
This may seem to be sheer sentimentality; but it can only seem
so when we do not properly understand the nature of love. In
another place I have attempted to provide what might be
styled a phenomenology of love (*Love Looks Deep*, Mowbrays,
1969). In that book, written for the general public and not for
scholars, I suggested that love includes the following elements
or aspects: commitment, mutuality, fidelity, hopefulness,
union—and that its goal is fulfilment in and with another or
with others. It is obvious that none of us is a 'perfect lover', for
none of us achieves anything like perfection in these several
ways in which love *is* and in which love *expresses itself*. But the
question to be asked is not whether we are thus 'perfect'. The
answer to *that* question is plain enough. The question which
ought to be faced is whether we are *moving towards* fulfilment,
with our fellows, in the several ways which love includes in
itself. In other words, are we *becoming lovers*? Is our actualization of the potentialities within us in the direction of our
becoming more committed, more open to giving-and-receiving,
more faithful, more hopeful in relation with others, more in
union with them? And we have only this mortal span in which
to *become* in this way, for death always stands as the end, the
terminus, of our loving and of our mortal learning to love.

Our human responsibility is to become what we are intended
to become. Thus that responsibility is that we shall become the
lovers we were meant to be. Our tragic situation is that we fail,
at so many places, in so many times, and in so many ways. It is
not only that we are frustrated in this. The frustration may be
due to the concrete conditions in which our existence is set;
about that we can often do little or nothing. Nor is it found in
the fact that within the space of years which is ours we are
frustrated in another sense, the sense (namely) that we do not

have time, as we say, to bring to fruition that which we would
wish to accomplish. The frustrations such as I have just mentioned, and other frustrations like them, are inhibiting factors
but they are not the decisive factors. What is decisive is whether
we are or are not open, within the imposed limits, to the loving,
the receiving love, the life in love, which will make us into
authentic men whose very authenticity is in their 'becoming
in love'.

It is astounding to notice that popular songs, so often con-
temptuously dismissed by the sophisticated and so frequently
condemned as cheap or vulgar or sentimental or lustful by those
who think of themselves as 'religious', have got hold of the
truth which I have been suggesting, while the sophisticated
and the self-consciously 'religious' fail to see what this is all
about. It is so easy to dismiss this sort of lyric because it is
usually replete with sexual allusions. Yet this may be the
importance of the popular song—and that for the reason that
human sexuality and the capacity to love (in all the aspects
which I have listed) are closely associated. Repression of sexuality can produce precisely the lovelessness which is man's
chief trouble, while the expression of sexuality, under the
control of love in its aim to be related in mutuality to another
or to others, can be a way for realizing love—and realizing it
both as a matter of consciously grasped experience and also as
a concrete movement towards the fulfilment of self in association with others of our race.

I may refer here, perhaps immodestly, to the book which I
just mentioned, where I have sought to show how this comes to
be, while in still another book, *The Christian Understanding of
Human Nature* (Westminster, Philadelphia, and Nisbet, London, 1964), I tried to relate the theme to Christian theology in
a wider sense. Daniel Day Williams, too, in his *The Spirit and
the Forms of Love* (Harper and Row, New York, and Nisbet,
London, 1968) has worked on the same lines. With these books,
and especially Dr Williams's, in mind, I shall not pursue this
subject here.

I must make one further point, however. We are thinking about the traditional scheme of the last things and we are doing this as those who in some fashion would wish to confess ourselves as Christians. For us, then, the faith in God enters the picture in a special way. God *is* love, we have said; He has declared this love in His loving action in the total event of Jesus Christ. Let us not forget that this love, declared in action, went to the limit of identification with humanity. Not only is God present in and with men, through his activity in the man Jesus—and elsewhere too, in varying degree and mode. God is also participant in the death which every man must die. To put it mythologically, as nowadays many would phrase it, God in Christ experiences everything in human existence including the death which puts an end to it. 'He learned by the things which he suffered'—and the Greek of that text suggests that what is meant by 'suffered' is what we should call 'experienced' or 'underwent'.

So the love which was worked out in human terms in the life of the Man of Nazareth was a love which knew mortality in its fullness, of body and of soul. It knew the responsibility of becoming itself, completely authentic and therefore entirely free, under those conditions and in that fashion. It is our faith that in that Man it did not 'fail', not because it had peculiar privileges or unique divine prerogatives, but because it held fast to its 'initial aim', making that its own 'subjective aim' and thus through 'the travail' which mortal existence imposed upon it finding the 'satisfaction' or fulfilment which was its destiny. To participate in that love which is humanly worked out in Jesus is truly to live in authenticity. Christian life, I should urge upon you, is just that authentic life in love. Because it is 'life in love', shared with Jesus Christ as the One who did thus realize and actualize love-in-action, it is also 'life in Christ'. And since life in Christ, shared with His human brethren, is both the reflection of and participation in the life which is truly divine—*God's* life—such 'life in love' is 'life in God', for God *is* love.

But none of this is possible without our facing the reality of our dying, any more than it was possible for Him whom we call our Lord and Master. To put it figuratively, the triumph of Easter Day is achieved in and on the Cross of Good Friday—it is not some 'happy ending' which cancels out the suffering that preceded it. Easter triumph in love is God's writing his 'O.K. That's the way things are and that's the way I am'—writing it across the tree on which Jesus hung on that fateful day.

For us this means that we must undertake the responsibility of loving, for that and that only makes possible the authenticity of living. In some lines that W. H. Auden once wrote, in *Letters from Iceland*, there is a compelling statement of this responsibility as it reflects itself in the call, so well known to us today, to social action in the world where we live out our days.

> *And to the good, who know how wide the gulf, how deep*
> *Between ideal and real, who being good have felt*
> *The final temptation to withdraw, sit down, and weep,*
> *We pray the power to take upon themselves the guilt*
> *Of human action, though still as ready to confess*
> *The imperfection of what can and must be built—*
> *The wish and power to act, forgive, and bless.*

FOUR

Judgement

In speaking of the momentous significance of the fact of death, not only as the *finis* or clear terminus of earthly life for every man and for the whole race of men, but also as the event which qualifies and colours each life, we introduced in our conclusion the possibility and the necessity of love.

Man is made to become a lover, we said. In this mortal existence, known as such by reason of our dying, this 'becoming' is frustrated by factors which prevent its complete realization, but much more importantly for each of us the failure in loving is due to our own incompetence and our own impotence in accepting love, both as a giving and as a receiving of self in the mutuality which love is. For this we must somehow shoulder the responsibility, since we know deep within ourselves that we *are* indeed responsible. However difficult it may have been, however many obstacles circumstances set in its way, man senses that he *could* have loved more than he did. A mature man is prepared to accept the responsibility for his not having responded to the opportunities of loving which in various ways, some great and some small, were open to him. Death is there; and it makes it plain to each man that during his mortal span he has both the opportunity and the duty to love.

What on earth and sky can *judgement*, with which in this chapter we are concerned, have to do with *love*? Perhaps that is the first question which we may feel obliged to ask. My answer would be in the Pauline phrase, 'much every way'.

45

One of the reasons, if not the only one, that this question can be asked is that we are the victims of a sentimentalized notion of love and its manner of working. I have commended popular songs for their stress on love and I have said that one thing about them that I find valuable is their association of love and sexual desire. This is commonly regarded as what is wrong about them; on the contrary, in my view, this is what is right about them. The thing that I believe is often wrong is not their use of sexual images and their talk about sexual desire, but the tendency (in some of the songs at least) to sentimentalize love. By this I mean to make it seem soft, cosy, sweet, comforting, and nothing else.

But it is not in such songs that we discover the worst manifestations of this tendency. It is in the devaluation of the very word itself, which for so many of our contemporaries, and even in many Christian circles, has come to suggest a kind of sloppiness, a simple and quite uncritical acquiescence in anything and everything. In that common misunderstanding of love we discover exactly the softness, the cosiness, about which I have spoken. Thus love becomes niceness. It is taken to be sweet, which indeed it is, but it is not grasped as being 'bitter sweet', if I may use here the title of one of Noel Coward's songs, found in a musical play of the same name. It has not seen the truth in the Spanish folk proverb, that 'to make love is to declare one's sorrows'; nor has it noticed that the deepest expressions of love are not only painful to the one who loves but can also make inexorable demands on the one who is loved —demands which are not arbitrary and certainly not coercive in their manner of expression, but which are inexorable none the less, since they expect of the beloved the full and complete realization of all his possibilities as a lover.

The sort of love about which I was speaking in the last chapter is such love as was shown in Christ, who 'having loved his own that were in the world, loved them unto the end' . . . the end of death on their behalf, which demanded (again, let us recall, in no arbitrary and coercive way) the response from them of a returning love which would show itself in their loving one another. The discourses put in Jesus' mouth by the Fourth Evangelist and the remarkable summary found in the fourth chapter of the first Johannine epistle are very pointed here— love is seen both in its wonder of identification and its mutuality in giving and receiving *and* also in its strange inexorability.

Love *hurts*, too. The identification to which I have just referred is no easy affair; it implies and it involves such a total sharing that the pain experienced by the one who is loved is also the pain of the one who loves. And even more profoundly, the anguish in such identification is the more terrible when the lover knows deeply and inescapably, as in all honesty he must, the failures of the one who is loved. These too he shares; and the anguish is compounded when, knowing these failures— these defects and lacks, shall we say?—he *still* loves. As St Paul tells us in the most famous of all the bits of his epistles, 'there is nothing love cannot face; there is no limit to its faith, its hope, and its endurance'. And he adds (I am using in my quotation the New English Bible) that 'love will never come to an end'—it never fails, as we more usually quote the Pauline passage. Or, in our own idiom, 'love can and does *take it*'.

Once we have come to understand that love is like that, we shall never be guilty of sentimentalizing. We shall see that love is comfortable in the meaning of that word in Elizabethan times: it is strengthening and invigorating. It is thus comfortable precisely because it has 'gone through many waters' which have not defeated and cannot 'drown it'; it is 'terrible as an army with banners', not because like such an army it uses force, but because it is in itself the only really strong thing in the whole world and in human experience. It is strong *because* it is patient, not strong in spite of its requiring patience.

Now all of what I have been saying ought to be perfectly obvious to anybody who professes and calls himself a Christian and who has learned what love is from contemplation of the figure of his Lord and Master. God is love *like that*—indeed we ought to put it more forcefully and say that such human love as we see in Jesus is the very reflection of the reality of divine love on the stage of human affairs. That is the way the world goes; the grain of the universe is exactly like that, however the appearances of things may seem. I should say that the basic affirmation of Christian faith is just there: the commitment of self to a love like that as the disclosure of how things go, most profoundly, and the 'life in scorn of consequence' (in Kirsopp Lake's grand words) which follows when such commitment is undertaken.

But if that is 'the disclosure of God's nature', known through his 'agency in the world', as Whitehead would put it, then it is also true that each man is intended to actualize in his own existence that love. He is to 'live in love' because to live so is truly *to live*. The English recusant poet Robert Southwell wrote lines that I delight in quoting: 'Not where I breathe, but where I love, I live.' He spoke not for himself alone but for all men—as all men, once they have been opened up to the understanding of themselves, may be brought to see. This is 'the life which is life indeed'.

It is with this background in mind and in this context that we can see why judgement is related to love. Although the word 'judgement' is not a happy one, as we shall see, what it intends to say is utterly integral to love. The relationship is no incidental or accidental one; it is tied in with the very reality of loving in itself. Indeed we might put it briefly by saying that love always *is* judgement, in the meaning which I shall try to give to that not too satisfactory word which traditionally has been employed to denote what I am talking about.

But what *am* I talking about?

Simply, one could state it in these words: I am talking about the honest recognition or facing of things as actually they are, with the consequences they have had, exactly as those consequences have been. I am talking about a brave and fearless *appraisal* both of the situation and of those who are in the situation. So I shall use the word 'appraisal' in the remainder of this chapter, rather than the word 'judgement'; the latter fails seriously, for us today at any rate, because it is so tied up with notions of law-courts, assizes, and the other parapher-nalia of 'justice' in the legal sense. *Such* notions have little or nothing to do with love; they are a matter of human justice which *may be* a mode of love's expression in certain situations but they are also very misleading because love is ultimately not concerned with 'justice' in the vulgar sense—it is *above* justice, whose interest is either retributive or distributive, for the interest of love is with *persons*, persons in society with their fellows, and the fulfilment of selves in the giving-and-receiving which is mutuality or union.

Furthermore—and this I wish to stress—the rewards and punishments motif is not part of the kind of appraisal that I think love entails. The only reward that love can offer is more opportunity to love; its only punishment can be failure on the part of the lover to continue in loving. If we import into our thinking ideas about rewards and punishments, as these are commonly understood, we turn God into 'the ruthless moralist' who, as Whitehead once remarked, is one of the false 'gods' that men have worshipped to their own frightful hurt. I say this with full recognition of the fact that in the gospels we find something of the rewards and punishments motif. But if one looks at what is said there, interpreting it in the light of what Jesus Himself *was*, as the community of Christian faith remembered Him and His impact upon them, we shall see that the reward promised to those who love God or do His will is really the presence of God and the joy of 'seeing him'; while the punishment is the alienation from His presence and that joy, the result of not loving which the victim has imposed upon himself. In any event, as we shall see when we discuss the meaning of the heavenly promise, as part of the scheme of the last things, it is not genuinely Christian to think that anybody can want God *and* something else. In having God, or better in being had by God, we have *all* that 'we can desire', as the collect puts it; it is not a matter of 'God and a lollypop', as I have heard it said. St Francis de Sales once commented that 'he who seeks God in order to have something more, does not know what he is seeking'. To seek God *is* to seek all good; and to live 'in God', which is to live 'in love', is in itself the *summum bonum*.

As mortal life in its finality, death introduces into our mortal existence the fact of appraisal. This is a concept which many have sought to remove from our thinking about human life. The reason for this is not only that it seems to give a somewhat unpleasant note to the portrayal of that life. Rather, as I see it, the reason is two-fold. First, the pictures of 'judgement' have been drawn so often from law-courts and the like that they bear little relation to the Christian insistence on God as love. Hence when that insistence is taken with the utmost seriousness, the whole idea is dismissed as mistaken—once again, to use the familiar aphorism, 'the baby is thrown out with the bath-water'. But second, the understanding of love itself has been sentimentalized, as I have said, and hence it has been thought that love has nothing to do with appraisal, evaluation, and the honest recognition of things as they are and persons as they are, however much we may love them.

Whether people like it or not, appraisal is a genuine and persisting factor in human existence. Appraisal means that each man is responsible for his life and for the decisions which he has made in the course of it; and it means also that each man must be prepared to give what traditional thinking describes as 'an account of his life'—in the face of whatever ultimately determines and assesses true values in the whole scheme of things. If that 'ultimate' is love, as Christians believe, the appraisal is all the more searching and it is all the more terrible to be aware that one must face it. 'It is a terrible thing to fall into the hands of the living God', we read in *Hebrews*. On which we may comment that it would indeed be 'terrible' to fall into the hands of one who is what Whitehead styled 'the ruthless moralist'; but it is even more 'terrible', in the most profound sense of that word, when one must look at the love which we have pierced by our own lovelessness, the cosmic Lover (as I like to put it) whose readiness to give love and to receive love is so devastatingly complete. The Love 'that moves the sun and the other stars', in Dante's final words in *La Commedia Divina*, cannot be faced with nonchalance or ease.

Appraisal, in the meaning I am giving to the word, is not necessarily 'final', if by this is suggested that it is not also *present*; indeed I would wish to say that it is essentially present, in this and in every moment. Every man, day by day, is appraised. The question which is being asked is insistent in all moments and in every moment of our existence: 'How do I "stack up" against the way things really "go"?' That question is asked, I have said. But by whom?

It is asked by each man of and for himself. That is the measure of our human responsibility and thus the determinant of our humanly moral earnestness, precisely as death is the measure of our humanity as mortal. And by 'moral earnestness' I do not mean the sort of moralism which centres itself in obedience to codes or laws or sets of commandments, whether they be ten or of any other number. These have their place, doubtless, in the living of human life; but it would be wrong, I think, to assume that 'moral earnestness' means only a meticulous 'keeping of the commandments' in as devoted a manner as possible. Christian, or even human, 'obedience' is not exhausted by anything like that. 'One thing you lack', Jesus is reported to have said to the 'rich young ruler' after that youth had said, doubtless in complete honesty and with entire accuracy, that he had kept the commandments all his life. What was lacking was genuine 'obedience', not to a set of moral requirements imposed from on high, but in a certain quality of spirit. And I think that the 'Follow me', in that *pericope*, is not simply a call to be a disciple in the obvious meaning of the word. It is a call to be *like Jesus*—which is nothing other than to be a lover, to become what one is intended to become, and thus to find oneself fulfilled as a man.

Thus our self-appraisal is in terms of our love. The question comes down to this: in what ways, to what degree, have I or have I not opened myself to love, to give love and to receive love, to commit myself in utter faithfulness, to live in real mutuality, to look at others with 'eager expectancy' (as Baron von Hügel defined 'hope'), and thus in the truest sense to have been *a man*? It is obvious that when this question is asked, by each of us for himself, the answer must be in terms of failure. Yet the *direction* which we have taken, the aim which has been ours, is the determinative factor. Is *that* the end which has been ours?

But none of us really knows himself completely. It is not to us that hearts are open, even our own; desires known, even our own; no secrets hid, even our own. Nor is it to our fellowmen, who also appraise. This is true, whether we are thinking of the contemporaries whom we know and who know us, of the wider society of which we are a part, or of history in its great sweep. By each of these we are evaluated; but none of these can know the complete truth about us. The appeal to the 'judgement of society', like the appeal to the 'judgement of history', is an appeal which is inescapable; whether we like it or not, that appeal is always being made. But because the society of our fellowmen, intimate or remote, is marked by the same mortality which is ours as persons, while the whole sweep of history as we experience and know it is also a mortal history—under the sign of death—any appraisal made in this way is also limited and partial.

The point is not that such appraisals are made 'in time' and not 'in eternity', as some would like to phrase it; I have already tried to make it clear that such a dualism will not serve us and that God himself is 'temporal' although in what we may style 'an eminent manner'. The point is that the human capacity to understand, in the most profound sense of the word, is so slight that nobody ought to venture to make what he can never in fact make, 'a final judgement' about anybody else, or even about himself. 'Judge not, that ye be not judged'; no man, no society of men, and no long historical sequence of men in society, knows enough or knows fully enough to make any appraisal that can claim to be entirely accurate and that can suppose itself to have seen everything that should enter into the making of such an appraisal.

But *God* is 'the fellow-sufferer who *understands*', as Whitehead says. *His* understanding is the supreme wisdom which knows things as they are; and it is unto him 'that all hearts are open, all desires known, and from whom no secrets are hid'. This is simply another way of phrasing the Christian faith itself—the faith which declares that God *is* love and that we are assured of this because he *acts* lovingly, above all has acted lovingly in the total event of Jesus Christ. People often smile when it is said that only love can really see another person as he is; we are inclined to think that love is 'blind', failing to see defects and always ready to discover values and virtues. This is indeed the case with human love, which is mortal and under the conditions of that mortality cannot be 'perfect', while at the same time it is under the 'condemnation' of failure. But the divine love, God himself as cosmic Lover, is in a different situation—or so a Christian must believe. That love *knows*; and knowing, that love *understands*.

I claim, therefore, that the only 'just' appraisal, the only 'judgement' which can take *all* the facts into account, is God's. And only He can make a 'final' judgement. His appraisal will be accurate, while at the same time it will be merciful. In stating it in this way, I am trying to indicate what seems to me the insight in the traditional view that God is just, not in the human sense of meting out, distributively or retributively, the proper rewards or punishments according to some prior set of laws or regulations, but in the divine sense (if I may say it this way) of complete understanding. Further, I am trying to indicate, by the word 'mercy', that God's appraisal is more than accurate, in terms of complete understanding; it is also characterized by God's *chesed*, his 'loving-kindness', his never-failing mercy, which always makes the best out of every situation and finds the best in every person. In saying this about 'the best', I do not intend the idea that this is read into the situation or the person. On the contrary, I suggest that precisely because God does know all desires, the secrets of human hearts, and the depths of each situation, He also knows there the 'initial aim' which in the first instance He gave, the entire condition of things which was there present, the possibilities which were offered, the efforts that were made, the failures that were experienced, and *everything else*. Knowing that, God's appraisal is 'charitable' appraisal in the true sense of that word—that is, it is *really* loving and thus can both see the best that is there and be prepared to use that best in the augmenting of good in the creative advance which is the cosmic process.

To speak in this way leads naturally to some further considerations in which (as I think) process philosophy can be of great assistance to us. In Whitehead's works there are two words which I wish to mention: one is 'decision'; the other is 'prehension', both negative and positive. I believe that these words, and the ideas that are associated with them, can be fruitfully used at this point of our discussion.

'Decision' means, of course, 'cutting off'. It should not necessarily imply conscious activity of the sort that we know in our own experience, when our 'decision' is or may be made with awareness of what is being done. If, as Whitehead claims and as process thought in general would assert, the element of 'decision' is found everywhere in the creative process, this should not be taken to mean that a quantum of energy, say, knowingly 'decides' for this or that among the relevant possibilities that are 'offered' to it. Similarly, the view which I share that 'subjective aim' is not only present at the level of conscious human movement towards the actualization of potentialities, in a dynamic process, but is also found at every level and at every point in that process, does not imply that such an 'aim' is consciously, knowingly, with full awareness such as we may assume is ours, 'subjectively' apprehended when the various occasions or occurrences or 'entities' in the order of creation move towards their own appropriate mode and degree of actualization.

For these reasons I think that Professor Hartshorne's use,

at one time, of the word 'panpsychism' was misleading, although I agree completely with what Professor Hartshorne was really concerned to assert. 'Panpsychism' (pan = all, psyche = soul) suggests some kind of *vitalistic* view, in which 'entelechies' (i.e. souls as opposed to bodies) are operative at all points and on all levels, after the fashion of the vitalistic biology of Hans Driesch and others. What I should claim, however, is that in a manner appropriate to the particular level and in a fashion suitable for the particular occasion, however 'large' or 'small', there is such 'decision' as entails a 'cutting off' of this or that possibility for actualization and an 'acceptance' of this or that other possibility. It is in this way that the creative advance goes on. Thus I think that human decision, in the self-conscious sense in which commonly we use the term, is related to and part of a general movement in which 'decision' is always a determinative factor. In this sense it is one of the 'metaphysical principles' which we require for our understanding of how things go in the world, even if in exactly that phrasing it is not part of a given categoreal scheme.

At the human level, with which we are concerned, such decision is made with some awareness of what is involved in it and certainly with a degree of self-consciousness in the making of it. This is part of what is intended when we speak of human responsibility. In any given situation, each human person brings with him from his past the totality of what has gone into making him what at that moment he is; this is his 'memory', in the most serious meaning of that word, including not only conscious and (as we might say) sub-conscious factors which might by the process of psychoanalysis be brought to the surface, but also the organic, physical, yes the physiological factors, which are 'viscerally' 'remembered'; including also the whole series of past prehensions—of graspings and being grasped—which have had their part and contributed their share in making him what he is *now*. Each human person too is *in* his relationships, contemporary with him although there is some slight span of time between their origination and their reception by him. And each human person is *towards his future*, as he moves in the direction of realizing or making actual the 'subjective aim' which is his on the basis of that 'initial aim' which has been provided for him in his beginnings.

Human decision is the way in which choice is made, among all possibilities offered at a given instant, so that actualization may occur. This happens constantly, since every occasion or occurrence is involved by necessity in the process of 'going on'. Most of the decisions may seem relatively insignificant or unimportant, but some of them are different—these are the decisions which respond to this or that possibility that may be strikingly determinative of the future direction to be taken. As such, they are responses to certain lures or solicitations of a peculiarly intensive sort. Every decision is a response to a lure or solicitation; that is how God effectively 'acts' in a creative process from which he is nowhere absent, by permitting things to 'make themselves' as decisions are undertaken that 'decide' the degree and kind of actualization that will occur. But *some* decisions are peculiarly significant; they are the response made to what is proposed as *important*, to use another Whiteheadian word. For a Christian, the event of Christ is important, in that sense, as providing a clue to 'the nature of God and his agency in the world'; the decision made for or against that clue is important, since it is determinative of whether or not life will be lived—that is, man will move towards becoming himself—in terms of the love which is there both manifested and released.

The decision may be negative or positive, because, in the process, prehensions, or graspings both of and by each occasion, may be either in terms of a 'yes' or a 'no'. A negative prehension means that the occasion rejects this or that which is offered to it, a rejection which may be made for a variety of reasons, the details of which we need not here investigate. A positive prehension means an accepting of what is offered, a receiving of it into the occasion which is presented with it as a possibility to be grasped, and this also may be made for a variety of reasons about which we shall not speak. But the *fact* of such rejections or choices is highly significant; and above all, to put it in a form of words, it is highly *important* that the *important* which is offered to each occasion as a possibility shall be decided for or against in an *important* way. Which is to say, in a decision that signifies commitment or determination against commitment.

What has been said in the last few pages may seem to some to be illicit metaphysical talk. But I would remind any who think this that it all depends on what one means by 'metaphysics'. I do not believe that what I have been saying is anything like the erection of some grandiose scheme in which super-terrestrial realities are being set up and the whole apparatus of a quasi-Hegelian metaphysic is proposed. On the contrary, I should claim, what I have been saying is metaphysical in the second sense of the word which I proposed in an earlier chapter; it is the making of wide generalizations on the basis of experience, with a reference back to verify or 'check' the generalizations, a reference which includes not only the specific experience from which it started but also other experiences, both human and more general, by which its validity may be tested—and the result is not some grand scheme which claims to encompass everything in its sweep, but a vision of reality which to the one who *sees* in this way appears a satisfactory, but by no means complete, picture of how things actually and concretely *go* in the world.

But to return to decision as an enduring factor in the world process. In men, that decision manifests itself in self-conscious choice. With choice goes the responsibility for what is chosen— granted that there are qualifying and conditioning factors, that human freedom is limited in many respects, and that what we deeply *desire* is much more significant than what we may perhaps have been able effectually to accomplish in consequence of our decision. In the perspective of Christian faith, what is suggested here is that in the appraisal which is part of human mortal existence, we ourselves can be at best but partial judges. History, as well as the society of our contemporaries, is in the same case—not enough is known of human 'depths', as the psychoanalysts put it, for any appraisal to be entirely accurate. But God, who *is* love, who is 'the fellow-sufferer who understands', and whose wisdom penetrates all that is actual and is aware of the relevant possibilities (but *as* possibilities, not in whatever may be made actual among them, for that is 'open' until it happens and God's omniscience cannot mean that He knows, hence must determine, what will occur *before* it occurs), can make an appraisal that is both accurate and merciful—that is 'just' and loving.

The appraisal that God makes is worked out in what He does—or, in words that describe the creative advance as we know it, the appraisal is worked out in terms of what is taken into, and what is rejected from, the 'consequent nature' of God, God as He is affected by what occurs in the world; and then, in what use is made of what has been thus taken or received in the furthering of the project or purpose of God, the implementation of good 'in widest commonalty shared'.

What did this particular life contribute to God's experience, we might then ask, as God receives into Himself what that life has been on the way to becoming and what it has achieved as it has proceeded on that way? In a similar manner, we might ask the question, What has the total life of the human race contributed to this ongoing process of good? At every moment, such an appraisal is being made, in the most serious sense— not as a juridical pronouncement, but as acceptance or non-acceptance. When death comes, appraisal must also be made in the same way, for the total pattern of a given human life, made up as it is of a particular 'routing' of occasions bound together in the fashion we indicated earlier, has also contributed, or failed to contribute, in its very totality, to the creative advance in good. Indeed the whole of the created order, as we style it, is also being appraised in the same way. Each man, each community, humanity as a whole, the range of historical development, the realm of nature . . . all are knit together in an organic totality; all have played, or failed to play, their part in the good which is being achieved by God. God, however, is not aloof from His creation; He is 'in the world or nowhere at all' and by virtue of this He is participant in, identified (but not identical) with, and enriched—or, maybe, impoverished—in His own life by what has gone on, does now go on, and will go on, yet remaining always unsurpassed by anything not Himself. He is the supremely worshipful because that is true of Him and of no other. He is also supremely worshipful because He is the love which is both the depth and the height in all occasions and the enticement or lure which leads those occasions, by their own free decision, to their satisfaction or fulfilment in the context of the wide social pattern which is the world.

God can and does 'make even the wrath of man to serve him'. That means that in every way and in every place, God makes the best of everything, including human lovelessness and the failure which it entails. But the evil is still evil, the wrong is still wrong, the lovelessness is still lovelessness; this is no case of 'partial evil, universal good', in the cheery phrase of Alexander Pope's. While evil is not radical, if by that is intended 'at the root of things'—for it *cannot* be, if God is love and is Himself 'at the root of things' through His creativity at work in them—it is most certainly not to be dismissed or minimized or talked away. Yet God in the creative advance can be trusted, says Christian faith, to use whatever is usable for His purpose of love; and some of us may be surprised to see how this is possible to do when the use is made of what may seem to us extremely unpromising material. But when we judge in that way, we are ourselves appraised for the unloving creatures we are.

Finally, the divine appraisal very likely has little to do with what we would think to be the 'religious' areas of experience. Those are necessary for us; so I should wish to insist, in opposition to the contemporary writers who regard *all* religion, in any sense, as necessarily bad. But God's appraisal, because He is what He is, disclosed in what He actively does, and precisely because the world is what it is, in terms of what happens in it, is an appraisal of real worth, wherever it may be found and however it may be expressed. By this I mean that since God lures, entices, invites, and solicits His creation towards the actualization of its 'initial aim' which becomes its 'subjective aim', in each of its occurrences or occasions, so also He appraises—takes into Himself and receives and uses, or must reject because it is un-usable—whatever is done, including the doing which is man's 'becoming', in a very great diversity of ways. Most of them, doubtless, are 'secular', not specifically 'religious'.

The lure of God is known in every channel and area of existence, not just in those that have a 'religious' tinge. And in those 'secular' channels or areas, God is working 'secularly', as Whitehead put it long before 'secular theologians' appeared on the scene. When He works in such a way, His 'incognito' is to be respected, not denied. But none the less it is *He* who is 'acting' there—and God always acts in love, to secure a freely given response from those who are made to be lovers too and the appraisal of whom is in terms of the degree of their contribution to love's purpose in the creative advance of the cosmos.

St John of the Cross, using the word 'judgement' where I prefer the word 'appraisal', put in one sentence what I have been trying to say: 'In the evening of our days, we shall be judged by our loving.'

FIVE

Heaven and Hell

Man dies and his death is both the end of his life, biologically speaking, and the qualifying characteristic of his life, marking him out as mortal, as aware of mortality, as responsible in that mortal existence, an existence during which he is intended to actualize himself as a lover, becoming what he is made and meant to be. He is under appraisal, both by himself and his fellows and by the God who has provided for him his 'initial aim' and who will either receive the good which his becoming has achieved or find necessary the rejection of that which does not contribute to the creative advance at which God Himself aims.

And each man, in every age and at every time, like the whole race of men, and indeed like the whole creation, is faced with two possible 'destinies', one or other of which will turn out to have been his, in terms of the direction he has taken in his mortal existence. Nor am I speaking of 'destiny' here in a merely futuristic sense, as if it were coming after a long time or at 'the end of the days'. It is in the *now* that these destinies are made present as possibilities. For just as the myth of the creation of the world is significant in its existential confrontation of man with his dependence and with the equal dependence of the world, so the talk about the last things is *essentially* a matter of *existential* import, if I may be permitted that odd combination of words.

The possibilities which are presented are blessedness which

comes from self-fulfilment and the acceptance by God of that self-fulfilment—all of this, of course, in relationship with others and not in any presumed human isolation of selfhood—or the disintegration or failure which comes from self-destruction or rejection by God because there is nothing to be received by God in His consequent nature for the furthering of His purpose of good in the course of the process of creative advance. If ever this double-presentation of possibilities has been portrayed in literature, it is to be found in Dostoevski's *Brothers Karamazov*. In that novel, the great Russian writer shows Ivan, Aloysha, and Dmitri as caught in this dilemma of choice; and they are appraised, in their personal quality, as *blessed* or *damned*, as we might put it, not by the arbitrary *fiat* of a *deus ex machina*, but by the ineluctable working out of what they have made of themselves, what they have become, as this is evaluated in terms of what in an earlier chapter we called whatever ultimately determines and assesses true values in the scheme of things.

Thus for each of us, the exacting and inescapable question, which must be faced and answered, is the question of our total mortal life as we are now living it, a question which arises from our mortality with the responsibility which that entails, which puts itself to us in the form of our measuring up to the possibility of becoming authentically ourselves, and which issues in our realization (not so much in thought as in deeply felt experience as *existing* men) of blessedness, as we know ourselves becoming what we truly are, *or* in destruction or damnation, as we know ourselves both frustrated men and failures in our human fulfilment. Heidegger in his own way has made this point about men—not about men in the 'mass' or 'lost in the crowd', but about each and every man—although he has made it in his own way. So also have others, many others. They have seen that each of us is a mortal project, so to say, responsible for our actions and for the character which both reflects them and which they reflect, and hence either 'blessed' or 'damned'.

The Christian faith speaks to men who are in this situation.

When it is true to itself it does not gloss over the facts, nor does it sentimentalize them. Above all it does not deny them. On the contrary, it is exactly at this point—in the context of such facts as we have been outlining and with full awareness of the concern, the uncertainty, and even the despair which can come to every man as he looks at himself with unblinking eyes and in utter honesty—that the Christian gospel has its special relevance and the faith which it awakens has its special significance. In the sequel we shall say more about this. At the moment it will be useful to speak of the presuppositions with which that faith starts in giving its account of men in such a situation.

I wish to notice three of these presuppositions, although I am aware of the fact that they are not exhaustive. The three which we shall consider are: (a) that man is indeed a 'sinner' but that he is also capable of 'redemption' and hence of 'glory'; (b) that history is not a senseless enterprise—someone has described it as 'meaningless meandering'—but a purposeful movement; and (c) that the natural world, in which history and each human life in community with other human lives have their setting, is not evil but good and also shares in 'redemption'.

As to our first presupposition, or (a), the truth of man's sin is surely given in our experience. Only a little observation and a little introspection are sufficient to bring us to see this. The associated traditional doctrines of 'the Fall' and 'Original Sin', with all their historical absurdity and however much we may wish to put in their place some better way of stating what they affirm, tell the truth about man. He is indeed a sinner, fallen from 'grace'; he is not 'able of himself to help himself'. This is *not* a statement of 'total depravity', at least as that idea has been commonly interpreted; what is at issue is the patent reality in every man's experience of something very seriously wrong with him. In the sort of language we have used in these pages, man knows that he should be on the road to love, but he finds himself frustrated on that road; while at the same time he knows very well (once he is honest with himself) that he has so decided, often against his better judgement and in contradiction to his deep desires and purpose, to reject the opportunities to love and to receive love, that he is a failure. Oddly enough, as it may seem, it is precisely those who to others appear most adequately to have realized in their lives (to have made actual) their possibility of love—it is precisely *those* who are most conscious of themselves as failures.

The truth about man is that while he is indeed created 'in the image of God', he is in a state of spiritual insufficiency so pervasive and so disturbing that he cannot live authentically as a man, much less as a 'son of God'. In the divine intention, he was made for the fulfilment of himself, with others, in free and open relationship to his Creator. In actual fact, he lacks that capacity for communion with God and his own fulfilment —which are the same thing, seen from different angles—and in his concrete humanity he is frustrated *and*, what is more important, he is responsibly aware of having made himself, by accumulated decisions, incapable of right relationships with his brethren. In this way he has succeeded in putting himself in the position where he is *privatus boni*, 'deprived of good', and *vulneratus in naturalibus* 'wounded in his natural human existence'. Of course he is never completely 'deprived' of the good which is God, nor is he destroyed in the 'wounding' of his human existence. But his situation is such that he feels this most intensely; and in consequence he finds himself possessed by a tendency which makes him rest content (save in moments of deep awareness) with the lesser 'goods', with the immediately obtainable goods, a tendency which perverts his best instincts, and which prevents him seeing things 'steadily and whole'.

But this is only one side of the Christian picture of man. As someone has put it, if the first volume of a study of man's existence is about his 'fall' the second volume is about his 'redemption'. Indeed the whole point of Christian faith is here, so far as human experience is concerned. Man can be redeemed; or rather, man has been redeemed. Man's possibilities are tremendous. He was indeed created 'in the image of God'; that

Heaven and Hell

image has been damaged but it has not been destroyed. When St Irenaeus wrote about this he took the text from Genesis: man as created 'in the image and likeness of God'. He distinguished, in bad exegesis, between 'image' and 'likeness'. The Reformers corrected the exegesis but they did not see that despite his exegetical mistake St Irenaeus had hold of a profound truth. For he had said that the 'image' is not lost, but the 'likeness' *is*. In traditional terms of Christian theology, what he was asserting was that man still has the capacity, but he lacks the power, to be 'righteous'—that is, to be authentic. To say that the capacity is lost would be to denigrate God's creation of man as *good*.

Thus when we have admitted all that we must admit concerning man's helplessness in his concrete situation, we must go on to affirm all that we can affirm concerning man's possibility of perfection—which means, in this context, his potentiality for becoming completely ('perfectly' or in full actualization) the man who loves. Human mortality shows plainly enough that this 'perfection' is not achieved in the span of our mortal life and under our present circumstances; that is true enough. But it remains *as* the possibility; what is more, Christian faith declares that God already accepts those who acknowledge their failure and commit themselves utterly to Him—so that they are already, as we might put it in mythological language, 'in heaven' or in other words discover themselves to be 'blessed'. Hence no Christian can despair of any man, even of himself; for each man is 'a sinner for whom Christ died', each man is loved by God, each man can direct his life in response to that love made manifest in diverse ways but 're-presented' (in Schubert Ogden's word) in Jesus Christ. Therefore each man can 'work out his salvation in fear and trembling, for it is God that worketh in him both to will and to do his good pleasure'.

A silly optimism about man, such as we knew 'between the wars' and in the 'golden days' of the liberal era, is not Christian. Our contemporary theologians often appear to wish to revive that optimism, perhaps in violent reaction from the

65

other extreme which appeared between the wars in certain of the dialectical or 'neo-orthodox' theologies. But they are lacking in realism. On the other hand, the total pessimism of much traditional Reformed theology, whether Calvinist or Lutheran, and its more recent revival, as well as the perverse denigration of humanity not stated but implied in Catholic penitential theology with its fear of human impulses and its dread of sexuality, is not Christian either. I think that one reason for this, on both sides, is that a look at man, as he is, may give us too much confidence when we are superficial in our looking or too much despair when we only regard man's condition as 'cabin'd, cribb'd, confined' and as failing so terribly in its accomplishment. If by 'heaven' we mean the possibility of blessedness, whatever else we may find it necessary to say on the matter, it might be asserted that if we do not believe in the possibility of heaven, we shall not believe in the possibility of good for man. But more about this will be suggested at a later point.

Our second presupposition, or (b), was that history is a purposeful movement. The origin of that presupposition is deep in the Jewish conviction that 'God is working his purpose out', despite everything that appears to deny or impede that activity. Once again, in reaction from a notion of 'progress' which was a secular substitute for this Christian conviction when Christian faith had become an absurdity to so many, recent theologians have 'given up' this belief to all intents and purposes. Not all of them, but some of them, have transferred 'the divine far-off event' to some realm outside history altogether. They, more than any other thinkers perhaps, have indeed 'emptied out the baby with the bath-water', to return to the image we have used earlier. But it ought to be clear that 'the increasing purpose' is neither automatic progress without relapse or defection, nor 'heaven' *in the sense of a completely non-historical state*. 'The hope of heaven', as I shall argue, need not mean this at all; I should say, *ought not* to mean this. Too often it is taken to do so. But the purposeful movement in history signifies that every moment *counts*, every moment makes its contribution of the divine life, and every moment is related to God who is intimately concerned with all the variety and content of history. Furthermore, it signifies that something is being accomplished in history, even if it is not always obvious to us.

Mother Julian of Norwich relates that in a 'shewing' she saw the entire creation as 'a little hazel-nut'. She asked how it could continue, since it was so tiny, so insignificant, in relation to the vastness of God. The answer came that it continued 'because God made it, because God loves it, because God keeps it'. In respect to history, then, we may say that God sustains its every event and is the chief (not only) causative principle behind all causation. God loves His world and everything in it; He is *there*, in the world, with cherishing care 'tending it' and bring-ing it on towards final good, while at the same time He redeems it from triviality and frustration. The movement of history is part of that care. Finally, God keeps His world—there is His purpose which sustains it and moves through it, towards 'the manifestation of the sons of God'. Whatever may be the remoter intention of God in the awe-inspiring stretch of space and time, it is all of a piece with what He is doing in the historical experience of men—in a way, that is what the *homo-ousion* of the Nicene Creed affirms. In the historical realm, as in the natural order (if the two may properly be distinguished in this way), God's activity is two-fold: first, to secure from each moment and each event the good which may be actualized there; and second, to work towards such a 'completion' of the process of creative advance that He may say of it, with a joy that includes but transcends all suffering, that it *is* good.

Thus the historical realm is characterized by a purpose which is nothing other than God's incredibly cherishing love, shared with His creatures and moving through their free decisions towards a great end. And when things go wrong, as they do, God is like the sculptor who can turn an artisan's mistaken and distorting chiselling into a lovely figure. His purpose can make history meaningful even when man has done his utmost to destroy its meaning.

The third presupposition, or (c), insists that the natural world is good and that it shares in redemption. Like the second presupposition, this has its origin in the Jewish insistence, found so clearly throughout most of the Old Testament, on a *positive* understanding of the creation. As against all Manichean or dualistic philosophies, as also against all those religions which offer escape from the world into an ethereal realm of pure spirit, Christianity has denied that the world of *things* is evil. It is good, because God created it; it is good, because He loves it; it is good, because He is in it and works through it—to repeat Mother Julian's 'shewing'. Nature is an instrument for the divine purpose, not something alien to that purpose and hence to be rejected or denied.

On this matter the theology of the Eastern Orthodox Church has much to teach the rest of us. For that theology, the whole cosmos is 'to be redeemed'; everything in it, from the very dirt under our feet to the loveliest configurations and harmonies, has its place in that redemption. There is no reason to fear or hate 'dirt', to sniff at 'matter' or material things. These may be misused and they can be abused; but in themselves 'dirt' and 'matter' and the whole world of nature, to which we as men in our history are organic, are 'good stuff' and must not be despised nor rejected.

It is interesting in this connection to compare the two greatest English poets of our time. T. S. Eliot seems never to have overcome his dislike of the material world—he was not like Aldous Huxley, who dismissed it all as illusory, but he hardly appears to have *included* it in his great vision. On the other hand, W. H. Auden, in his *Christmas Oratorio*, writes superbly and lovingly of the possibilities of the natural world and speaks tenderly of man as *there*. The conclusion of that work, with its use of a Whiteheadian theme, is magnificent witness to what I am urging here. Auden writes: 'At your marriage/All its occasions shall dance for joy.' It is the marriage of man with God, with his fellowmen, and with the world itself that he has in mind.

We cannot picture or describe or even imagine the way in which the whole creation serves as 'the body of God'. But to be afraid of that phrase is to be afraid of the deepest intention in what Christian faith has to say about creation and about redemption. The cosmos, as God receives it and uses it, is *what the world means to God*, in terms of what has been done in it and with it, in terms too of the response made in and by the cosmos. And although what I have been urging is based upon Christian faith, as I anyway understand it, and is immediately related to human experience (for it is from that experience, in its context, that anything we say must begin), the corollary is that the cosmos has value *in itself*, not just as a stage of man's existence and for man's redemptive possibility. Such a cosmic setting for, involvement in, and relationship to what we know by faith about ourselves gives the Christian faith a sweep and range that saves it from the charge of parochialism or mere anthropocentrism. As I have said in the second chapter, this is one of the ways in which a process conceptuality seems to me to be of enormous use in Christian thinking.

I hope that this long discussion of presuppositions has not seemed an unnecessary intrusion into the subject of this book. I do not think it is an intrusion, since it has provided for us some ground on which to stand as we return to the particular topic, heaven and hell, with which we are immediately concerned.

Some years ago a novel appeared with the title *All This and Heaven Too*. I have completely forgotten the novel but the title has stuck in my mind. When one hears a discussion of Christian faith as promising abundant life, giving meaning to present-day existence, and substituting for broken personality the authenticity of an integrated and forgiven, accepted and accepting personality, one thinks of that title. Can it be, one wonders, that the 'heaven too' has significance for us today? I think that it does have such significance. And perhaps I can get at what I mean by recalling a popular saying of some years ago. When young people who wished to convey the idea that something was superlatively good, splendid, and *real* ('That's *for real*', they also said—and it is a significant phrase), they would often use these words: 'It's out of this world'.

Now that *might* have meant that this good, splendid, and real experience or thing was quite literally 'out of' the concrete world and in a completely spiritual realm which made that world irrelevant and ridiculous. But such was not the intention with which the phrase was used by young people. What they intended by it was something like this: Here is an experience in which we have found a wonder and glory, a beauty and splendour, such that it seems to be *more than*, although most certainly not opposed to and in flight from, the day-by-day experiences which are so familiar. I do not wish to exaggerate, but it might be suggested that in the famous line, 'bright shoots of everlastingness', something of the same sort is being said. There is a suffusion of ordinary experience with a glory that is very much present, very much here and now, yet unexhausted by the here and now and in a strange fashion evocative of a certain reverence. I am convinced that this 'more' in man's mortal existence is known to people of every type and under every condition, although they do not quite know how to express it. At any rate, it is plainly the case that they do not experience it *or* express it, for the most part, in specifically 'religious' terms.

It is easy enough to interpret what I have been describing in 'other-worldly' fashion. It is easy to speak of it as if it had to do with 'pie-in-the-sky-when-you-die'. A good deal of Christianity has been vitiated by this very unbiblical way of interpreting human life; as one of the recent popes said, 'true life' or 'real life' is not here but 'beyond death'. I am paraphrasing here some words of Pope Leo XIII in his very this-worldly encyclical about social justice, *De Rerum Novarum*; in his writing about that demand and necessity for social justice he could not emancipate himself from this false 'other-worldliness'. Nor is he alone in this, for it has been very much a part of traditional Christianity as commonly taught, preached, and understood. Yet it constitutes what Professor Bethune-Baker once described as the greatest 'apostasy' in Christian thought, for it made it possible to think that we could put off to 'another world' what it was our duty to do in *this* one. But if it is easy to fall into that sort of escapist 'other-worldliness', it is also easy to exhaust the significance of the experience to which I refer by entirely 'humanizing' or 'mundanizing' (if I may coin the word) what it delivers to us. Above all, it is possible to exhaust what the gospel has to say by talking about and working for the immediacies, assuming that there is in that gospel nothing more than an imperative for better relations among men, classes, races, and nations, with the building in the not too distant future of a society in which opportunity of fulfilment will be guaranteed to everybody.

I do not wish for a moment to decry the stress on the 'secular' import of the gospel nor to seem ungrateful for all that men like Harvey Cox and Gibson Winter, to name but two, have been teaching us. Nor do I wish to reject the truth of Bonhoeffer's insight about the gospel being concerned with *life*, right here and right now, rather than with some 'future life' which is promised to those who are 'saved'. To put it vulgarly, I am *all for* this recognition of the 'secular' import of the gospel in its impact on a society that is becoming more and more 'secularized'. And I agree that this relative autonomy of the 'secular' is a consequence of the whole development of the Jewish-Christian understanding of God and of history and of the world.

At the same time, I believe that precisely *in* the 'secular' as we live it in a 'secularized' society, there is something 'heavenly'—if I may phrase it so. But I must explain what I am trying to say, lest I be completely misunderstood and my meaning misinterpreted. Perhaps I can best do this by commenting on a passage from one of St Augustine's sermons (Sermon 256, section 3). He used these words:

71

'O the happy alleluias there . . . There, praise to God; and here, praise to God. But here, by those who are filled with anxious care; there, by those who are freed from care. Here, by those whose lot is to die; there, by those who live eternally. Here, on the way; there, in our fatherland. Now, therefore, my brethren, let us sing—not for our delight as we rest, but to cheer us on in our labour. As wayfarers are accustomed to sing, so let us sing and let us keep on marching. For if you are going forward, you are *indeed* marching; and to go on marching is a good thing, if we go on in true faith and in right living. So, brethren, sing, and march on.'

That is a beautiful passage, as we shall all agree. But what is wrong with it? I should say that what is wrong with it is that it seems to urge that the 'there' is *after* this existence and *only so*. But we need not to read it in just that way, although doubtless that was the way St Augustine intended it. We can just as well read it as speaking of the double nature of human experience as men exist in 'true faith' and as they seek after 'right living'. In the very *here* of our existence there may be the *there* of blessedness; and if perhaps something is added about what happens *after* that, it is no contradiction of what happens *now*, *here*, in this *present* moment of our Christian belonging. There is more in man and in man's experience, there is more in history, and there is more in the natural order than meets the eye. There is 'the whole creation groaning and travailing in pain', as it is being 'delivered from the bondage of corruption into the glorious liberty of the children of God'. *All* things, as St Paul says in another place, are somehow of God, for God, to God, 'whether they be things in earth or things in heaven'; and the 'heaven' need not be seen as a 'beyond' which is not also in the world in its travail, moving as it is in creative advance under and in God who is love.

Exegetes may say that St Paul did not 'mean' what I have been saying, any more than St Augustine meant what I have said is a possible way of using his words. Very well, I admit this. But just here I recall to you what I have urged earlier

about the need for 'in-mythologizing', in the attempt to make
clear to ourselves, what the case actually is as we can see it, if
men like that, in their time, under their conditions, with their
patterns of thought, spoke as they did. At the very least, I
should claim, what I have been saying is a *possible* interpretation, for ourselves, of what they were driving at in their own
way and in their own terms. So far as I can see, this is the only
way in which we can be delivered from a literalism of the text
which so often prevents us grasping what might be styled 'the
deep intentionality' which is there. What is at stake, in my own
conviction, is the seeing that it is not so much *beyond*, as it is
in and through, 'the flaming ramparts of space and time' that
redemption, re-integration, and the fulfilment of the divine
purpose of love takes place. It is in *this* way that I should wish
to understand the point of that eschatological motif which is so
much a part of the biblical picture.

Christian faith affirms that man's action and character in
this world have a determining quality in respect to himself,
history, the world, and God—or so I am convinced. This confronts us again with those two 'destinies', those two 'ultimate
possibilities', for man.

The first possibility which we shall consider is that he shall
so terribly and persistently fail, in his ignorance and impotence
and in his own decisions, that he must suffer a continuing
rejection. That is hell; by definition, it is the absence of God.
Hell is always a real and live possibility, although I shall wish
to qualify this later and to say something on behalf of 'universalism'. None of the Church's theologies, however it may have
been with this or that particular Christian writer, has con-
signed any single person to that fate. But the possibility of
wilful alienation from God, and persistence in that alienation
by free decision, is there. And since God cannot, by His own
nature, coerce any man, but must win that man by His love,
there is always the possibility that the offer of acceptance may
be declined. Notice that I have said, throughout, 'the *possibility*'.

The other possibility is enjoyment of God, in which God accepts and receives into Himself the man who, in his ignorance and impotence and by his free decisions, has yet b een possessed of the kind of 'becoming' which makes him thus acceptable and able to be received by God. Everything that was said in the last chapter is relevant here, in respect to these two possibilities or possible destinies. We are not talking about some state 'after this life'; we are talking about the negative and positive prehensions by God of what is going on *in* this existence. That granted, the traditional scheme was *right* in speaking of 'heaven' as it did, with the 'beatific vision' and the bliss or happiness which is granted through that vision. Furthermore, popular hymnody was *right*, however unfortunate its images, in picturing this in terms of full satisfaction; it took the *best* moments of contemporary experience and used them in an eminent fashion to describe what this would mean. Homely fields in *Green Pastures*, the 'heavenly city', 'being with those I love', 'gardens and stately walks' in the Elizabethan lyric—all these were symbolic and suggestive of fulfilment. 'When I wake up after his likeness, I shall be satisfied', says the Psalmist. Such pictures need be misleading only if they are taken to be purely futuristic in reference, as if what was meant by 'heaven' was only compensation for the pains of earth. But we have already rejected any such way of understanding the deepest intention here.

The assertion of hell and heaven in the out-worn scheme of the last things confronted men with these two destinies or possibilities. But what about that other, found in Orthodox and Catholic theologies—'the intermediate state'? I believe that this too says something important and meaningful. I should put it in this fashion. *If* any occasion or 'entity' is accepted by God, for His own enrichment and for His use in the development of further good in the process, it is accepted with and in its obvious imperfections and its partial but real failures. It requires 'purification'; which is to say, it requires the negation of those elements or aspects or factors which are *not* acceptable and which would not enrich God nor provide material for His employment in the creative advance towards further and fuller good. To say it figuratively, those who might be prehended in an entirely negative way are those who have in them *nothing*—but are there any such?—which is enriching and useful. Those who are acceptable, precisely because there *is* a good which is enriching and useful, are not however *perfectly* 'good', as they themselves would willingly and honestly admit in the light of the appraisal with which our last chapter was concerned. Yet they can be accepted and received, they can be enriching for God Himself, and they can be employed in His purpose—but only if and when, in a phrase of Rupert Brooke's (in a different context but not entirely unrelated), 'all evil' is 'done away'. That 'evil' is *negatively* prehended; but the occasion as it is constituted, because it has such 'good' in it, is *positively* prehended. Nor do I think that such an interpretation is fanciful; indeed, I believe that it is precisely in this manner that the creative advance does go on, under God and with God participant in it, with God Himself 'in process' (if I may again use here the title of a book of my own which sought to say this in a relatively popular manner).

The very natural and very human desire to 'pray for the departed' might also be fitted into this pattern. Such prayers need to be cleansed from the medieval superstitions about them, to be sure. But if they are genuinely 'remembrance before God' of those whom we have loved, they are by way of adding our strong desire for such use of accomplished good as may be possible by the great cosmic Desire-for-Good which is God Himself, for such reception to God's enrichment, and for the 'communion' of those who have prayed with that same God, so that they too may have their share in that movement of love which is what God is up to in His world.

Finally, we must speak of the imagery of the 'resurrection' and of the 'consummation'. This rich imagery, found especially in I Corinthians 15, cannot readily be transposed into the language of prose, yet if it is taken literally it seems to most of

75

us impossible and absurd. Traditional theologians attempted to put what the images portrayed into a system of concepts that hardly fit together and that for us today are as absurd as the literal pictorial presentation. Yet *something* is being said here, something which is integral to the Christian faith.

I suggest that the important thing that is being said is that the love which God manifested in the life, death, and victory of Jesus Christ is indefeasible. What is even more important, in the way in which the picture is presented to us, is that this love is indeed victorious—the story of Christ, we may recall Whitehead's saying, is told 'with the authority of supreme victory'. Love, 'the love of God which was in Christ Jesus our Lord', *reigns*—but reigns as love can only reign, not in the grandeur of some oriental Sultan's court nor with the coercive omnipotence of a dictator, nor as a 'ruthless moralist' who imposes his righteous will, but in the sheer fact of loving faithfully and unceasingly, through all anguish that His creatures know and that He shares. The 'joy of heaven' incorporates and transmutes but it does not deny that anguish.

Second, I suggest that the talk about 'resurrection of the body' is an assertion that the totality of the material world and of human history, as well as of every man in that history who, with his brethren, has achieved good in his existence in the world, is usable by God who through it has been enriched in His own experience without changing in His supremely worshipful deity—the God unsurpassable by anything not Himself, but open to enrichment in being what He is and in terms of what He does.

Thirdly, I suggest that the 'body' which is 'raised' is *Christ's* body. I do not mean here the chemicals, the biology, of the flesh which walked in Palestine two thousand years ago. I *do* mean the wholeness of that which Christ was, taken into, received by, enriching to, and usable for, 'the glory of God the Father'. Those who have shared in the life of Christ as the diffusion of His love in the world are by that very fact 'members incorporate in his mystical body', as the Prayer Book phrases it. Which is to say, they live in *his* love and they are a part of *his* life. The resurrection is for them a sharing in Christ's being taken into, received by, enriching to, and usable for God the Father. Thus the resurrection is not something that will take place in the distant future, when the 'scroll' is opened and a grand assize held. It is a present reality in the faith of the Christian. The 'Christian hope', grounded in the Christian faith, is a present experience; indeed, that hope, like the love which is participant in Christ, *is* in that faith. The living in Christ—by which I mean, as I have indicated, living 'in love' as a human possibility which has been 're-presented' for us in the Man Jesus—as Christ lives in those who respond and hence know what love is: this *is*, at this very moment, 'our hope of glory'.

What this comes to in practical experience needs to be said, as we close this chapter. It means courageous trust in the God who 'raised Jesus from the dead' and has given us confidence and hope. It means profound concern for and dedicated action in the world, yet with a certain 'detachment' which gives us perspective on what we undertake. It means the adoration of God as our 'refuge and strength', with the implementation of that adoration in daily experience, so that the faithful man becomes 'an other Christ' in this mortal existence, a personal channel through whom the 'Love that moves the sun and the other stars' is an almost tangible reality in the affairs of life. It means a life which, in New Testament idiom, is 'in the heavenly places' even while it is lived here; for belief, worship, and action are seen as worthwhile, since they can never ultimately be frustrated or useless—*God* receives them, enjoys them, employs them, to 'his greater glory', which is nothing other than His continuing loving action in the advance of the creative process towards the good. He is indeed the supreme affect, as well as the giver of all initiating aims.

SIX

Question and Hope

At several points in these chapters I have spoken of God as 'supreme affect'. This term I have borrowed from Schubert Ogden, who uses it in his fine book *The Reality of God*, a book to which I acknowledge my debt in the preparation of these chapters. At the same time I acknowledge him as the author of this phrase. In Ogden's book there is a chapter called 'The Promise of Faith' and I should like to commend it to you, for it seems to me that with a rather different approach, yet much more adequately, Ogden says in it much that I have been trying to suggest in what I have been putting before you.

Ogden's essay concludes with an honest statement that he does not, at the time of writing, see that such a portrayal of 'the promise of faith' as he has drawn—and I remind you that since he and I have said much the same thing, this would be true of my own presentation—necessarily entails what he calls 'subjective immortality', the persistence beyond death of the conscious self. Yet the portrayal still holds good, he claims; and he goes on to say that it is precisely because he is trying to think and write as a responsible Christian theologian that he feels obliged to affirm that such personal persistence is not in and of itself, by necessity, utterly integral to Christian faith. And I agree with him.

But the very reality of 'the promise of faith' raises the question of such personal persistence beyond death—raises it *as a question* which should be discussed. And it does not exclude the possibility that such persistence, in some mode, may be a legitimate consequence of the indispensable 'promise', even if it is not absolutely entailed by it. Interestingly enough, the fact that in so many prayers used in the Christian fellowship and in so many books dealing with Christian theology, this is actually spoken of *as* 'the Christian hope', or 'a reasonable, holy, and religious hope' (in one familiar prayer), may have its lesson to teach us. At least it warns us against the wrong kind of confidence on the matter, and it prevents us from succumbing too easily to that odd variety of self-centredness, in the worst sense, which demands 'immortality' because it is determined to play 'dog in the manger' in God's universe.

In this chapter I plan to discuss the *question* and to say something about the 'hope', although I know that I cannot provide an adequate answer to the former and I am in no position to speak with certainty about the latter.

In his recent study of process theology, Peter Hamilton has noted that he has found among the young people with whom he has worked as a chaplain and teacher of divinity a willingness to consider very seriously the reality of God but a feeling that talk about 'personal immortality' makes no sense. That book, *The Living God and Modern World*, is the most important British study of process theology; and it should be read. Furthermore, Mr Hamilton's remarks on this particular subject should be considered with care, for he represents, I think, in his comment about his own students what is also a prevalent attitude in other circles as well. I mention this for what it is worth, realizing quite well that what people think is no indication of what is true; realizing also that Christian faith is not to be 'cut' to the measure of popular opinion. None the less, if it should turn out that one *can* be a Christian without holding firmly to personal persistence beyond death, this is significant; and since, as I have just been saying, I think that such is indeed the case, I believe that nobody ought to *require* acceptance of some variety of personal persistence as a pre-requisite for a welcome into the Christian community which is grounded on that faith in God in Jesus Christ which the community exists to make available to men and women in every age.

But this may be beside the point. Let us proceed to the question and to the possible 'hope' and see what may be said about them.

First of all I should like to set side by side a negative and a positive consideration, each of them relevant to our question. The negative consideration has to do with that kind of selfishness to which I have already alluded. The positive one has to do with the intrinsic value of personal human existence.

I think that there can be little doubt that a good deal that is said in support of personal persistence after death is based upon a strong individualistic stress on the self. One can have no sympathy with the variety of humility which turns itself into a doormat and invites others to walk on one, in a manner which becomes a strange sort of self-pity masking as humility. Nobody is asked to be Uriah Heep! But it is also possible to be assertive about the self in a less obvious and equally unpleasant fashion. *I* am what matters; *my* destiny is the important thing; if God does not preserve *me*, the universe is a mess and nothing is worth while. 'Glory for me', the old gospel-hymn is supposed to have sung—but the very words show that the hymn is not about *the gospel*, for the gospel speaks of 'Glory to God', in whose 'glory' all good is contained.

There *is* a concern about the self which is healthy and, as a matter of fact and observation, essential to each of us; but there is also a concern about the self which is vicious and un-lovely—and also, I should say, destructive of the very thing it seeks to assert. In the Christian tradition, *that* sort of concern about the self, 'the glory for me' variety, serves as part of the picture of hell. I introduce here, both for a little 'light relief' and because it makes my point so accurately, a poem by Rolfe Humphries which he entitled *Hell*. It may be found in his *Forbid Thy Ravens*, published some years ago by Scribners (New York):

Hell is a place of solitude enforced
On the great host, cut off by sorrow, going
Under a wind intolerably cold,
A wind from no direction, always blowing.

Hell is a place of everlasting noise,
Where voices, plaintive and obnoxious cry
Over and over again their favourite word
In constant iteration: I, I, I.

Hell is a place where mirrors are black water,
And rivers salt, and atmosphere like leud,
Where suffering is all the rage and fashion,
And everything is dead except the dead.

Hell is all right to visit, if we have to,
And hard enough to miss, in any case;
But, I insist, I would not like to live there,
Not if you gave me all the God-damned place.

It is the 'I, I, I' that I find significant in that poem. We all 'visit' hell, as Humphries has it, from time to time; it is indeed 'hard enough to miss', as the possible destiny to which I have referred. But the horror of it, the death in it, and the 'solitude' known there, are all summed up in those words 'in constant iteration: I, I, I'. That is why hell is a 'God-damned place'. William Morris was right in calling fellowship heaven, and lack of fellowship hell. Sometimes I incline to think that those who selfishly seek for personal persistence, for their own sake, and in the demand that they shall not 'lose themselves' in the 'love and service of God', are really asking for hell—and if that is what they are asking for, the *kind* of person who does ask in this way has already obtained what he sought. He is already in hell.

The positive consideration which I should set alongside this negative one has to do with what I have styled the intrinsic value of personal human existence. This is not a matter of concern for *my*self; it is basically a concern for the value known and the love seen in others. John Baillie has written eloquently about this in his *And the Life Everlasting*, where he speaks movingly of the incredibility to him of the thought that this or that friend, whose love has been shown towards him, shall not be accepted as being indeed a lover, with a worth that nothing can destroy. It is for his friend, for the one he loves, that Baillie asks personal persistence beyond death, not for his own self such as it is.

However we phrase this, there is a point here. And I think that within the systematic statement of process theology, a place has to be made for that profound feeling. If, as we shall be arguing in a moment, we may be sure of 'objective immortality', the taking into God's life of every good that has been achieved in the creative process; and if, as that understanding of the world order implies, *one* of the goods is the agency by which these given goods have been achieved, including at this point the human agent as a peculiarly significant focus—may it not be the case that not only the good which has been achieved but the agent who has achieved it (himself good, despite defect and the instances of his failure in this mortal existence) will be preserved beyond the 'perishing of occasions'? If value is never lost, as Whitehead claimed in his Ingersoll lecture on *Immortality*; and if value is always associated, in the process, with fact—may it not be that exactly in receiving all that has been done which is valuable, the doer of the valuable is also to be received? May not something like the 'communion of saints', in the divine life and usable by the divine agency, be a possibility? After all, 'personality' *is* in relationships.

I put these two considerations side by side, for what they are worth. At least they help us to see what the *question* is asking. Now I wish to make three statements which seem to me to be plainly true, either from a serious acceptance of the conceptuality which I have been assuming or from the deliverances of the Christian faith itself. These will help us to get the question in even more accurate focus.

My first statement is simply a repetition of what I have just said about 'objective immortality'. That each and every occasion or occurrence, each 'entity', makes its contribution, negatively or positively, to the creative advance is clear enough. The *way* in which this is done is by the good which has been accomplished being taken into God's 'consequent nature'— God as concretely he is, not abstracted from the world but in unfailing relationship with it. Everything that can thus be received *is* received; we might say that God is a good husbandman who wastes nothing. Anything not received, anything that is negatively prehended, is utterly use-*less*; it is 'cast as rubbish to the void', in Tennyson's words, because it can make no contribution to the abiding good and its implementation in the creative advance.

Is there anything that is like that? Obviously we do not know. Equally obviously the horror of evil, in all its forms, is not to be denied. But again with equal obviousness, God's capacity to transmute and transform what is most certainly evil into an opportunity for good cannot be denied by any Christian who has contemplated what we say God did with Calvary. Love such as God is, demonstrated in what God does in *that* instance, is able to 'work wonders' with the very worst of events and (may we not believe this?) with the very worst that men can do and even, I dare to say, with the very worst that men can be. 'Nothing is lost that can be saved'—is there anything or anybody who *cannot* be saved? Not against its or his free decision, that is to say; for in that case it would be coercion and hence literally nothing worth doing would be accomplished. But love can solicit, invite, lure, entice, in so many different ways and through so many different channels, 'secular' and 'religious', that one need not be hopeless about the matter. I have said that the only *really* strong thing is love; and I now add that the divine persuasion, working tenderly yet indefatigably, may very well be able, in the long run, to win free consent. That free consent would be to *God*, yes; it would also be the realization or actualization or fulfilment of creaturely potentiality.

My second statement has also been intimated at an earlier point. The 'resurrection of the body of Christ', in the sense in which I have presented it, is an assurance of faith. I do not need to develop this further, since I have already discussed it at some length.

And my third statement is simply a reference to what I have borrowed from Schubert Ogden, about God as 'supreme affect'. To him, into him, all good is a contribution. He knows, as such affect, the sting of anguish; he also knows the reality of joy. He takes them all, accepts them all, uses them all, in so far as there is any usability about them. And he does this *now*, not in some remote future. Mortal men strive and struggle, labour to do their best (and fail), move in the direction of fulfilment through the decisions they make. They die . . . 'and with God be the rest', as Browning puts it. To be able to say that, in complete confidence, *is* Christian faith; and 'the promise of faith' is the assurance that this *is so*. Thus the theocentrism so basic to the biblical witness is reaffirmed. As from God all initiating aims were derived, so to God all fulfilment must go as its 'final rest'.

Having made those three statements, I must confess that for me personally this is *enough*. But I have left it still as a 'question', not as a complete answer—the question, namely, whether or not there can be and is *personal* (*viz.*, conscious) persistence after the death which is the terminus of our mortal pilgrimage. Yet there is what I have called 'the hope'. I must say something about it.

John Baillie, in the book to which I have referred, places the grounds for this 'hope' in two Christian convictions. The first is that God is good—that He is 'pure unbounded love'. The second is the resurrection of Christ. For him it is inconceivable that a genuinely good and loving God would permit the annihilation of those persons whom He has created, whom He has so lovingly sustained, and upon whom He has showered such superabundant grace. And it is inconceivable to him that the communion with the 'risen Lord', which the fact of resurrection has made possible, should ever be brought to an end—a communion like that, in which love is shared so richly, has about it the quality of everlastingness, even (as Baillie would doubtless say) of eternity. Nothing, certainly not the moment of mortal death, can destroy it.

I believe that Baillie has singled out the two *big* matters, thus reducing any other 'arguments' to triviality. In effect, he says that if God does permit the annihilation of human personality, in its self-conscious awareness as recipient of God's love, there is something oddly selfish about God Himself. Now I should wish to say that it seems to me that this is a very strong point. If God is truly love, and if love is relationship, and if relationship means sharing, then it would be more like God as He relates Himself to the creative process to wish to 'share' with others that which is good, that which is being done towards good, and that which leads to enjoyment in good. Whether this means also something like the 'communion of saints', where the divine love is indeed 'in widest commonalty shared', I do not know. But I may be permitted to *hope* that it does.

As to the resurrection of Christ, I have already spoken about what this means, at least so far as I can understand its meaning. It is life 'in Christ', triumphantly victorious over everything evil—which is to say that it is life 'in love', of a type that does indeed have about it the quality of everlastingness and even, maybe, of eternity, although I dislike that word because of its suggestion that temporality is a lesser good or perhaps an evil. If one should seem to be thinking only of those who have 'encountered' the historical Jesus, then there would be a kind of unlovely and unlovelike selectivity which would make such talk seem a little absurd. But if one is thinking of life 'in love' as an authentic possibility for every man, wherever and whenever he has happened to live out his mortal existence, then I must say that I both understand and find strength in the argument.

As so often, a human analogy helps; and although some

contemporary theologians have been chary of using such analogies, one can be encouraged by the dominical employment of them and continue to find them useful. When I think of the love that I know so well between a particular person and myself—and I am in fact thinking of one particular person with whom I am so bound in love that it remains for me a source of wonder and joy—I am aware, in a fashion that words cannot adequately express, that there is something so *enduringly* real in our mutuality in giving and receiving, in our commitment one to the other, and in our hopefulness one about the other, that the thought of its having a terminus cannot enter my mind. 'This thing is bigger than either of us or than both of us', lovers often say in one form of words or another. The *thing* that is 'bigger' in such love is the activity of God Himself, I should dare to affirm. Yes, but the two lovers *share* in that; and by their sharing, they seem also—at least to themselves, each for the other—to share in the sort of endurance through all vicissitude which is characteristic of God who is never-failing love.

I do not know whether this also means conscious and personal persistence beyond the death of either partner or of both of them. But I may be permitted to *hope* that it does. And quite seriously I must add, 'with God be the rest'. Which, by the way, is exactly what Browning was prepared to say for himself and for his Elizabeth.

We have seen the question, in all its depth. And we have heard about the 'hope', with its poignancy and longing desire. It is almost time to end, but I wish to say one or two things more as I bring these chapters to a close. Since I have just used the word 'desire', I want to speak of it for a moment—or rather, to speak of what it is pointing towards. Then I want to return to that grand 'shewing' of Mother Julian of Norwich which I quoted earlier.

Desire . . . how much that word has been abused and how much derided! Yet it points towards something that might almost be taken as a definition of what it really means to be a man, even of what it means to speak about God. To say this may seem ridiculous; to many it will seem the sheerest sentimentality. But I wonder if it is either ridiculous or sentimental. In fact I do not really wonder; I flatly deny both charges.

For consider what desire is, as we know it in ourselves, in all our own 'desiring'. Often desire is used to signify sexual impulses, which are thought to be evil or at the best not very worthy. I have already indicated my rejection of such a view and my conviction that all love, so far as we know it humanly, has a physiological sexual aspect. The only question, in respect to sexual desire, is how it should best be expressed, both for the fulfilment of each person and for the best shared life of the community. Thus sexual desire is a good enough place to start when we think of what desire comes to, in our experience. To say briefly what I believe that to be, let me put it this way: desire is the yearning, affective, deeply-felt urge for fulfilment. It is how love works, when it is not a chilly matter of 'rational approval' or a Kantian affair of willing the good—both of which, in my judgement, are so absurdly inadequate that they need no further comment.

If this be what desire in man comes to, what about desire in God? Here I wish to contradict the thesis of Anders Nygren's great work *Agape and Eros*. As you will recall, Nygren insists that in God there is no *eros* (the Greek word, by the way, for what I have been calling 'desire', which significantly also in Greek means 'love'); in God there is only *agape*, which Nygren interprets to mean the love which gives without regard either to the value of the recipient or the urgency on the part of the giver to receive a returning love. I believe that this notion is biblically unsound, in view of much that is said about bride-and-bridegroom, husband-and-wife, lover-and-beloved as symbolic of God's relation to the world. I know that it is psychologically untrue; I am sure that it is existentially nonsensical. Theologically, it is disastrous. God *is* love; and in His loving He both gives and receives. He shares; He opens up and delights in mutuality. Unless this be the case, the

Christian faith is sheer absurdity and should be rejected out-of-hand, for the God about whom it is talking cannot be the God Nygren presents. In fact, as somebody has pointed out, Nygren's God of sheer *agape*, in the meaning he gives that word, is a moral reflection of the untouched, unmoved, self-sufficient deity as *ens realissimum*—note the neuter gender—which Christian theologians have tried to join with the living, loving, caring God of the Hebrew-Christian scriptures—and have failed.

God as *desire*, or as I have put it earlier as the great Desire-for-good, is the yearning God, seeking to fulfil others in relationship with them, and by that very token seeking their returning love, which because it is given to Him freely is also His own fulfilment, His own enrichment. A view of God as one who can receive nothing because He already has or is everything is a pagan conception; it is an idol which no Christian should pretend to worship. Nor does he, since worship can be given only to the lovable, the perfectly lovable. Cringing fear is appropriate in the presence of such an 'absolute' as sometimes has been named God and only humiliating cringing is appropriate in the presence of a deity conceived after the analogy of the worst type of man we know—namely, the one who is so self-contained and unrelated that he wants and needs and welcomes nothing, since he is entirely self-sufficient. Aristotle's so-called 'magnanimous man', in the *Nichomachean Ethics*, seems to me a ghastly model for God, with that man's 're-markable condescension' but with his incapacity genuinely to *share*.

Furthermore, as G. K. Chesterton once acutely remarked, the Buddhist image of Gautama is a squatting man, with eyes closed, absorbed in inner thought, and possessed of the kind of peace which is had through rejecting all desire. On the other hand, the Christian symbol is a Man hanging on a Cross, with His eyes wide open, embracing in passionate yearning the whole of the world. So George Tyrrell wrote. The contrast is significant. Certainly the one God is at work in Buddhism, but it must be *in spite of* that image of Gautama. Yet the Buddha was right in saying that desire is the cause of the world's suffering. It is, because to love with desire *is* to suffer. He forgot to say that it is also the cause of the world's joy, since to love with desire is the only way to abiding happiness, in the true meaning of that much mis-used word. God both suffers and rejoices—and the picture of Him as experiencing both is the unique thing about the Christian affirmation of Him.

Now I must say something more about that quotation from Mother Julian: that the world continues because 'God made it, God loves it, God keeps it.' It seems to me that we have here the basic grasp of 'how things go' which enabled Mother Julian also to see that 'all shall be well, all shall be well, all manner of things shall be well'. The two together give us the ground for the ultimate optimism which in Christian faith conquers all provisional pessimism. She knew that 'the world is in God's hands', as the negro spiritual says—God made it, God loves it, God keeps it. Everything is safe that is worth saving. So no Christian need fear. Hence, as I have quoted Kirsopp Lake as saying, faith is not 'belief in spite of evidence', although the evidence from time to time may be very powerful and disturbing to us; it is 'life in scorn of consequence' and it is an adventure and a risk and a challenge.

Faith is an invitation to become lovers. That is what it works out as, in practical experience, when its significance is rightly apprehended. It points to God as cosmic love and cosmic lover, who gives to everything its beginning by providing its 'initial aim'. It points to God as active lover as it sees Him supremely active in the Man Jesus and in all who participate in His Spirit. It points to God as the lover who not only gives but receives and cherishes what He receives, as it sees Him to be 'the supreme affect', in whom all good finds its home. It points to Him as love faithfully and everlastingly at work, as it recognizes that He will use whatever good He receives, along with His own urgent desire for good, in furthering the expression of love in the creative advance which is the world.

The traditional scheme of the last things will no longer serve us, I have said; yet that scheme did confront men with the Christian faith and it did make them face 'reality' with honesty and humility. The purpose of this book has been to suggest ways in which what that traditional scheme did for our ancestors may still be vital for us today. That is all I tried to do; and I hope that with all their inadequacies and imperfections, these chapters have brought to your attention some, but not of course all, of those consequences of the faith which we share.

Let the conclusion be, not mine, but Robert Browning's, from *A Death in the Desert*:

> *For life*
> *With all it yields of joy and woe*
> *And hope and fear . . .*
> *Is just our chance o' the prize of learning love,*
> *How love might be, hath been indeed, and is.*

SEVEN

The ⟨...⟩ ove

Almos⟨...⟩ ⟨a⟩go Professor Dorothy Emmet
wrot⟨e⟩ ⟨...⟩ature of Metaphysical Thinking:
'In ⟨...⟩, and pre-eminently in Christi-
ani⟨ty⟩ ⟨...⟩is directly relevant. The religion
d⟨...⟩ ⟨i⟩n developing the content of the
f⟨...⟩ of the founder is held to be one of
⟨...⟩ ⟨per⟩haps the crucial moment, of history,
⟨...⟩ ⟨relati⟩on to the transcendent has been estab-
⟨...⟩ ⟨re⟩gion seeks continually to re-affirm and
⟨...⟩ ⟨i⟩n rite, celebration, meditation, way of
⟨...⟩ makes it the key to an interpretation of
the world⟨...⟩ ⟨p⟩. 155–56).

I believe that ⟨wh⟩at Miss Emmet said is of enormous importance; and I wish to apply her words to the contemporary
theological situation, especially in regard to the various 'radical'
movements of our day.

The first point is that in all significant groups working
towards the re-conception of Christianity today, Jesus Christ is
taken to be 'directly relevant'. If there is any one fact univers-
ally present in today's Christian thinking, in all quarters, that
fact is its 'christo-centric' character. All too often, it seems to
me, the christo-centrism is exaggerated, so that Jesus stands in
complete isolation from everything else; He is often regarded
as being, not the central or definitive fact, but the *only* one
which needs to be considered. This is a great mistake, for it

removes Him effectively from His context, de-historicizes Him, and hence reduces (perhaps even negates) that 'direct relevance' to which Professor Emmet refers. None the less, Jesus *is* taken with utmost seriousness.

Furthermore, thanks to the work of a hundred years of biblical study, we no longer regard Christianity as simply 'developing the content of the founder's teaching.' It is His *life*—the whole reality of what nowadays it is fashionable to call the 'Christ-event'—which is seen to be 'crucial'. So we are delivered from the 'imitation of Jesus' type of theology and from that kind of reductionist thinking which interpreted Christianity as 'following a great prophet' and nothing more.

All this is on the positive side. But I think that a considerable number of 'radical theologians' are not prepared to go along with Miss Emmet when she says (rightly, I am convinced) that the 'life of the founder', in this instance Jesus, must in authentic Christianity be seen as both establishing 'some new relation to the transcendent' and making that life 'the key to an interpretation of the world'. It is not only that some of the anti-metaphysical theologians, not to speak of the American 'death of God' writers (theologians I will not call them, for to do so is to engage in a contradiction in terms), reject any reference to 'the transcendent' and hence can hardly talk meaningfully of a 'new relation' to it. What I have particularly in mind is that while there is much talk about taking Jesus as a key to the interpretation of *human* nature, as it is often phrased, or to the meaning of *human* life, or to the point of *man's* existential situation, there is a lamentable tendency to stop there and not to go on to talk about 'the world'—by which Miss Emmet meant, I assume, the totality of things including physical nature; in other words the cosmos in its basic structure and its chief dynamic energy.

Existentialist theologians, for example, seem to forget entirely that human existence, about which they talk so much, has a location in time and space and in a given part of the natural order. As I have put it elsewhere, all history has a geography. I find that many others, too, appear to be content to see Jesus as relevant to human affairs but hesitate to draw any conclusions about His relationship to the cosmic situation in which such affairs take place.

One of the reasons that some of us have been attracted to process-thought is its emphatic insistence on the cosmic structures and the cosmic dynamic. Process-thinkers have seen that man is a product of the evolutionary movement, just as much as anything else. If that is true, as obviously it is, the natural order must be interpreted in such a fashion that it permits us to account for human life—and if we do that, we must account also for the fact that in human history there has appeared the Man Jesus, with whom also we must come to terms. Or arguing in the other direction, if we take Jesus as significant for human life and history, He must also be seen as having some relationship to the setting of that life and history—the natural order—and hence be as much a 'disclosure' of that as He is of *man's* existence.

Historically the Christian tradition has spoken of Jesus as the incarnation of God, the manifestation of the divine reality 'in the flesh'. It has not presumed to think that we can get to that divine reality by some escape from the human situation; nor has it taken the view of a friend of mine who once said, to my astonishment, 'Let's look at this as God Himself sees it'. We cannot do anything of the sort; we are men and our knowing of anything whatsoever is as men and in terms of human experience. As Aquinas said, all knowledge is *ad modum recipientis*, and the 'mode' of our human receiving is the human mode, which is tautological but none the less true and never to be forgotten. This truth of our human situation is met, in Christian faith, by the claim that God 'has come in the flesh'. Hence, in St Augustine's words, 'we do not need to climb up to heaven to find him (we could not do that, in any event), since he has come to us where we are'.

But it is *God* who has come to us where we are, not just the truth about human life in supposed isolation from 'the transcendent' and from 'the world'. I am convinced that until and unless the modern theologians who are calling for a 'radical' reconstruction of Christianity recognize this, they will fail us utterly in our need to see Christian faith afresh. The *way* in which this was done in an earlier day certainly cannot be ours in this time; but the vision, insight, intuition, conviction—call it what you will—that Jesus Christ establishes with the transcendent a 'new relation' into which 'in rite, celebration, meditation, way of life' (to use Miss Emmet's phrases) we are permitted to enter and to have it made our own—notice I did not say 'make our own', which would deny the divine priority in this event—*is* Christianity. And the consequence is a 'key to the interpretation of the world' which includes *everything* and not simply human life in a presumed separation from that 'everything'.

Somewhere in *Appearance and Reality* the English idealist philosopher F. H. Bradley remarked that 'the man who, transported by his passion, feels and knows that only love gives the secret of the universe', is not engaging in proper metaphysical discourse. That is rubbish, in my view. I do not think that a Christian can for a moment accept Bradley's pejorative judgement. Precisely *that kind of man*, 'transported by his passion'—in this case his being caught up into a relationship with God in Christ, although it may very well be true in other ways as well, since to be 'transported' by passion is to enter upon the most profound experience possible to human beings —precisely such a man does feel and know what is nothing other than 'the secret of the universe'. The secret is that *God is love*; and it carries with it the corollary that God who is love 'works in all respects for a good end to those who love *him*', in the natural order as well as in history.

Of course this does not mean that everything becomes sweet and cosy; the fact that Love incarnate suffered crucifixion negates any such sentimentality. The 'good' towards which God works 'in all respects' is not comfort; nor is the Christian religion 'a research after comfort' (Whitehead properly denounced such a conception). None the less it *is* a 'good': it is, indeed, the Kingdom of God which is the sovereign rule of love into which those who respond to God's love are admitted— and in being admitted given the task of conforming this world of human affairs to the pattern of the Love 'which moves the sun and the other stars'.

Thus I am obliged to say, with H. H. Price, that theism, at least in a Christian sense, is 'a metaphysics of love'; and with this, I am obliged to affirm that 'the world', including nature in its farthest stretches as well as in the intimacy of human existence, is given its proper 'interpretation' only when 'the key' to it is found in Jesus Christ. That, essentially, is what Christian faith is all about—it has a cosmic sweep and is not to be accepted as an affair of human importance only. Its message, accepted on the grounds of faith and in the continuing activity of utter self-commitment to that which is spoken forth in the event of Christ, is precisely that 'love is all and more than all', in E. E. Cummings' telling phrase.

The tragedy of Christian theology is that this faith, this message, has not been given the central place which it not only deserves but demands. For far too many of the great theologies of the Christian tradition, the recognition of love has been a peripheral rather than the central concern. This manifests itself not only in the way in which Aristotelian notions of the 'unmoved mover' or neo-Platonic ideas of 'being-subsisting-from-itself' have been taken to be the proper definition of what is meant when we speak of 'God', but also in liturgical language where all too often the basic concept implied or (as most often seems to be the case) affirmed is the utter immutability of deity, along with the rigidly legalistic moralism which it is suggested should mark those who claim to 'obey' the divine mandates. Of course I have exaggerated here. There are plenty of instances, in the traditional liturgies, of emphasis on the sheer love of God, His being affected by human attitudes and responses, and the tender relationship which He intends between Him and His children. Yet I think that I do not exaggerate when I say that the chief impression received by an observer is precisely the divine impassibility, the intransigence of the divine demand, and the requirement from men of a servile obedience rather than life in 'the glorious liberty of the children of God'.

At the same time that Christian theology has so emphatically insisted on the divine absoluteness (taken in the sense which I have indicated), there have always been elements in that theology which have suggested another idea. In some of the greatest of the Church's teachers there has been a strange ambiguity. In St Augustine, for example, the personal relationship of man with God, as well as the deepest nature of God Himself, has been interpreted in terms of a love which the theological structure would seem to render almost absurd. St Thomas Aquinas was also a 'double-man', in that while he accepted and sought to develop a Christian interpretation of Aristotelian ideas in which Aristotle's 'unmoved mover' was given priority over the relational view of God, at the same time in his own sermons, prayers, and occasionally throughout his writings there is the stress on exactly that relational view. This kind of internal contradiction seems to run through much traditional theology; it finds explicit expression in Luther's dichotomy between the terrible God, who put him not only in awe but in utter terror, and the tender and loving God whom he knew in Jesus Christ as the saviour, the loving friend, and the gracious Father of men.

The real question is whether we are to make absolutely central in our thinking the 'love of God which was in Christ Jesus our Lord' or in one way or another regard that love as so adjectival to the divine substance that it appears to be irrelevant. Indeed, to talk of 'substance' here is in itself misleading; for the use of that term, despite all the protests of the neo-Thomists and others, is certain to bring us to think of God in terms of unchanging and unchangeable inert *stuff*—and to do that is to deny, *ab initio*, the possibility of a God who responds in complete faithfulness and with the utter integrity of His own nature, yet with deepest awareness and sympathy. In other words, we find it difficult if not impossible to move from the model of deity as primarily substantial being, existing in and of itself, to the model of deity as genuinely participant and really affected by what goes on in His world.

It is the purpose of this chapter to argue, from many different sides, that another way is required. This is the way which is provided if we adopt, not the so-called 'classical' view of God, but the 'neo-classical' view—a view which stresses the relational aspects as being much more than *merely* aspects—as being, in fact the basic reality of God Himself. Unquestionably this will present very difficult problems for Christian theology and especially for the sort of theology which has been conventional during most of Christian history. Yet there is nothing sacred about that theology as such; for what is abiding in Christian faith is not this or that theological formulation, however widely accepted, but exactly what Professor Emmet has said: 'the life of the founder', the 'new relationship to the transcendent' which that life has disclosed, and hence the total impact of Jesus Christ on men, in all its richness and depth. If *this* is the abiding Christian 'thing', then theologies may be subject to change, as we come to understand more and more adequately what is being disclosed to us in the person of Jesus Christ. And what is being disclosed, I repeat, is the utter centrality of love.

We need not *blame* our fathers in the Christian tradition for what they did, although we may regret much of it and wonder how ever they could have said what so often they did say. What is required is to understand how, under the particular circumstances which were naturally theirs, they took the positions they did. But this does not entail *our* taking those same positions, especially in respect to such a central point as this one. The requirement from us is to do for our time, in the light of a deeper apprehension of the centrality of love, what in their own way they sought to do in their time. This will mean, I am certain, that we shall be obliged to give up that model of deity which, with the best intentions, they accepted from the general philosophy of the time. But it will not mean that the true 'intentionality' (as I may phrase it) which was theirs will be forgotten.

If we have available a philosophical conceptuality which is more congruous with Christian love, we shall be prepared to use that conceptuality in the task of theological re-construction. Yet in doing so, we must have the wit and wisdom to discern that in their insistence on the divine changelessness and even on the divine impassibility, they had hold of something important. We cannot phrase it as they did; but we can see that what they were talking about was the utter reliability of God, His faithfulness to His purpose, His inexhaustibility, His never ceasing to be and to act in accordance with His undeviating purpose of love. If *they* felt themselves forced to express this 'intentionality' in terms of a philosophical concept which for us is incredible, this must not suggest that the 'intentionality' in and of itself was wrong. There is a difference between the deepest instinct and desire which was theirs and the particular language (and with that language, the philosophical notions which it entailed) which they employed in stating that instinct and desire.

In any event, the point of this chapter, intended to prepare the way for further discussion of what I have styled 'another' (and I am convinced a *better*) theological approach, is simply to insist that we can only be loyal to our ancestors in the Christian tradition, but above all loyal to the chief stress in the faith which that tradition has conveyed to us, if and when and as we are ready to put stress on love's centrality—and to use *that* as our key to the whole theological enterprise.

Now almost all Christians would agree that Wesley was correct in writing of God that 'his nature and his name is love'. It would seem obvious to them that this is the Christian claim and many of them would say, if they heard us stress the absolute centrality of this assertion, 'Of course, that is taken for granted'. Right there, I think, is the problem. We simply cannot 'take it for granted' that 'God is love' and let matters rest there. Failure to go further, failure to see the shattering nature of that assertion, is the reason for an enormous amount of misunderstanding and the occasion for an even larger amount of misinterpretation of the Christian doctrine of God.

This was brought home to me not long ago when, after a lecture on the subject of 'process-theology', in which I had stressed the Johannine text, a member of my audience rose to put the following question: 'Of course it is the Christian faith that God is love. But unless God's love is backed by His power, what guarantee have we that it will triumph in the end and that Mother Julian's conviction that "all shall be well" will be vindicated?'

The short answer to the question would have been that my questioner obviously did not himself believe that God's love is very important. *If* love, in order to be truly effective, must be associated with coercive force—as he indicated was to him essential—then it is apparent that love is *not* recognized as supreme. What *is* supreme is power. He was saying that love is a very fine thing, that there ought to be more of it, that in some way or other God does care, but that in the long run the really effective instrument in God's control of the world is His capacity to coerce. It is as if someone offered us, with his left hand, the gift of love; and then, with his right hand, made a fist at us and said, 'If you won't accept love, I'll knock you down'. In other words, in such talk love is *not* the basic dynamic in the world; it is *not* the deepest and highest reality; it is *not* the essential definition of God. And so all the verbal assertions that 'God is love' really amount to nothing; they are *only* verbal assertions, with no genuine grounding in the structure of things and in how things go in the world. In my judgement, this is a denial of the central insight of Christian faith; it is the ultimate treachery.

Part of the problem, of course, lies in the meaning of *power*. If by power we intend to signify, as most often *is* intended, the use of coercive measures whether these be overt or subtle and hidden, then it would seem that to ascribe such a quality to God as His chief characteristic—as in fact, if not in word, is suggested when people talk as did my questioner—is a denial of the point of Christ's disclosure of God. Yet there is a sense in which love itself is powerful. By this I mean that although love will not use coercive measures, driving people to do what they will not do otherwise, *making them* (as the phrase has it) act in contradiction to their own freely chosen decision, love is the *most* powerful of all agencies in the world. This is because love can win response when nothing else can do so; it can lure, elicit, attract, incite—and in this way it can accomplish its ends.

Yet at the same time the ends which love would accomplish are not the selfish sort which would imply that the lover is seeking his own fulfilment without regard for the loved one. On the contrary, the ends which love seeks to accomplish and which only love can accomplish are always ends which are mutually shared and in which the loved one finds his fulfilment too. In other words, when love is central to the picture, we see *ends* and *means* to be 'of a piece'—the end is loved shared, the means is the sharing of love.

I believe that considerations of this sort are of quite enormous significance today. It might be said that the history of the past half-century is the story of human attempts to secure world-community, the triumph of righteousness and justice, the establishment of understanding among the peoples of the earth, but always through the exercise of some variety of coercion. The result has been anything but what was initially desired. The utter bankruptcy of power, in the coercive meaning of the word, is apparent.

This, I take it, explains the revulsion of so many young people—to take but one obvious example—from the political game, their contempt for warmongers and their unwillingness (as in the United States) to participate in a conflict which they feel will accomplish nothing save further suffering. Hence there is a surprising rediscovery of love among modern youth as the only means to the end, and at the same time an insistence that love is *also* the end to be sought. We may dismiss these young people as 'idealistic', even when at the same time they are criticized for being too 'realistic' in (say) their approach to human relations, especially in sexual matters. We may dismiss youth as being unwilling to be, as we think older folk are, starkly 'realistic' about the fact of power and its necessity in national, international, social, economic, industrial, and other areas of human society. But such criticisms, either of the 'idealism' of youth or of their 'unrealistic' appraisal of the situation, come very ill from people like ourselves. It is precisely *our* settling for the use of power, *our* unwillingness to 'try love', and *our* cynical distrust of the possibilities in love as means towards love as an end, which has brought us to the state we are in.

That force must sometimes be employed is not to be denied —very likely there was no other way in which Nazism, for example, could have been defeated in the short run; I am not advocating complete pacifism in every situation. But I am insisting that for Christians at least their religious conviction should be clear and the consequences of that conviction in their list of priorities as to means should be equally clear. If we *must* use coercion, then let us know that we are doing so; let us admit honestly that insofar as this is done we are not obeying the perfect divine will; let us recognize that at best the use of such force is a *pis-aller*, not the entirely right thing. And if and when force is used, let us not hallow it by thinking of *God* as essentially such coercive power. Above all, let us be repentant of the use we make of force and let us act, once force *has* been used, in such a manner that its evil sting is (if not removed then) drawn and the poison which it injects into the life of men is drained out by the renewed employment of loving action, concern, caring, and self-giving. Only so can we in any sense justify the force which we may have felt impelled to use in this or that given circumstance—we can never *glory* in coercion.

But I must return to the main point of this chapter, which is that we must decide, once and for all, whether we are to give priority in our thinking about God to the concept of love or to the concept of power. Yet that is not quite the right way to put it, since we are not dealing with concepts (which are abstract ideas) but with what nowadays would be called 'models'. What *model*, then, is to be chosen? If we chose power for our model, thinking of God in terms of a person known to us who exemplifies this quality (we must think in this fashion, however anthropomorphic it may appear, although we must carefully 'qualify' our model), it will follow that love will be adjectival and in a secondary place. On the other hand, if we decide for the model of love, thinking of God as more like a human lover (but with defects, imperfections, frustrations, distortions removed), it will follow that whatever power *is* exercised by Him will be loving in its essential quality.

This theological decision has consequences in practically every area—I should venture, even, to say in *every* area—of faith. An obvious instance has to do with the relation of grace and freedom. For centuries, men have worried about this problem: *if* God's grace is indeed His activity, coming before and present in every good human act, how *can* such acts be truly free and responsible acts on the part of the human agent? If God acts, then man's response is not truly his own. If a human act is genuinely free, then where does God come into it? So the problem has been posed. But surely that way of stating it presupposes that God's grace is coercive power. The model which has been assumed, before the problem is discussed, makes possible only the absolutely over-riding quality of God's action, man being only a puppet in God's hands. Or, from the other side, it is human agency which is in control and God can 'enter in' only as a sort of extra.

If the model of God is taken from the realm of loving relationships, however, things are seen very differently. In that case, God does not force His human children, nor do they act in entire independence of God's concern. The divine love is prevenient to, active in, and unfailingly related to everything that is done by men; but the way in which love works is through the luring, attraction, solicitation, invitation, to which

we have referred. God's action is first, since He always loves
men and surrounds them with His loving action—but it is
genuinely loving action and hence not pressure of a coercive
type. On the other hand, man too is active, but his activity is
also in love; he responds freely to the love which is given him
and in that response he knows that he is truly 'being himself',
for he was intended by his creation to be a responding lover
and in no sense a marionette pulled by strings manipulated by
God—certainly not the victim of the divine coercion.

One could go through the catalogue of Christian doctrines
and discover how in each of them a radical alteration will follow
once we have decided that love, not power, is the decisive fact
in God's 'ways with men'. It is obvious that a corollary is the
recognition that love is always a *relationship*; and a relationship
involves two who are in it—God to man, man to God—in which
each of them is not only acting in a causal manner but also being
acted upon in an affective manner. How different would be our
thinking about the Atonement in such a context—to take but
one other example. To take still a third, the understanding of
the Incarnation would no longer fall into the dangerous trap of
either 'God-made-man' or 'only' a very good Man who knows
and serves God in a unique fashion.

Thus we can see that many, if not all, the most difficult
questions in theological discussion have been vitiated by a
peculiar variety of what Gilbert Ryle has taught us to call the
'category-mistake'. We have taken a set of ideas from one
category—the force category—and have applied them almost
without qualification to another category—the God-man
relationship. What we should have done is to see that in the
'Galilean vision', as Whitehead called it, we have the clue to
the proper category for use in the God-man relationship; the
category is 'love in action', the divine Lover acting and the
human intentional lover acting too. And then we should have
found that the situation was very different from what it seemed
to be when power was used as the interpretative key. Once
accept the disclosure of God in Christ (and in all that is

christ-like in human experience, for we ought not to be exclusively christo-centric in the narrower sense); once take that disclosure with utmost seriousness—and then God as 'pure unbounded love' becomes central in our thinking. It makes *all* the difference—and in my judgement, this difference is what Christian faith *is about*.

To take that key with such utmost seriousness and to use it with equal seriousness in the re-framing of Christian theology, will obviously require some very drastic changes in our ways of envisaging what the theological enterprise is all about. We may fear such changes; there is a tendency on the part of theologians to like things to continue as they have been. Yet risk is an element in life and it is also an element in all faith that is worth anybody's having. But on the other hand there would be a wonderful release of energy in thus accepting love's centrality, since love *is* a releasing (as well as a demanding and dangerous) matter.

Let me close with a little story—one which happens to be true in essence, even if there is a bit of embroidery in the way in which it was told to me many years ago. Perhaps it will illustrate my point about love and at the same time show that this emphasis is not entirely new in Christian thought.

In the reign of Charles I there was in Scotland a covenanting minister Samuel Rutherford, who was minister of Anworth in Galloway. One Saturday evening he was catechizing his children and servants. There was a knock at the door. He went to it, and the stormy wind blew in so that the tall tallow candles flickered and he could hardly see a venerable old man who stood muffled up in the rain. 'May I come in?' said the old man, 'And wouldst thou give me shelter for the night?' Rutherford at once said, 'Yes, right gladly. Come in and we will give thee porridge, but not before we finish our catechism.' 'I thank thee', said the stranger, 'and I shall be glad to take my share in the catechism with the others, if thou wilt.' So Rutherford went on asking questions around the family circle. It so chanced that when he came to the stranger, the question was, 'How many commandments be there?' 'Eleven', answered the stranger. 'Alas, sir', said Rutherford, 'I had thought that one so wise and venerable of aspect would have given a better answer. There be but ten.' 'Nay, kind host', replied the stranger, 'in truth there be eleven commandments.' Said Rutherford, 'But that cannot be; there are but ten.' The stranger then went on, 'Hast thou forgotten? There was One who said, "Behold, I give you a new commandment, that ye love one another." ' Rutherford sprang to his feet. 'Who art thou?' he gasped. 'I am James Ussher', said the stranger, 'and I have come hither in private that I might have speech with thee.' It was the famous Archbishop Ussher, Primate of Ireland and one of the most eminent scholars of that day. 'Welcome indeed thou art', said Rutherford, 'thou wilt remain here, but tomorrow thou wilt preach in my church.' 'Yes, gladly', said the Archbishop; his eyes twinkled as he added, 'I think I have chosen my text already. Shall it not be from St John's Gospel, Chapter 13, verse 14?'

The text which Archbishop Ussher proposed runs like this: 'If I, then, your Lord and Master, have washed your feet; ye also ought to wash one another's feet.' It is found in that place where the Fourth Evangelist gives the account of the foot-washing in the Upper Room and where he cites the words of Jesus about the 'new commandment'. It is based on, indeed made possible by, the earlier words which the Evangelist writes as he begins this account: 'Jesus, knowing that the Father had given all things into his hands, and that he came from God and was going to God . . .' And *that* sentence assumes the truth of the even earlier words in the gospel narrative: 'Jesus . . . having loved his own which were in the world, he loved them unto the end . . .'

The Lord came from God precisely in order to love, in order to be the humanly visible instrument of the divine Charity. Christian theology, in my conviction, is nothing other than the explication and application of what that statement *means*.

EIGHT

After the 'Death of God'

The furore over the 'death of God' theology seems to have died down in the United States, but to continue undiminished in Britain. Perhaps this is because the publication in Britain of the writings of the advocates of this position was rather delayed; hence the impact which they make is very much a present reality. In the States, William Hamilton, among the first who talked and wrote in this vein, has said that the 'death of God' emphasis belongs to the past—the recent past, surely—and that today we must go beyond it. Whatever may have been the contribution it made, the contribution *has been* made; what comes next?

I do not myself subscribe to the view that theology works in the fashion which Hamilton's remark suggests—a sort of drunkard's progress, with no real direction and without obvious continuities. But I agree on three points: first, that the 'death of God' literature has made a contribution to theology, even if it is not the contribution which its spokesmen might think; secondly, that the movement is just as dead as its leaders said that 'God' was dead; and thirdly, that we must go forward to a doing of theology, in the Christian mode, which will take account of what that particular literature had to say. I wish to speak about these three points.

The talk about the 'death of God', I believe, was an extraordinarily misleading, even if highly provocative, way of saying something important. For what was really involved in the talk was the death of certain concepts of God, rather than a supposed death of God himself. One realizes that this interpretation has been denied by Thomas Altizer and other advocates of the view; they insist that they are talking about a genuine death of God as an historical occurrence. But even they show that the contrary is the case, as Altizer himself demonstrates when he claims that he is talking about the absolute immanence or 'presence-in-this-world' of the Word or Spirit, in consequence of the radical *kenosis* or self-emptying of the transcendent deity usually denoted by the word 'God'. That Word or Spirit most certainly is *not* dead; and Altizer's 'gospel' is precisely the reality in human experience and in the world-order of that Word or Spirit with whom men must reckon whether they wish to do so or not.

I am convinced that what has died, that whose death has been announced, is a series of models, images, pictures, or concepts of deity which for a very long time have been taken by considerable numbers of people to be the Christian way of understanding God. It is important in this connexion to note that each of the three leading advocates of the position is in reaction against a notion of God that represents just such a series of models. Paul van Buren was a disciple of Karl Barth, under whom he wrote his excellent doctoral dissertation on Calvin's teaching about Christ as the true life of men; Hamilton was an opponent of natural theology in all its forms, even if he studied at St Andrews under Donald Baillie—but it was the so-called 'neo-orthodox' line which had attracted him, theologically; Altizer is a slightly different case. He worked under Paul Tillich and with Mircea Eliade, but his reaction has been *against* the aspects of Tillich's thought which stressed 'being-itself' in God and *for* those aspects which emphasized the need for radical re-conception of Christian thought.

Whitehead, to whom I shall return, wrote in *Process and Reality* many years ago that the Christian theological tradition has tended to conceive of God in three ways, each of them mistaken: as 'the ruling Caesar, or the ruthless moralist, or the unmoved mover'. It has failed to give central place to what he styled 'the Galilean vision', in which God is shown as persuasion or love. Hence, in his striking phrase, 'the Church gave unto God the attributes which belonged exclusively to Caesar', seeing him 'in the image of an imperial ruler', 'in the image of a personification of moral energy', or 'in the image of an ultimate philosophical principle'. With certain qualifications I should say that Whitehead stated the facts here.

In various combinations and with differing emphases, the concept of God with which many Christian thinkers have tended to work has been composed of exactly those ingredients; absolute power, stark moral demand, and unconditioned (essentially unrelated, in the sense of a two-way movement) 'being-itself' as the ultimate cause of everything not-God, but not in any way affected by that which was not itself —and the neuter here is highly significant, *ens realissimum*. Great theologians, like Augustine and Aquinas (to name but two), have worked in this fashion; but they were also strangely discontented in doing so, since their *real* faith was in the biblical God of unfailing love-in-action, effecting his purpose of love in nature and history, and most profoundly open to and receptive of what went on in the world. Hence the ambiguity which (as I think) one can see running through so many of the great theologies.

But it was the stress on power, on 'ruthless moralism', and on transcendence in the sense of non-relationship, which many took to be demanded when one talked of God, although one might also add, as a kind of afterthought, 'Oh yes, he is also loving'. I do not parody here, for I myself have found often enough that when I have tried to present a theological point of view which made the reality of love absolutely central, and put the other so-called divine attributes in a place secondary to that love, I have been met with the response, 'Of course God is loving, but we have to begin with His omnipotence, or His transcendence, or His aseity (self-contained and self-existence), or His absolute righteousness with its consequent demands on men'.

This procedure seems to me to be entirely wrong, however traditional it may be. What we ought to do is to start with God self-disclosed in human affairs as love-in-action. Then, and only then, can we use (adverbially, as it were) the other so-called attributes. God as love-in-action is more than any particular expression of His love (hence He is transcendent); God as love-in-action is always available (hence He is omnipresent); God as love-in-action is able to envisage every situation in its deepest and truest reality and accommodate Himself to it, so that He can indeed achieve His loving ends (hence He is omniscient and omnipotent); God as love-in-action is unswerving in His love, unfailing in its expression, unyielding in His desire to confront men with the demands of love (hence He is righteous). If we had worked in that way, we should have been saved from many of our supposedly insoluble theological problems, most of which are based on taking the other, and as I think wrong, approach.

However this may be, the fact is plain that for contemporary men and women, not only of a sophisticated sort but also of quite ordinary attainments, the notion of God as absolute power, as unyielding moral dictator, and as metaphysical first cause never Himself affected, has gone dead. There are many reasons why this has happened; this is no place to discuss them, but among others we may mention scientific constructions, psychological discoveries, awareness of sociological conditions, and all that Bonhoeffer summed up in saying that man has 'come of age' (by which he did *not* mean that man is an entirely mature and adult creature who now can take the place of God, in a fashion not unlike the claim made by the Provost of King's in his recent utterances; but he *did* mean that we now know our own responsibility and that God treats us, not like slaves nor like little children, but like sons to whom He entrusts such responsibility). This 'going dead' of the notions I have mentioned is stated plainly for us in the writers who speak of 'the death of God'.

So much for my first point. My second is that the movement

called by that name is now itself a matter of the past; it has made its contribution and that is that. It has taught us something, and by now we ought to have learned what it had to teach us. Of course the learning has not been done simultaneously in all parts of the Christian world or anywhere else. Hence for some of us, it might be said, the situation is still *pre*-'death of God'; and, for those who are in this situation, the lesson is still to be learned. But for those who have got an inkling of what this is all about, who have learned the lesson, the situation is *post*-'death of God'; we must now go on to the constructive task.

I shall not spend time in showing how and why we are in that 'post' era. I only call in witness the remarks of Hamilton which I have already cited. He at least feels that the 'calling in question', the denials, the stark affirmation of the 'end of sheer transcendence, sheer moralism, sheer power' (as I like to put it), has been accomplished. So the problem for us, as for him, may be phrased in a typically American way: 'Where do we go from here?' And it is with that question that the remainder of this chapter will concern itself. But the one thing that is quite clear is that we do *not* 'go back', as if we could return to the older ideas and concepts, quite unchanged by what has happened during the past few decades. If we cannot retreat, rest content in the denials, the 'calling in question', and the like, neither can we into one of the theologies of the past. If I may say so, this is what I find troublesome in the writing of Dr Mascall on the subject. He is usually very sound in his criticisms of the 'death of God' school and, indeed, of the whole 'radical theology' which in one way or another is associated with it. But because of his failure to understand *why* such a theology in its various forms has appeared, he is unable to see any other solution than a 'return'. Leonard Hodgson, in his review in *Theology* of *The Secularization of Christianity*, made this point about Mascall; and he made it with such clarity and precision that I need only mention it here.

In going forward, then, with Christian theology *after* 'the death of God', we have several options. Let me mention some of them, assuming that we cannot work with Thomism (either 'classical' or 'revised'), nor with that peculiar Anglican affair known as 'liberal Catholicism' in the style of *Essays Catholic and Critical* or the writings of Charles Gore, nor with 'liberalism' in its reductionist form as found in Harnack or Harnack *redivivus*, nor in sheer biblicism in its fundamentalist dress. So I mention the following possibilities, getting some of them from an excellent little book of lectures given in Chicago a couple of years ago, *Philosophical Resources for Christian Faith*: (1) existentialism in some mode; (2) phenomenological (and in that sense non-metaphysical) enquiry; (3) analytical philosophy and its talk about *bliks* and various 'language games'; (4) process thought in its several forms. To these four I should add the so-styled 'secular theology' often advocated today, with a side-glance at revived and restated 'biblical theology'. Here are six possibilities.

Of some of them I must speak very briefly. For example, the kind of 'biblical theology' sometimes advocated assumes that we should go forward by taking with utmost seriousness the biblical images or motifs—not the literal, textual stuff of Scripture, which would involve us in a kind of new 'fundamentalism', but the main-line of biblical images. I am very much in sympathy with this approach, so far as it goes. For Christians the biblical images and patterns are of *first* importance, since it is from them that the Christian picture of God takes its rise. But it must be pointed out that these images and patterns are most diverse; further, they belong, in their explicit shape, to ages in which we do not ourselves live. Hence what is required is just what Leonard Hodgson has so often, and rightly, demanded: we must ask ourselves what the case *really is*, so far as we can grasp it today, if people who thought and wrote *like that*, phrased it in the way they did. Otherwise we shall be using the Scriptures in a very wooden and unimaginative fashion, even if we do not succumb to literalism in its obvious sense. Furthermore, if we wish to communicate the deepest meaning of those images and patterns, we dare not rest content with them as they stand. That would be to resemble the Chinese who, when shipwrecked on a desert island, made their living by taking in each other's laundry. We must translate if we wish to communicate.

Again, the use of analytical philosophy will help us enormously in the way in which we use words. It will enable us to clarify our language, to avoid contradiction, to stop talking sheer nonsense, to look for some kind of referent which will give the necessary verification to what we are saying as Christians. All this is of great importance, lest we fall into the temptation to use high-sounding words for the evasion of difficulties. It has been said that whenever some older theologians got to a hard place they simply quoted a few lines of Wordsworth or Tennyson, thinking that ended the matter; or they made a few biblical citations as if that were the complete answer; or (at worst), when the attack was most fierce, they used the word 'mystery' as a kind of 'escape-hatch'. But analytical philosophy is a neutral discipline—for which we may be grateful—and it gives us no working conceptuality for the statement of the theological implications of Christian faith with the claims that faith makes about 'how things really go in the world'.

The kind of phenomenological method which is often advocated is of a non-metaphysical type; that is, it is interested in description, in terms of how living religion, as a matter of deepest intuitive observation, effectively operates in human experience in the world where men live. This seems to me to be most valuable; a van der Leeuw, an Eliade, and others like these, can help us a great deal. How does faith function, what embodiments does it have, what attitudes does it demand? These are questions which ought to be answered. But I cannot think that their answer will provide the general conceptuality which we require if Christian faith is to be grounded in the stuff of reality and if the case for it is to be made in a manner which speaks meaningfully to the men and women for whom it exists and to whom it is supposed to address itself.

We are left with three possibilities: 'secular theology', an existentialist theology, and a process theology. I shall say something about each of them—and, as my ordering indicates, I shall come down in favour of the last of the three, as offering us the best conceptuality available today as we go forward from 'the death of God'.

The phrase 'secular theology' may be taken to mean one of two things: either a theology *of* the secular or a theology which *confines itself to* the secular realm. Since I have spoken critically of Dr Mascall I am glad to say here that I believe that he has written admirably about this distinction in the last part of his recent *Theology and the Future*. He has pointed out that a theology which is strictly *confined* to the world of 'here and now' cannot take account of the ultimate questions which men must ask, whereas every sound Christian theology is required indeed to speak of that 'here and now', but to relate it to God as a creative principle and to see God at work in the immediacies of human existence in the whole range of what we style 'secular existence'. In other words, I agree that Christian faith must see God *in the world* but that it cannot remain content with 'the world' as if it exhausted all there is of God. Whitehead once said that 'God is in this world or he is nowhere'; that is entirely sound. But Whitehead also said that the world and God are not identical; and I should interpret this utterance, along with others by him, to mean that there is in the divine life an exhaustibility which makes possible the wonderful novelty which the created order manifests, disclosing what Gerard Manley Hopkins named 'the dearest freshness deep down things'.

In any event, if a 'secular' approach to theology thinks that it avoids all metaphysical conceptions, it is profoundly mistaken. Of course one can mean what one wants by the word 'metaphysical'. If one intends to speak of a grandiose construction in terms of supernatural entities, with a schematic ordering of everything according to some superimposed pattern, metaphysics may very well be denied. It seems to me that the present-day attack on metaphysics is nothing more than an attack on idealistic constructions of this type, after the fashion (say) of Hegel or Bradley. But metaphysics can also mean—and process thinkers would say that it ought to mean—the inevitable human enterprise of generalizations widely applied, on the basis of a particular point or event or experience taken as 'important', to the rest of our experience of the world and the world which we surely experience. It can mean, then, the development of those principles which most adequately express what we experience and know, in the full range of our human encounters; and the result is a 'vision' which can be tested by reference back to experience and to the world experienced. Metaphysics in this mode is not some highly speculative system imposed on the world. It is an induction from what is known of the world. Everybody engages in this, usually in a very naïve manner; the 'philosopher', so styled, is only one who in a more sophisticated and critical manner engages in this attempt at making sense of things, including human experience.

But the self-styled 'secular theologian' is doing exactly that. You have only to read Gregor Smith, whose untimely death we all lament, to observe this. Both in *The New Man* and in *Secular Christianity* Gregor Smith is actively setting forth *this* kind of metaphysics, taking as his 'important' moment or event the historical encounters of men, specifically with Jesus, and from these developing a view of the generalized situation of man-in-the-world which, in my sense of the word, is inescapably metaphysical, even if he himself rejects the word and thinks that he is also rejecting the enterprise. What he is rejecting, it turns out, is only that 'supernaturalistic' species of metaphysics which idealistic philosophers have set forth in a pretentious claim to encompass in their thought all things in earth and heaven.

Thus, as I see it, the options which remain are in fact two: either an existentialist approach or a 'process thought' approach, since the 'secular' theology in itself does nothing more than deny a particular kind of metaphysic and leaves us open to the possibility of interpreting the secular world, and everything else in human experience, in some appropriate manner.

The existentialist approach in contemporary English-written theology has been associated with two names: one is Paul Tillich, the other John Macquarrie. I cannot mention the name of Tillich without reverence, for that great and good man was a dear friend of mine and I respect, honour, and love him, though he has now gone from us. His theology was an attempt to combine an existentialist analysis of the human situation with a Christian faith interpreted along the lines of German idealistic thought; he himself confessed that Schelling had been his great master. His method of correlation is, I believe, very suggestive and helpful; his masterly analysis of what it is like to be human is almost beyond criticism. But his final 'system', as he used to call it, seems to me to be too abstract in its statement to convey the Christian gospel, although in his preaching he was anything but abstract. I think that Professor Macquarrie's efforts, especially in *Principles of Christian Theology*, offer a much more 'available' approach for most of us. His insistence that every existential analysis presupposes and includes ontological affirmations seems to me right and sound; his way of using Heideggerian thought is instructive. He takes the biblical images with utmost seriousness and employs them effectively as being determinative of the total picture of God–world–man in the light of Jesus Christ.

If I were to make any criticisms of this existentialist mode of theologizing it would be to say that it is not sufficiently regardful of nature, in the strict sense of the physical world and the material stuff of things. And I should add that it lacks something of the dynamism which I believe is required of any Christian theology, not only because of the dynamic quality of biblical thought itself but also (and more significantly) because of the evolutionary way of things which men like

Teilhard de Chardin have so insistently pressed upon us. But I confess that *if* I did not find process theology more appealing I should opt for Macquarrie's approach. At the same time I must say that if those two criticisms of mine were met sufficiently, there would not be too much (I think) to differentiate *his* way from the one to which I now turn in conclusion.

It is not necessary for me to outline my reasons for preferring process thought; I have already indicated these in my book *Process Thought and Christian Faith*. It will suffice if I note that process thought regards the world as a dynamic process of inter-related (and hence social) organisms or entities, whose intentional movement is towards shared good in widest and most inclusive expression; and that it interprets deity along *those* lines. God is no unmoved mover, dictatorial Caesar, nor 'ruthless moralist'; He is the cosmic lover, both causative and affected, 'first cause and final affect' as Schubert Ogden has so well phrased it. He is always *related*, hence always *relational*; He is eminently *temporal*, sharing in the ongoing which *is* time. His transcendence is in His sheer faithfulness to Himself as love, in His inexhaustibility as lover, and in His capacity for endless adaptation to circumstances in which His love may be active. He does not coerce; He lures and attracts and solicits and invites. He waits for free response from the creaturely agent, using such response (which He has incited by His providing 'initial aims') to secure the decisions which enable the agent to make actual his own (the agent's) 'subjective aim'. In the historical realm and in human life He discloses Himself, precisely as love-in-action, in the total event which we name Jesus Christ. Since His love-in-operation is His essential nature—He *is* love, which is His 'root-attribute', not *aseity*, as the older theology claimed—the other things said about Him (transcendence, immanence, omnipotence, omniscience, omni-presence, righteousness, etc.) are to be understood, as I have already argued earlier, as adverbially descriptive of His *mode of being love* rather than set up as separate or even as distinct attributions.

We live in a 'becoming' world, not in a static machine-like world. And God Himself is 'on the move'. Although He is never surpassed by anything in the creation, He can increase in the richness of His own experience and in the relationships which He has with that creation. He is the *living* God; in that sense, we may say (as the title of a recent book of mine dares to do) that God is 'in process'. In other words, the basic point of the biblical images of God as the living, active, loving, personalizing agent is guaranteed.

But above all, since He is no dictator after the model of Caesar, no self-contained being after the model of the worst sort of man we know, no moralist after the model of the puritanical and negative code-maker, He is truly to be worshipped. Worship means 'ascribing worth'; and this we can do only to a lovable because loving One. We cringe before power expressed coercively and arbitrarily; we tremble in the presence of rigid moralism, when we do not react against it in wild and desperate efforts to be ourselves; we can only be puzzled by the kind of absolute essence which is without affects from what goes on around and about it. But we can worship, truly 'ascribe worth', to the perfection or excellence which is love in its eminent and supreme form. God is that; hence He is adorable.

What is more, He is imitable. And with that affirmation I must end. We are to imitate God; both Aristotle and Plato said so, whilst Jesus gave it content by saying that we were to be 'like our Father in heaven'. Known as love-in-action, disclosed as that love by the event in which Jesus is central, caught up into life 'in love' (which, if 1 John 4 is right, *is* life 'in God'), we are enabled to become what God intends us to be, created lovers. That is why we are here; that is our destiny—or else Christianity is a fraud.